Apocalypse and After

APOCALYPSE
AND AFTER
Modern Strategy
and Postmodern Tactics in
Pound, Williams, and Zukofsky

Bruce Comens

The University of Alabama Press

Tuscaloosa and London

Copyright © 1995
The University of Alabama Press
Tuscaloosa, Alabama 35487-0380
All rights reserved
Manufactured in the United States of America

∞

The paper on which this book is printed meets the minimum requirements of
American National Standard for Information Science-Permanence of
Paper for Printed Library Materials, ANSI Z39.48-1984.

Library of Congress Cataloging-in-Publication Data

Comens, Bruce, 1953–
Apocalypse and after : modern strategy and postmodern tactics in
Pound, Williams, and Zukofsky / Bruce Comens.
p.   cm.
Includes bibliographical references and index.
ISBN 0-8173-0732-X (alk. paper)
1. American poetry—20th century—History and criticism.
2. Literature and history—United States—History—20th century.
3. Williams, William Carlos, 1883–1963—Criticism and
interpretation.   4. Zukofsky, Louis, 1904–1978—Criticism and
interpretation.   5. Pound, Ezra, 1885–1972—Criticism and
interpretation.   6. Apocalyptic literature—History and criticism.
7. Postmodernism (Literature)—United States.   8. Modernism
(Literature)—United States.   I. Title
PS310.H57C65   1995
811'.5209—dc20   94-5843

British Library Cataloguing-in-Publication Data available

For Jean and George Comens

Contents

Acknowledgments

In the course of working on this book I received help from many people. I would particularly like to thank Peter Quartermain of the University of British Columbia; Bob Creeley, Neil Schmitz, Bill Sylvester, and the late Jack Clarke of the State University of New York at Buffalo; and Susan Stewart, Lyn Tribble, and David Watt of Temple University; all of whom read and commented on portions of the manuscript. The comments of the two readers for The University of Alabama Press, Charles Bernstein and Burton Hatlen, also improved the book considerably. Grants from SUNY Buffalo and Temple University provided time for research; on one of those occasions Kate and Byron provided generous hospitality. I'd also like to express a more general gratitude to the faculty and graduate students of the Department of English at SUNY Buffalo for the stimulating intellectual community in which this project was first conceived. And I'll mention Bob Creeley once again: beyond his specific contribution to this book, his continuing interest, encouragement, and support have meant a good deal more to me than these words will say.

PERMISSIONS

Ezra Pound

William Carlos Williams

Louis Zukofsky

Abbreviations

Pound

ALS	*A Lume Spento and Other Early Poems*
America	*America, Roosevelt and the Causes of the Present War*
C	*The Cantos of Ezra Pound*
CEP	*Collected Early Poems of Ezra Pound*
Confucius	*Confucius: The Unwobbling Pivot, The Great Digest, The Analects*
GB	*Gaudier-Brzeska: A Memoir*
GK	*Guide to Kulchur*
JM	*Jefferson and/or Mussolini: L'idea statale: Fascism As I Have Seen It*
LE	*Literary Essays of Ezra Pound*
P	*Personae: The Collected Shorter Poems of Ezra Pound*
PD	*Pavannes and Divagations*
PJ	*Pound/Joyce: The Letters of Ezra Pound to James Joyce, with Pound's Essays on Joyce*
Poems	*Poems 1918–1921*
Radio	*"Ezra Pound Speaking": Radio Speeches of World War II*
SC	*Selected Cantos*
SL	*Selected Letters, 1907–1941*
SP	*Selected Prose: 1909–1965*
SR	*The Spirit of Romance*
T	*Translations*
VA	*Ezra Pound and the Visual Arts*

Williams

A	*The Autobiography*
CP1	*The Collected Poems: Volume I: 1909–1939*
CP2	*The Collected Poems: Volume II: 1939–1962*
EK	*The Embodiment of Knowledge*

I	*Imaginations*
IAG	*In the American Grain*
IWWP	*I Wanted to Write a Poem: The Autobiography of the Works of a Poet*
P	*Paterson*
PB	*Pictures from Brueghel*
RI	*A Recognizable Image: William Carlos Williams on Art and Artists*
SE	*Selected Essays*
SL	*The Selected Letters of Williams Carlos Williams*

Zukofsky

A9	*First Half of "A"-9*
B	*Bottom: On Shakespeare*
CF	*Collected Fiction*
CSP	*Complete Short Poetry*
P	*Prepositions: The Collected Critical Essays*
PZ	*Pound/Zukofsky: Selected Letters of Ezra Pound and Louis Zukofsky*
T	*A Test of Poetry*

1

From Modern Strategy to
Postmodern Tactics

One, two, three. Time, time!
—*Cymbeline*, II, ii, 51

"THE BOMB," wrote William Carlos Williams, "has entered our lives" (*PB* 168). That deceptively simple statement conveniently focuses my central concerns and primary dilemma in what follows. For the Bomb—the capital does signify, as I will shortly explain—both exerts a considerable influence on our lives and provokes a tremendous fascination, providing occasion for dramatic pronouncements and grandiose gestures, and inviting apocalyptic thought with an ease that makes the millennial almost commonplace. The period after Hiroshima saw a resurgence of enthusiasm for eschatological visions that continues to the present, a resurgence the more remarkable in that it is now a readily accepted, almost typical response.[1] Whether we are swayed by overtly apocalyptic rhetoric or quietly concede that total nuclear war has become "the absolute referent, the horizon and the condition of all the others," such responses, however significant, can be dangerous (Derrida "No Apocalypse" 28). They can all too easily dwarf, blot out, "our lives," in discourse as on earth.

As corrective, it is useful to recall that in her last work, written in 1946, Gertrude Stein professed complete indifference, beginning "they asked me what I thought of the atomic bomb. I said I had not been able to take any interest" (*Reflection* 161). Titled "Reflection on the Atomic Bomb," the piece in fact exemplifies and in a sense justifies Stein's refusal to engage in strenuous, "serious" reflections—a refusal begun by the title's insistence on *literal* reflections, both visual ("-on", "on"; "-om-", "-om-") and, with suitable nursery-rhyme accent, aural ("reflection on"—"atomic bomb"). That insistence on childish play continues in the syntax and diction of this brief work, culminating in the seemingly outrageous deliberate naivety of the final sentence, "this is a nice story." But we should not mistake this sophisticated naivety for ignorance; nor should we simply dismiss Stein's quite sophisticated response to the Bomb.

Indeed, Stein's interest also lies in "our lives," in the particularity of diverse human practices. If, she says, the Bomb is "really as destructive as all that," there will be no one to take interest, or to take interest in. And if it is not "all that" destructive, then it is not much different from other deadly technologies, "just one of the things that concern the people inventing it or the people starting it off." Those involved may take interest, may find it useful to their own ends, but the rest of us, uninvolved, "have to just live along like always." In sum, "machines are only interesting in being invented or in what they do, so why be interested." We live "our lives" between the invention and, we hope, the use. Stein next attempts to generalize her feelings—"really way down that is the way everybody feels about it"—but the reiterated denials of the remainder of the paragraph seem excessive, overly protesting: "They think they are interested about the atomic bomb but they really are not not any more than I am. Really not. They may be a little scared, I am not so scared, there is so much to be scared of so what is the use of bothering to be scared, and if you are not scared the atomic bomb is not interesting." If we see in this passage a childlike denial of an uncomfortably intrusive reality, we do no more than recognize a consciously used technique. Gertrude Stein is "not so scared," which admits that she *is* scared. But why, then, does she counsel us to "just live along like always"?

The answer to that question finally depends on a fuller understanding of the bomb and its relation to culture. For the moment, however, it will suffice to note that Stein's indifference, her playful but determined insistence on the priority of human interests and human practices, constitutes a defense against the Bomb. If we are alert to and intent on human interests—and that repeated word acquires extra resonance when considered in relation to the newly important "American interests" of 1946—the Bomb will not be of interest and therefore will not be used. Stein does not deploy the rhetoric of argument—the events of the preceding years, culminating in August 1945, had shown only too well what that rhetoric can bring. Instead, Stein's insistence on human practice in the face of a strategy that culminates in the Bomb is reflected in her own textual practice: she takes advantage of whatever opportunity presents itself to engage in playful, disruptive tactics. As we have seen, the title provides one such opportunity; note too how the final sentence undercuts the argument she begins to develop in the final paragraph: "Everybody gets so much information all day long that they lose their common sense. They listen so much that they forget to be natural. This is a nice story." Argument, clearly, is not "natural"; instead of producing a "nice story" it leads to steadily more powerful means of winning—an escalation that leads, finally, to the Bomb.

"Defense" and "attack," then, as I have used them above, need to be dissociated from the notion of distinct "places"—geographical or rhetorical—which one defends or from which one attacks. From such a place one implements a strategy designed to take over an opposing place, but, without hope of ever possessing a distinct place, one can only use tactical interventions to prevent total domination. Since this distinction goes well beyond the singularities of Stein's work, to provide, as I will argue, a focus for the shift from modernism to postmodernism, it is worth considering in some detail.

*

The distinction between strategy and tactics has a long but often rather confused history in military thought. Generally, tactics are subordinate to strategy as strategy is subordinate to policy. As Liddell Hart, the great British theorist and historian of both world wars, paraphrased von Clausewitz, strategy is "the art of distributing and applying military means to fulfill the ends of policy" (qtd. in Howard 101). Elsewhere he first distinguishes among three levels of operation, "as tactics is an application of strategy on a lower plane, so strategy is an application on a lower plane of 'grand strategy,' " and then adds that "grand strategy" is itself subservient to "the political objective of the war—the goal defined by fundamental policy" (qtd. in Eccles 45–46). This neat hierarchy of command, with each level implementing the decisions of the higher level, is doubtless a useful military model, though one wonders how accurately it describes actual practice. The assertion that tactics merely implement, or at least should implement, strategy also seems questionable. Even in a traditional battle, specific incidents do not always aim to secure the strategic goal, as we can see even in the origins of Western tradition. The *Iliad*, for instance, has room for many motives beside the conquering or defense of Troy, and even those aims were not entirely subordinate to the restoration or retention of Helen. Sometimes other motives coincide with the strategic object, as Achilles' revenge against Hector, but at other times they do not: in any case, those diverse motives are precisely what give the poem its human dynamic. In more recent history, the spontaneously organized truce of Christmas 1914, during which the German and allied troops met in No Man's Land to chat, trade cigarettes, and play football, demonstrates a distinct unconcern with overall strategy—as their commanders immediately realized, expressly forbidding such activity in future (Robbins 38; Fussell 10).

Furthermore, as Liddell Hart's distinction between "strategy" and "grand strategy" would indicate, his distinction between strategy and tactics is based on degree. The terms mark relative positions along a continuum rather than a qualitative difference. Although he begins with a similar distinction, Herbert Rosinski soon shifts to another, more fruitful opposition. Strategy, he writes, "is the comprehensive direction of power," while tactics "is its immediate application" (qtd. in Eccles 46). Tactics is subordinate to strategy, but the two have begun to polarize in relation to "comprehensive direction." *Control* thus becomes the key concept in strategy, as Rosinski's subsequent elaboration makes clear: because strategy must take into account "the multitude of possible enemy counteractions . . . it becomes a means of control. *It is this element of control which is the essence of strategy: Control being the element which differentiates true strategic action from a haphazard series of improvisations*" (qtd. in Eccles 46). Here Rosinski seems mindful of the origin of "strategy" in Greek *strategos*, "general," a focus of power and control. Note, though, that his opposition has shifted: he now opposes strategy not to what he calls tactics (the implementation) but to "a haphazard series of improvisations." The judgmental "haphazard" is, I think, ill-chosen. Improvisations may appear haphazard, but only to an observer, someone external and nonparticipant. And they will especially appear haphazard to someone in, or striving for, a position of control, since improvisations are likely to disrupt any overall strategy. From a participant's point of view, however, improvisations are merely opportunistic, events occurring "outside" an overall control, but which are not therefore entirely meaningless or purposeless.

In contrast to traditionally conceived tactics, then, which may be subsumed under strategy as merely a further, more detailed implementation of the will of the *strategos*, I use the term to denote largely improvisational practices that do not adhere to an overall strategy. The practice of such tactics does not constitute an implementation of control through the comprehensive direction of power; nor does it aim to achieve such control. In fact, such practice constitutes, explicitly or implicitly, a reaction against the autocratic, totalitarian implications of strategy. As Rosinski clearly realizes, his conception of strategy is by no means limited to purely military applications: "Thus, strategy in contrast to haphazard action, is that direction of action which aims at the control of a field of activity be it military, social, or even intellectual. It must be comprehensive in order to control every possible counteraction or factor" (qtd. in Eccles 46). Unfortunately, Rosinski does not link this control to totalitarianism (political or discursive), any more than he develops or even fully articulates the opposition between strategy and improvisation. Precisely these concerns, however, are at the center of Michel de Certeau's study of contemporary society, *The Practice of Everyday Life*.

As de Certeau theorizes it, the distinction between strategy and tactics has considerable generality. By "strategy" he denotes "the calculus of force-relationships which becomes possible when a subject of will and power (a proprietor, an enterprise, a city, a scientific institution) can be isolated from an 'environment.' A strategy assumes a place that can be circumscribed as *proper* (*propre*) and thus serve as the basis for generating relations with an exterior distinct from it (competitors, adversaries, 'clientèles,' 'targets,' or 'objects' of research)" (xix). That is, a strategy is deployed by an external, objective power aiming to control its entire field of operation. So far, de Certeau's chief distinction from Rosinski is in his choice of a more abstract and currently fashionable discourse. As his parentheses suggest, de Certeau applies this model to spheres well beyond the purely military, for, as he says, "political, economic, and scientific rationality has been constructed on this strategic model" (xix). Later he asserts an even higher level of generality: "In sum, strategies are actions which, thanks to the establishment of a place of power (the property of a proper), elaborate theoretical places (systems and totalizing discourses) capable of articulating an ensemble of physical places in which forces are distributed" (38). It is important to note that strategic systems and "totalizing discourses," however remote from the military or political spheres, still articulate and therefore control physical places and actual forces.

In the face of these totalizing discourses, this threatening and overwhelming rationality, human practice relies on the tactic, which de Certeau defines as "a calculus which cannot count on a 'proper' (a spatial or institutional localization), nor thus on a borderline distinguishing the other as a visible totality. The place of a tactic belongs to the other. A tactic insinuates itself into the other's place, fragmentarily, without taking it over in its entirety, without being able to keep it at a distance" (xix). It is precisely characteristic of improvisation to use materials to hand, materials that likely belong to quite distinct systems. De Certeau does not focus on improvisation, but does stress its concomitant, time: "because it does not have a place, a tactic depends on time. . . . Whatever it wins, it does not keep. It must constantly manipulate events in order to turn them into 'opportunities' " (xix). While strategy privileges space, and stable, spatial relations, tactics "gain validity in relation to the pertinence they lend to time" and fleeting temporal relations (38).

Analogous to the strategy-tactics distinction—in fact, what provides a basis for de Certeau's theorization—is the Saussurean distinction between the abstract, systemic *langue* and the concrete, individual speech acts comprising *parole*. We speak within a larger order that we can never transcend, within a discursive space that we can never, ultimately, possess. At best, so the argument runs, we can deconstruct others' pretensions to such possession. But by means of *parole*, by means, that is, of the individual, always improvised speech act, we can fleetingly use that order—which is to say, *any* totalizing discourse—to our own human purposes. Any speech act is a tactic, improvising a combination of elements from various systems (various discourses, and beyond those, extralinguistic systems). (This analogy points to the possibility of a "strategy" that is not imposed from an external point, as no one can manipulate or utter *langue*: a strategy without a *strategos*, one that simply occupies, creates the available space.) Like any other tactic, the speech act is opportunistic, characteristically taking advantage of the "chance" devices afforded by the temporality of language: cadence, rhyme, repetition, consonance, assonance—in short, all the devices generally associated with the poetic dimension of language in contrast to the rational, discursive dimension.

Indeed, poetry may be seen in one sense as consisting largely in the use of such playful devices to disrupt (but not replace or eradicate) the hegemony of rational discourse, ultimately the systemic referentiality of language. As we have seen, Stein uses precisely such disruptive devices to prevent "Reflection on the Atomic Bomb" from being entirely dominated by a discursive argument. In a 1946 "Transatlantic Interview," she explained Cézanne's importance: "up to that time composition had consisted of a central idea" subordinating all else, whereas "Cézanne conceived the idea that in composition one thing was as important as another thing." While other artists "fell down on it, because the supremacy of one interest overcame them," Stein would attempt to give each one—person, thing, word—"the same value" (15–16).[2] We may reflect, too, that a *reflection on* some object is ideally performed by an objective observer, an observer having his own place outside the observed system. Like the act of naming (the sign of Adam's dominion over creation), to reflect on an object is to control and thereby possess it. Stein's refusal to reflect with proper sobriety, her disruption of her own argument *about* (circling, containing) the Bomb, thus marks a perception—perhaps not fully or even consciously articulated—that to attempt to possess the Bomb is to be possessed by it. For the Bomb culminates all—and any—strategy, including that which seeks to dominate it.

*

It is time, then, to turn to the Bomb itself, to consider its significance, to discover what meanings it attracts to itself. First a definition: by "the Bomb" I refer to the possible total annihilation of the human race—and therefore the world—in a nuclear Armageddon, as symbolized so powerfully in the mushroom cloud of any one explosion—Los Alamos, Hiroshima, Nagasaki, and Bikini being the most famous. How probable such annihilation may be, or whether it be initiated purposefully or accidentally, or how it may be effected (by explosion, radiation, starvation, climactic conditions, etc.)—all these are immaterial, for our purposes, to the singular imaginative impact of the present possibility of total destruction. The single, familiar image of the mushroom cloud subsumes particular details. Its power scarcely needs stressing, the image remaining remarkably vivid despite there having been no above-ground tests since the 1963 signing of the Test-Ban treaty. In fact, that treaty can provide a further symbol: as atomic bombs are now detonated in the interior of the earth, so have we internalized the Bomb. Even when not explicit, when not visible, its presence is felt, its effects real.

Historically, the Bomb's effect was both profound and immediately apparent. In 1945, only two weeks after Hiroshima, Norman Cousins proclaimed modern man obsolete in the *Saturday Review of Literature*. Less than a year later Bernard Brodie alluded to that claim in *The Absolute Weapon*, the first book on "atomic power and the world order," when he asserted that most observers, assuming "that war and obliteration are now completely synonymous," believed "that modern man must therefore be either obsolete or fully ripe for the millennium" (21). Brodie intended to establish practical guides for political and military decisions, but the significance of the book's title came to the fore at the beginning of his 1959 study, *Strategy in the Missile Age*. He begins that book by recounting the story of the war in Heaven in Book VI of *Paradise Lost*. After the first day of battle, Satan proposes and then develops new, "more valid Armes, / Weapons more violent" in order to take control of the war. The next day the rebel angels' infernal engines—field guns—threaten to conquer the field, but the loyal angels then use the absolute weapon, the hills of Heaven itself, uprooting them and hurling them at the rebels, who then "in imitation" seize upon the same weapons. The battle of absolute weapons thus threatens "all Heav'n" with wrack and ruin, until God directly intervenes by sending his Son. Christ, of course, casts out Satan and the others without difficulty, restoring order (6.406 ff.; Brodie 3–5).

Although the persistence and centrality of the Armageddon motif in a practically oriented book is striking, Brodie summarizes by drawing a simple analogy: "the war in Heaven dramatizes the chief dilemma which confronts modern man, especially since the coming of the atomic bomb, the dilemma of ever-widening inventions and his social adaptation to them" (4). The dilemma occasioned by the Bomb, however, pertains to the nature of strategy itself. For strategy seeks the maximum force to achieve control; hence wars and arms races constantly escalate. Any strategy thus culminates in the greatest force available, and will further ensure the development of even greater forces. As

Milton evidently foresaw, that force will ultimately prove too great to control, its use resulting in the destruction of both sides together with the territory in question.

There can be no doubt that the Bomb ultimately controls the field; its particular effect stems from the fact that no one controls the Bomb. Even those with power to deploy and use nuclear weapons do not control them, for they are part of the field the Bomb conquers by destroying. Thus a coherent, rational strategy cannot be used to "defeat" the Bomb; we must instead rely on tactics, on opportunistic improvisations that (unlike, say, guerilla warfare) thwart any tendency to become subordinated to an overall strategy. The Bomb thus alters our position relative to strategy, rather than transforming strategy itself. As the readiness and aptness of phrases such as "nuclear Armageddon" and "nuclear apocalypse" suggest, the Bomb affects us not by imposing a radically new structure but by taking control of an already existing structure. The hope of an eventual, but thankfully deferred, spiritual sublimation into the clouds of heaven has been entirely replaced by the threat of immediate, physical sublimation (vaporization) into *the* cloud. Since it can provide human activity with a determinate and valued end, the millennium is useful when perpetually deferred, but its threat overwhelms such use when it becomes a distinct possibility.[3] Implicit in the Bomb, as we will see in Williams' *Spring and All*, is a critique of the apocalyptic tendencies (and related asceticism) of religion.

The Bomb also implies a critique of Western rationality and science. This critique has first an immediate, practical, and familiar dimension. If the Bomb constitutes one of the great demonstrations of the power of rationality, of the ability of science to discover and exploit nature's secrets, then reason and science open themselves to a fundamental questioning as to their value and morality. Following Hiroshima, Milton's classification of science as an infernal art and his caution that humans should not transgress their limits began to seem all too significant. For reason and science can be seen as particularly powerful moves within larger sociopolitical strategies—moves so powerful, in fact, that they come to seem transcendent, somehow "above" or "beyond" more mundane sociopolitical struggles. As La Fontaine commented, "the reason of the stronger is always the best"; Michel Serres, in an article on "Knowledge in the Classical Age," significantly and accurately modifies this remark to "The reason of the strongest is reason *by itself*" (28). Plato's dialectic, after all, begins in public, oral argument and only later moves into the quiet, domestic pursuit of "objective" truth. The rather exaggerated rhetoric of Serres' summary should not obscure the clarity or accuracy of his point: "knowledge is a hunt . . . a strategy. These epistemologies are not innocent: at the critical tribunal they are calling for executions. They are policies promulgated by military strategists" (28). The model of rationality is agonistic both in origin and in context,[4] a strategy within a strategy. Discursive and military strategies are both structurally homologous and functionally equivalent. Within the larger social context, reason and war are equivalent moves, the choice between them determined by strategic effectiveness. But they ultimately coincide in the totality of their final end, the Bomb.

Of course, this latest fruit of the Tree of Knowledge in a sense only replays—"culminates" may be more apt—the original Fall: in a sense the Bomb marks the culmination of the destruction always implicit in science and rationality. Artists have been particularly concerned with this relation at least since Blake attacked Newton. More recently, the Futurists' critique of analytic Cubism was based on precisely this issue: Umberto Boccioni argued that while the Cubist "analysis of the object is always made at the cost of the object itself," the Futurists sought to "identify with the thing, which is profoundly different" (qtd. in Dasenbrock 48). And the account of Williams will be of particular interest in a subsequent chapter. For the moment, though, Heidegger's succinct formulation, not very far at all from Williams' thought in the twenties, can help to orient us: "Science's knowledge, which is compelling within its own sphere, the sphere of objects, already had annihilated things as things long before the atom bomb exploded. The bomb's explosion is only the grossest of all gross confirmations of the long-since-accomplished annihilation of the thing: the confirmation that the thing as a thing remains nil" (170). The Bomb's physical annihilation only confirms the annihilation of the concrete begun by science's necessary abstraction. Conditioned by science—and this is also the thrust of Williams' argument—we no longer perceive the thing as thing, or the person as person. Heidegger in fact demonstrates just such conditioning in his own derogatory reference to the Bomb as a "gross confirmation": he derides the "merely" physical atomic bomb in contrast to the evidently more significant realm of abstraction.

Elsewhere, in a passage particularly relevant to our consideration of strategy and control, Heidegger goes even further. He writes that the atomic bomb, "this particular death-dealing machine," is not itself deadly, for "what has long since been threatening man with death, and indeed with the death of his own nature, is the unconditional character of mere willing in the sense of purposeful self-assertion in everything" (116). Here science is clearly a strategy, deployed by "mere willing" to achieve "self-assertion"—that is, control. And total control for Heidegger is at least figurally equivalent to the Bomb, threatening not merely physical but also—and again, evidently far worse—spiritual death. The danger, then, originates in domination, i.e., strategy, rather than in abstraction, that particular form of strategy. Technology, the Bomb, rationality are all finally seen as aspects of the tendency to strategic totalization: "It is not only the totality of this willing that is dangerous, but willing itself, in the form of self-assertion within a world that is admitted only as will. The willing that is willed by this will is already resolved to take unconditional command. By that resolve, it is even now delivered into the hands of total organization" (117).[5] As noted above, Heidegger's assessment of the Bomb's importance seems determined by precisely the rationality he would attack. Although reason presents dangers apart from the atomic bomb, however, those dangers are fully realized, and fully apparent, only in the Bomb.

Hence, as Derrida acknowledges, "deconstruction, at least what is being advanced today in its name, belongs to the nuclear age," for only by the Bomb's light do the "characteristic structures and historicity" of the various strategies become recognizable ("No Apocalypse" 27). His corollary remark, however, that the Bomb is the "absolute referent" of all discourse, although presenting an opposite evaluation of the Bomb's import, nevertheless succumbs to the same overvaluation of abstraction as Heidegger. The Bomb can indeed provide the absolute referent, temporally as the ultimate End and also as the ultimate Signified that can anchor and close the system of language. No doubt on the psychological level, "lesser" fears and anxieties to some extent derive from the primary fear and anxiety occasioned by the Bomb. But such an assertion merely concedes the field to the Bomb, acknowledging its total strategic control. Having recognized its ultimate dominance, we should withdraw from the absolute, from strategy. For only the systemic *langue*—an abstraction posited for theoretical convenience—makes reference primary and therefore demands, entails, the closure provided by an "absolute referent." In the world of *parole*, of practical tactics, effect is primary, and therefore there are many other signifieds, many other referents. Those referents are closest to "our lives," closest to the practical, human world that stands, from the practitioner's viewpoint, self-sufficiently, without reference to an absolute, strategic End. The significance of the Bomb should be recognized, but not theatricalized.

*

One way we can try to avoid such theatricality is to see the Bomb as a historical process rather than a sudden, single event. Heidegger and Derrida, for all their differences, both see the Bomb as the final step in a long and continuing process, its inaugural moment being conveniently marked by Plato's constitution (and codification) of rational discourse. Since Nietzsche that process has become increasingly visible, leading to the popularity currently enjoyed by deconstruction—a practice of tactical disruptions of discursive strategies. This visibility leads Derrida to assert that "the nuclear epoch is dealt with more 'seriously' in texts by Mallarmé, of Kafka, or Joyce . . . than in present day novels that would offer direct and realistic descriptions of a 'real' nuclear catastrophe" ("No Apocalypse" 27–28). Certainly we can agree that the effects of the Bomb are more *visible* in those and other modernist writers than in many post-Hiroshima works explicitly dealing with the topic. We should recall that "the Bomb" refers to the possibility, the threat, of total annihilation, and that such a possibility may be evident long before it becomes physically practicable—as the long apocalyptic tradition, for instance, can testify, even in a more secular instance like Yeats' "Second Coming" (1921), with its "rough beast" troubling the poet's vision (185). These effects, of course, are foreshadowings from the realms of literature and ideas. As I have suggested above, however, the history of Ideas and the history of States meet and fuse in the Bomb. Politics, philosophy, religion, all strategies attempting maximal control, culminate in the one, pyrrhic expression of such control.

World War I, in any case, provides a more concrete foreshadowing, producing many imaginative effects similar to those produced by the Bomb. Interestingly, H. G. Wells' *The World Set Free*, written just before the war and published in 1914, its first year, details the future development of atomic power and its ability utterly to transform the conduct and character of war. With striking prescience, Wells shows how air power becomes determinant in war, and how war then threatens total destruction. During the first nuclear war, one participant remarks that "the atomic bomb had dwarfed the international issues to complete insignificance . . . to us it seemed quite plain that these bombs and the still greater power of destruction of which they were the precursors might quite easily shatter every relationship and institution of mankind" (146). It is easy to see Wells' dire prophecy as an expression of the ominous forces, the inner strains, that were building toward World War I. Less clear is the actual relation between that war and the Bomb. Although the experience of trench warfare and that of a nuclear war must necessarily be radically distinct, the imaginative effects of the two seem more closely allied. It was, after all, the first that was deemed the Great War, "the war to end all wars," the first war that marked a decisive break with the chivalric codes and genteel traditions, civilian and military, of the nineteenth century.

That rupture had of course several causes. The sheer length and scope of the war combined with its lack of any evident progress to strip away ideals through sheer weariness, a weariness that inevitably focuses on the trenches. After November 1914, when they were established as a 400-mile "line" extending from the coast of Belgium to the Swiss border, the trenches showed little variation—perhaps a few hundred yards, rarely a mile or more—for the next three years (Robbins 34). Paul Fussell has calculated that the actual trenches, including both sides, total about 25,000 miles (37). More significant were the immense numbers of men required to staff those lines (and of course the other "theaters"). In effect, the trenches constituted a large, underground city, akin to the *bolgie* of Dante's Dis, seemingly devoted to no other goal but the extermination of its constantly replenished inhabitants. All these factors contributed to the disillusionment, the sudden impersonality and inauthenticity, that were to characterize the new era.

Eliot's *The Waste Land*, of course, provides the most famous expression of the subsequent psychic desolation. The best work based on actual experience of the trenches, however, is David Jones' *In Parenthesis*, first published with an introduction by Eliot in 1937. In his preface, Jones carefully situates the work in the period from December 1915 to July 1916. The first date marks his arrival in France; the second "roughly marks a change in the character of our lives in the Infantry on the West Front." Jones' characterization of this change is worth quoting in full:

> From then onward things hardened into a more relentless, mechanical affair, took on a more sinister aspect. The wholesale slaughter of the later years, the conscripted levies filling the gaps in every file of four, knocked the bottom out of the intimate, continuing, domestic life of small contingents of men, within whose structure Roland could find, and, for a reasonable while, enjoy, his Oliver. In the earlier months there was a certain attractive amateurishness, an elbow-room for idiosyncrasy that connected one with a less exacting past. The period of the individual rifle-man, of the "old sweat" of the Boer campaign, the "Bairnsfather" war, seemed to terminate with the Somme Battle. There were, of course, glimpses of it long after—all through in fact—but it seemed never quite the same. (ix)

The loss of the intimate, the amateurish, and the idiosyncratic marks the eclipse of the individual in war, and accordingly the eclipse of the tradition, dating back at least to Achilles, of the noble death. Walter Benjamin expressed this shift in terms of a devaluation of individual experience, as a result of which "at the end of the war men returned from the battlefield grown silent—not richer, but poorer in communicable experience" (84). Indeed, the exaggerated, heroic aura surrounding fighter pilots seems a result of the more traditional nature of air battles: freely chosen, one-on-one combat, to those being anonymously shelled or gassed in the trenches, appeared the more glorious because a fantastic relic from a past only recently lost.

Significantly, Jones in his summary shifts attention to technology as he relates the change to the postwar civilian world: "Just as now there are glimpses in our ways of another England—yet we know the truth. Even while we watch the boatman mending his sail, the petroleum is hurting the sea. So did we in 1916 sense a change. How impersonal did each new draft seem arriving each month, and all these new-fangled gadgets to master" (ix). Or, as Benjamin puts it: "A generation that had gone to school on a horse-drawn streetcar now stood under the open sky in a countryside in which nothing remained unchanged but the clouds, and beneath these clouds, in a field of force of destructive torrents and explosions, was the tiny, fragile human body" (84). The vastly more efficient and more impersonal technology of death distinguishes the wars of this century as a whole from earlier conflicts: the machine gun, the tank, gas, the submarine, air warfare, all were invented or dramatically improved during the war. Hector was killed by a mighty blow from a mighty warrior, aimed specifically (and personally) at him as a unique individual; his death therefore earns his enduring name, defines his character, makes him what he *is*. A machine gun or mortar barrage, however, requires very little human effort at the moment of use, and is usually intended for no specific, nameable individual.[6] To judge from the frequency of reference, one of the more horrific details of the Bomb is "the button," the fact that so easy and so apparently insignificant an act as pressing a button could produce such a catastrophe. Moreover, those killed by shelling in the trenches were frequently engaged in harmless, "civilian" activities, not unlike those killed by area bombing in World War II or by atomic bombs in Hiroshima and Nagasaki.

Air power, especially its use to bomb civilians, provides a particularly significant link between World War I and the Bomb. Military analysts and theoreticians have generally seen the Bomb as a continuation of the development of civilian bombing in World War I.[7] In that war, of course, such bombing had little physical effect and no decisive psychological impact. The Germans largely hoped to weaken morale by bombing London, but since the destructive power was quite limited they probably succeeded only in stiffening resolve. Even so, the importance of air power was clear, and strategic bombing became a major part of World War II. The bombings of Hiroshima and Nagasaki, of course, continued the task of strategic bombing with vastly superior weapons, as ballistic missiles were subsequently to provide means of delivery far superior to the airplane. Inherent in the beginning, however, and clearly evident to contemporaries like H. G. Wells, was the possibility of general attack on civilians so devastating as utterly to destroy the basis of social structure. It was also clear that if both sides possessed this capability, war would be unwinnable.

In the light of Derrida's—and for that matter, Heidegger's—"deconstruction" of the Western philosophic tradition, a tradition epitomized in Hegel's philosophy, it is particularly interesting to observe L. T. Hobhouse's response to the bombing of London. A political philosopher and professor of sociology at the University of London, Hobhouse explained the genesis of his *The Metaphysical Theory of the State, A Criticism* (1918) in a dedicatory letter to his son. He asks his son to recall, "across the abyss which separates us all from July 1914," an idyllic time when they read Kant together in a Highgate garden. One morning three years later, Hobhouse continues, he again sat in the garden, this time alone and "annotating Hegel's theory of freedom," when the "jarring sounds" of "our strange new world" announced a bombing raid. When the raid ended, Hobhouse felt inclined to self-ridicule: "was this a time for theorizing or destroying theories, when the world was tumbling about our ears?" But then came the insight that, just as his son fought with the "weapons of the flesh" in the RAF, so he could fight with the "tools and weapons that he [could] use," the "weapons of the spirit," to make the world safe for democracy. For "in the bombing of London I had just witnessed the visible and tangible outcome of a false and wicked doctrine, the foundations of which lay, as I believe, in the book before me" (5–6). Hobhouse does not consider whether his tranquil vision of a scholar's pastoral may itself be partly implicated. Only a short step, though, separates the criticism of the metaphysical theory of the state from the critique of metaphysics. We may conclude that the impact of the Bomb gradually made itself felt, in various areas of life, over the course of the century.

*

This notion of a process, of a gradual impact, remains too vague to be of significant use; nor does it correspond well to the more definite distinction between strategy and tactics. There is, however, a logical structure to the process, two stages of development roughly corresponding to the periods following the two world wars. The first war seems to have compelled recognition that existing strategies in various fields—that is, political, social, economic, and artistic structures—were inadequate, corrupt, or both. The response to this recognition, while of course varying with the individual and the field, was generally not to discard strategy as such but to search for a superior strategy. Only after World War II, when the Bomb presented an actual and definite threat, did the abandonment of strategy in favor of tactics occur. Of course, that abandonment is by no means fully explicit or complete: indeed, after Hiroshima the ideal of world government, for example, enjoyed considerable support, although few in power paid it much heed. But the "decentered multiplicity" of postmodern society would be characterized by the absence of any overall strategy.

No linear causal relationship exists between the two wars and these cultural developments. Rather, a complex network of causal interrelations creates a field of coincident tendencies leading to parallel developments and parallel structures, as the coincidence of Wells' *The World Set Free* and World War I illustrates. Giulio Douhet's development of military strategy can thus provide a useful analogue for developments outside the military sphere. The experience of the largely immobile trenches of World War I convinced Douhet that technology had rendered land offensives impossible: no strategy could be developed that could overpower the defensive position. The Battle of the Somme, which for David Jones marked a decisive change in the character of the war, was the quintessential attempt at a "Big Push." It was later termed the "Great Fuck-Up," its failure demonstrating the futility of Allied (and German) strategy on the Western Front (Fussell 12, 29). Strategy, Douhet reasoned, must therefore turn to a literally higher level, air power. He felt that future wars would be determined entirely by one side's mastery of air and consequent ability to destroy the other side's social structures: "We must therefore resign ourselves to the offensives the enemy inflicts upon us, while striving to put all our resources to work to inflict even heavier ones upon him" (qtd. in Brodie *Strategy* 87). World War II proved that, although Douhet was correct to stress the importance of air power, he overestimated its ability and underestimated the offensive capability of land power. We can see in his argument, however, a clear attempt to develop a greater strategy to replace, or rather subsume, inadequate lesser strategies. That development culminates in the offensive capabilities of the atomic bomb. As Brodie summarizes, Douhet's "framework of strategic thought . . . is peculiarly pertinent to any general war in the nuclear age" (106). Indeed, the theory of nuclear deterrence is largely an extension of Douhet's thought: if both sides possess sufficient offensive air power to annihilate the other, then no offensive strategy can succeed.[8]

The political arguments and speculations of Hobhouse and Wells show a similar tendency. Hobhouse attacks the Hegelian state for its totalitarian aspect, its absolute subordination of the individual to the state, as opposed to the democratic principles of the British and their allies, wherein the state is merely a means to the betterment of "humanity." He insists on "going back from the large generality, the sounding abstraction, the imposing institution, to the human factors which it covers," but he does not advocate a return to anarchic particularities. We cannot "dissolve the fabric," for "men must continue to build, and on deeper foundations and with larger plans" (136). As his conclusion makes clear, Hobhouse criticizes the evidently dangerous strategy of the Hegelian state from the perspective of a greater strategy: "In the democratic view the sovereign state is already doomed, destined to subordination in a community of the world. In the metaphysical view it is the supreme achievement of human organization. For the truth let the present condition of Europe be witness" (137). The implicit ideal of a world government was popular at the time, though perhaps more so at the beginning of the war than at the end, when simple "peace" seemed enough to hope for. Wells proposed a similar solution in *The World Set Free*. The atomic war Wells envisions is called "the last war" because its extraordinary danger ultimately frees the world from war, first destroying existing sociopolitical structures and then forcing the creation of a new, greater structure to prevent any recurrence of war.[9]

The same line of reasoning led to the Great War's being termed "the war to end all wars" (Robbins 22). Unlike the Bomb, which threatens to end war by annihilating those who would participate, World War I would end war by uniting all in a common world—or so the optimistic thought. Indeed, that end seemed to many the only possible justification for the conflict—as many historians have indicated, the participating governments seemed to lose all sense of objective other than the nebulous, and to some extent purely honorary, "victory."[10] In another book published in 1914, this one a propagandistic essay called *The War That Will End War*, Wells distinguished between the cause of the war—"our honor and our pledge obliged us"—and the objects of the war, peace and disarmament. The war, he says, "aims at a settlement that shall stop this sort of thing for ever" (14). In his concluding chapter Wells goes so far as to assert that "this monstrous conflict in Europe, the slaughtering, the famine, the confusion, the panic and hatred and lying pride, it is all of it real only in the darkness of the mind. At the coming of understanding it will vanish as dreams vanish at awakening" (106). Such thoughts may have helped Wells to deal with the war; they seem unlikely to have comforted those in the trenches. In any case, we can see in both Hobhouse and Wells a tendency to reexamine and reevaluate the recent past—in Hobhouse's case extending back to Kant and the eighteenth century—in order to discover the source of error and then develop a new strategy. The Second World War, however, confirmed the inadequacy of attempts to derive and implement a "grand strategy" for the elimination of war, and thereby confirmed the real lack of purpose of the First.

In literature this framework corresponds, as I suggested above, to the distinction between modernism and postmodernism. Formally the works of modernism are characterized by a dissatisfaction with existing structures (strategies like the traditional lyric, epic, or novel), a dissatisfaction expressed in their fragmentation and evident play with the conventions of form. Pound's concern to "break" the pentameter, intimately related to his fragmentation of the traditional epic, should be considered part of a whole field of such concerns, a dissatisfaction with that moribund stasis of tradition most vividly symbolized by the trenches (*C* 81:518). The works of Eliot, Joyce, Pound, Jones, and others all reflect attempts to get at the basis of the problem by reconsidering the bases of existing strategies of art, thought, and discourse. Like Hobhouse's rejection of the sovereign state, however, modernist experiments do not stop at fragmentation. They follow it with reunification, attempting finally to develop a new and larger strategy that would revitalize art and society. Where *Ulysses*, in its refusal of traditional, seemingly self-evident structures, to some contemporaries appeared confused and confusing, perhaps bordering on schizophrenia, to Eliot—and us—it reaffirms a greater order.[11] Writing at the end of the twenties, Williams noted a twofold movement in modernism: the "violent torsions" of writers like Stein and Joyce are intended to "divorce words from the enslavement of the prevalent clichés" in a critical moment, whereupon "words used with a broader sweep of understanding" will function as restoration: "Nothing but poetry can readjust the understanding (sold to books) to a reasonable view of the world" (*EK* 143). We should of course understand "clichés" in a very broad sense here, not only as the symptoms of a moribund structure (or "understanding"), but also as the structure itself. Thus the modernists characteristically rejected their immediate past and searched the Western tradition for earlier formal conventions (the metrical and formal experiments of Pound and Eliot) and still earlier, mythic structures, out of which to formulate a new strategy or formal architecture—a word particularly appropriate for its sense of enclosure—for the modern world.[12]

That search for a greater strategy, a great architecture, finds thematic expression in the modernists' attitudes toward the history of Europe, in their diverse attempts to recreate Western culture and society. Their internationalism—indicated by the ease with which we can speak of a concern for *European* culture—suggests their dissatisfaction with narrow cultural nationalism.[13] Pound, an obvious example, seeks clues to a firmer basis for society in many earlier cultures, but he generally finds them in the early Renaissance (e.g., Malatesta's Rimini) and the Middle Ages (Provençe, Dante's Florence)—significantly, the two most important sources outside those periods, Kung and Jefferson, are also outside Europe. Though never as didactic as Pound, Joyce implies in his works (especially *Ulysses*) and elsewhere explicitly states a preference for the medieval over later culture.[14] Thomist modes of thought influenced more than merely his esthetic. Eliot's famous credo, "classicist in literature, royalist in politics, and anglo-catholic in religion" virtually speaks for itself, indicating clearly his affinities for the Renaissance and his rejection of all those cultural developments that might be supposed to have led to the modern world (*For Lancelot Andrews* Preface). Williams' rejection of Europe, as we will see, is more total and more programmatic; in many respects World War I proved forceful enough to propel him into the postmodern world. Notable, however, is his interest in specific Renaissance individuals like Botticelli,

Brueghel, and Shakespeare. In general, the modernists rejected the recent history of Europe in order to reestablish culture on the firmer ground of earlier (Medieval and Renaissance) but still largely European bases.

The formal and thematic concerns of the modernists are thus intimately related, each in fact necessary to the other. Indeed, the drive for a greater, more all-inclusive strategy implies a search for a higher integration of form and content. James McFarlane has recently drawn attention to this aspect of modernism: "The very vocabulary of chaos—disintegration, fragmentation, dislocation—implies a breaking away or a breaking apart. But the defining thing in the Modernist mode is not so much that things fall *apart* but that they fall *together* (recalling appropriately the derivation of 'symbol' from *symballein*, to throw together). In Modernism, the centre is seen exerting not a centrifugal but a centripetal force; and the consequence is not disintegration but (as it were) superintegration" (92). Finding the difficult center and then building on that basis a greater strategy—these are the driving impulses behind the modernist enterprise. Pound's lament in the late Cantos proclaims his failure to achieve these goals, established early in his career. Not until after the Second World War and the actuality of the Bomb do we find a general rejection of both the search for a center and the attempt at a superior strategy. That rejection is expressed formally in a refusal of totalizing structures and thematically in a much greater concern with non-Western (Eastern and "primitive") cultures—an acknowledgment of the limits of the West's ability to subsume other cultures.

*

As my sketch of the larger context suggests, many other writers could have been included in the discussion that follows: aside from those already mentioned, a number of other modern and postmodern writers could convincingly be included. Obviously discussion has to be more limited to be meaningfully specific. The choice of Pound, Williams, and Zukofsky is no doubt based partly on personal predilection, but there are other reasons. First, the very nature of their enterprises intimately involves them in the opposition between strategy and tactics. All three writers attempt sweeping visions of society and the world, and struggle to embody those visions in major forms—the *Cantos, Paterson, "A"*—that are necessarily implicated in strategy. Yet all three are deeply concerned with the implications of strategy, and are committed to developing alternatives—to a considerable extent by means of formal innovation, both large and small scale. This inescapable duality of focus, on strategy and on the critique of strategy, on large social issues and on details of syntax, makes Pound, Williams, and Zukofsky particularly significant to our understanding of the relation between the modern and the postmodern. This is especially the case, of course, with Pound, whose political involvement with fascism has been much discussed, but whose poetics, especially in the late works, has also had a considerable influence on later, left-leaning writers—including, of course, Zukofsky. The relation between his politics and his poetics will therefore warrant special attention here.

The three writers also provide a convenient means of gradually shifting attention away from military wars and away from the subgenre of war poetry, in which war is primarily a theme rather than a focus of formal innovation. Where Pound's early Cantos are obviously intimately related to World War I, and the Pisans arise directly from Pound's wartime involvement and postwar incarceration, Williams' works instance a greater distance from and refraction of the two world wars, and Zukofsky, too young to have been impelled by World War I—modernism had already been accomplished—shows a similar distance from World War II, along with a greater explicit understanding of the theoretical issues involved in postmodern poetics. As we move from the modern to the postmodern, we also move from the narrow domain of war poetry toward an agonistic understanding of the interaction among distinct discourses, or voices, in contemporary society. How to develop a harmony of such distinct voices, with no one voice subsuming all others, is a problem critical to these writers, and increasingly to contemporary society. Thus Pound writes of "the liberty of the individual in the ideal and fascist state," wherein "a thousand candles together blaze with intense brightness," and "no one candle's light damages another's" (*SP* 306). As Zukofsky proposes, however, the voices need not be dominated by a rigid order: "to the ear / Noises. / Or harmony" ("*A*" 231).

Finally, the three writers, for all their divergences—social, historical, and political—were to a considerable extent involved in a common enterprise, a struggle not merely to make new poems, but to transform their culture and society. Pound and Williams, of course, have long been linked in this manner, but increasing attention is now being paid to the long literary and personal friendships between Zukofsky and Pound and between Zukofsky and Williams. In 1927, when Zukofsky submitted "Poem Beginning 'The' " to Pound's *Exile* magazine, he and Pound began an extensive correspondence that continued, despite their political differences, through the thirties. Pound even sent Zukofsky money to help pay for the younger poet's 1933 trip to Europe, later dedicating his *Guide to Kulchur* to Zukofsky and Basil Bunting. Zukofsky's friendship with Williams began with Pound's introduction in 1928, the year Zukofsky began "*A*", and continued until Williams' death in 1963. Their close literary relation, based on mutual respect and support, was highlighted by

Zukofsky's extensive editing of Williams' *The Wedge* and his 1963 tribute to
Williams in "A"-17, "A Coronal For Floss."[15]

Particularly interesting from our perspective is Williams' review of Zukofsky's 1946 booklet, *Anew*. In "A New Line is a New Measure," Williams
bestows high praise on Zukofsky's work, declaring with an urgency perhaps
impelled by the recent war that Zukofsky's new line marks a vital breakthrough in his own search for a new measure. Williams' sense of "measure,"
of course, goes far beyond the realm of prosody; it is integral to his hope for a
new stance toward, or participation in, the world. Zukofsky's line constitutes
a revolution that could transform society, a discovery akin to the splitting of
the atom: "in a single poem the world can be shattered to bits," even though
the world "will not realize it for a hundred years" (*SS* 162). But this destructive
power, like that of the new nuclear physics, could also release a tremendous
creative power: "a revolution in the line, maintained by first-rate work, gives
a chance for vast revisions that potentially penetrate the very bases of knowledge and open up fields that might be exploited for a century. It is the key the
true key that will really turn a lock, the toughest lock there is. The poetic line
can be the key opening a *way* to learning, the hidden implement which could,
once learned and supported by great *work*, poems, make knowledge work—
though it lies in a stasis now" (164). *Anew* thus provides "a fleck of the bright
future," with which "a whole can again be imagined and the music picks up
again" (165). The war and immediate postwar years in fact saw a major shift
in Zukofsky's poetics, as he progressed from "A"-8 (1938) to "A"-12 (1950).
When we consider also the striking achievements of Pound's Pisan Cantos
(1948) and of Williams' own *Paterson*, we can better understand the urgency
and enthusiasm of Williams' claim to "hear a new music of verse stretching out
into the future" (165). That new music signaled a remarkable breakthrough in
the search for a new poetics, the search for new esthetic and new social forms,
to which the three writers had for decades devoted themselves. The development of a tactical poetics was thus the first step in the development of new
orders of knowledge, concomitants of a new social and political world that
would derive from tactical practices rather than from a single strategic order.

*

My own strategy, the structure I propose here of a shift from strategy to
tactics roughly coincident with the two world wars and constitutive of the shift
from modernism to postmodernism, is not intended to be absolute. To take
only one instance, the disruptive tactics we have observed in Gertrude Stein's
"Reflection on the Atomic Bomb" were used long before, finding early development in *Matisse, Picasso and Gertrude Stein* and full expression in works like

Tender Buttons and *Stanzas in Meditation*.[16] Also, such writers as Joyce, Pound, Woolf, Moore, Eliot, and Williams—not to mention the many other modernists—obviously do not espouse a party line in their distinct attitudes toward Europe and European history. Nor do I wish to subsume the striking diversity of postmodern writing under a single thesis, although I suspect that postmodernism may be in some respects more homogeneous than is commonly believed. Rather, I seek to provide a structure around which to organize, and thereby improve understanding of, the development of modernism into postmodernism. The structure also provides a means of understanding formal literary developments in relation to their social context, thereby freeing us from excessive reliance on overt, thematic statements. We will discover, in fact, a complex relation between form and theme—sometimes coincident, sometimes contrasting, always mutually conditioning. The structure, then, is not purely strategic, but exemplifies a tactical adoption of a strategy, a useful aid. In what follows it provides a reference and a guide, but we should not subordinate the various authors and works to a strategy as dominating and constrictive as those they sought to escape. The strategy of inquiry should find both its beginning and its end in the diverse practices of "our lives," here the diverse, singular practices of Pound, Williams, and Zukofsky.

2

Pound's War

This is my war all right, I have been in it for 20 years.
My Grandad was in it before me.

—Pound, 1942

The Great War and the Enemy

POUND'S WAR? We could as well speak of war's Pound, so caught up (and, in the end, so mastered) did he become. Reflecting on World War I in 1934—well before the frenzy of Rome Radio—he could write that "the real trouble with war (modern war) is that it gives no one a chance to kill the right people," the calm tone accenting the brutality of his assertion (*GB* 140). Such a statement—and there are others—may seem at a great remove from the largely esthetic battles that had earlier engaged Pound, and from the largely esthetic context in which his work has most often been considered. Yet it reflects accurately the critical importance of war to Pound's work, from World War I through World War II and beyond. The coincidence of the chronology, indeed, has long been noted. Before the first war, Pound had produced a few highly wrought, beautiful but slight lyrics, and some interesting but only in retrospect significant manifestos and esthetic musings. Within ten years of the first hostilities Pound had produced several masterpieces—the poems of *Cathay* (1915), "Homage to Sextus Propertius" (1919), "Hugh Selwyn Mauberley" (1920), and *A Draft of XVI Cantos* (1915–1923). We could add two of Pound's most significant critical statements, *Gaudier-Brzeska: A Memoir* (1916) and his edition of Ernest Fenollosa's *The Chinese Written Character as a Medium for Poetry* (1918). Following *A Draft of XXX Cantos* in 1930, however, *The Cantos* weakened (though there are bright spots, and though the material is of considerable importance) until the events of World War II produced another masterpiece, the *Pisan Cantos*.

The Great War's immediate, personal impact on Pound has also been well documented and remarked. The Great English Vortex, which seemed so active and so promising of future action on the eve of the war, dissolved in the face of other concerns; first Henri Gaudier-Brzeska and then Wyndham Lewis left London (and Pound) for the front; and Gaudier-Brzeska died in action when he seemed on the verge of great work. In 1918 Pound proclaimed Gaudier-Brzeska's death the arts' greatest single war loss, but interestingly also ascribed other, "peaceful" deaths to the war: Remy de Gourmont, Henry James, and Claude Debussy "must all be counted among war losses, for in each case their lives were indubitably shortened by war-strain" (*GB* 136). Pound's intense sense of loss, of particular lives and of the cultural potential of a whole era, was to remain with him for decades.[1]

But war is not simply an extraneous spur to Pound's esthetic or literary pursuits; his personal struggles are not taken up incidentally by a poetry essentially autonomous, engaged in other pursuits. In fact, Pound's first piece of art criticism, long before World War I, had been "a freshman theme" on Paolo Uccello's "battle picture," *The Battle of San Romano*, and if at the time he felt "largely attracted" by the medieval, we may assume that the battle itself at least contributed to his fascination—indeed, Pound's interest in the medieval period would seem inseparable from the attractions of war (*VA* 305). Even as the Great War spurred a transformation in technology as the combatants sought to develop more effective weapons, so did it effect a remarkable transformation in Pound's work. As contemporaries noted, the poems in *Blast* 1 (1914), despite Pound's theoretical advances, are embarrassingly old-fashioned compared to the work of the other Vorticists. During the war Pound's practice finally began to catch up to and fulfill his theory, to a great extent because the war spurred a significant reorientation of his aims. Where before they had been vague, largely esthetic, and only ambiguously connected to society, the war occasioned a new urgency that in turn greatly increased the specificity, scope, and significance of his enterprise. In its various manifestations, and of course mediated by Pound's own imaginative structuring, war was integral to his work, both forming and informing it. We need to consider not merely the effect of war on Pound's themes, but more importantly the varying but intimate relation between agonistics and his poetics. It will be worth considering in some detail, then, how World War I helped to structure his aims and consequently his poetics.

*

Curiously, Pound's immediate written response to the Great War was minimal—curious because the London artists' wars had been so much on his mind in 1914. In February 1914 he wrote that the artist, a humanist only out of reaction to the placid society around him, had "at last been aroused to the fact that the war between him and the world is a war without truce. That his only rem-

edy is slaughter"—and, lest we too quickly dismiss this last claim as hyperbole, that "this is a mild way to say it" (*VA* 180). In June, just before *Blast* 1
appeared, he wrote that in Wyndham Lewis' work "one finds not a commen-
tator but a protagonist . . . a man at war" (*VA* 188). Other, less extreme martial
references are frequent in Pound's writings in this period. No doubt the influence of Lewis, who would later refer to himself as "the Enemy," is evident
here, but the esthetic wars were real enough: to cap his ongoing struggles
against W. C. Williams, against "Amygism," and against the London publishing establishment, Pound was actually refused access to the prestigious (and
paying) *Quarterly Review* because of his association with so disreputable a magazine as the Vorticists' *Blast* (*LE* 357–58). And then there is *Blast* itself, largely
the creation of Lewis, but with considerable input from Pound. The magazine's
title strikingly prefigures the great blast to come, while the contents produce
the effect of a frenetic battlefield, assaulting and disorienting any who would
enter the fray. To be sure, artistic manifestos of the period are generally aggressive and antagonistic. In the pages of *Blast*, however, esthetic declamations
function as random artillery barrages—not so much advancing a position as
rendering any position untenable. It is perhaps to be expected that the magazine's first issue would offer a variety of incommensurable and even incompatible statements by individual artists, but *Blast* goes beyond this acknowledgment of internal diversity to present not one but two "general" manifestos of
the movement, thereby thwarting any attempt to fix Vorticism in a single place,
a proper place. And while it is of course significant that the second *Blast* manifesto, to which Pound was a signatory, attempts to define Vorticism through
an extended series of war metaphors, the relation to war those metaphors suggest is more subversive than the straightforward adoption of a position opposed to societal (or esthetic) norms. The manifesto does not really present a
Vorticist position; rather, it embodies Vorticism as a field of agonistics, irreducible to any single order. The Vorticists will use as their starting point "opposite
statements of a chosen world"; they advocate no cause because their "*Cause* is
NO-MAN's"; and they will therefore "fight first on one side, then on the
other," as "Primitive Mercenaries in the Modern World." The Vorticist, then,
is characterized by an absence of position, an embrace of and participation in
a field of turbulence, characterized by diverse, constantly shifting, vectors of
intention. Or we could say that the intent shifts as soon as it becomes know-
able—for the Vorticist, predictability is synonymous with entrapment. Hence
the emphasis throughout *Blast*, as in Pound's own Vorticist writing, on speed,
on the "constant rush" of ideas, and on the image as a transient, vortical node
of vectoral energies rather than a settled achievement or point of contemplation
(*GB* 92).

Appropriate to *Blast*'s aggressive tone, the first section ends with a barrage attacking both a soporific society and traditional concepts of comedy and tragedy:

(8) We set Humour at Humour's throat. Stir up Civil War among peaceful apes.

(9) We only want Humour if it has fought like Tragedy.

(10) We only want Tragedy if it can clench its side-muscles like hands on its belly, and bring to the surface a laugh like a bomb. (*Blast* 1, 31)

This rhetoric is not deployed in service of a specific policy; rather than seek to procure agreement with a specific position, it seeks to demolish the possibility of position, the possibility of remaining a "peaceful ape," displacing the space of conceptual discourse with its own explosive, atopic power. As Gilles Deleuze and Felix Guattari observe in their discussion of the "war machine," "linear displacement, from one point to another, constitutes the relative movement of the tool, but it is the vortical occupation of a space that constitutes the absolute movement of the weapon" (397). Unlike parody, satire, or irony, which are deployed as means to specific ends, *Blast*'s manifesto inhabits its own disruptive space. The speed of *Blast*'s laugh is precisely the absolute of the weapon—the absolute of the tactic, of *agon* apart from *strategos*.[7]

In *Blast* 2, the July 1915 "War Number," Lewis continues at this velocity. His essays deal with the war almost exclusively, deploying an at times brilliant humor. One essay on empire and war, for example, ends: "I fear that War won't go. It will be the large communities that make war so unmanageable, unreal and unsatisfactory, that will go. Or at least they will be modified for those ends" (*Blast* 2, 16). Elsewhere, in his "WYNDHAM LEWIS VORTEX No.1," he belies the cliché of his subtitle, "BE THYSELF," by again attacking the desirability of achieving a secure position: "You must talk with two tongues, if you do not wish to cause confusion. . . . You must catch the clearness and logic in the midst of contradictions: *not* settle down and snooze on an acquired, easily possessed and mastered, satisfying shape" (91). In this article, too, Lewis specifies the necessity of speed, but also presages Deleuze and Guattari's interest in nomads—"you must also learn, like a Circassian horseman, to change tongues in mid-career without falling to Earth"—and in machinic formations: "You can establish yourself . . . as a Machine of two similar fraternal surfaces overlapping. . . . Any machine then you like: but become mechanical by fundamental *dual* repetition." Deleuze and Guattari's writings on the "war machine" are particularly relevant to the general tendency, if not the eventuality, of the Great English Vortex. I would argue that Lewis' preference for his own "very intense and vertiginous Peace" over the superficial involvement in "regular military War" of F. T. Marinetti and the Italian Futurists in fact constitutes an early formulation of the "war machine" in contrast to the war state (26).

Pound's response to the Great War, however, is quiet and curiously distant. His three articles, concentrating on esthetic and narrowly cultural issues, in context seem rather precious, as he himself was perhaps aware (*SL* 69). His only direct reference to the discords of war is incidental to a defense of the discords of *Blast* 1: "while all the other periodicals were whispering PEACE in one tone or another . . . 'BLAST' alone dared to present the actual discords of modern 'civilization,' DISCORDS now only too apparent in the open conflict between teutonic atavism and unsatisfactory Democracy" (*Blast* 2, 85–86). Even *Blast*'s agonistics must be legitimated as a representation of the contemporary world—and the quotation marks around "civilization" mark Pound's disapproval of modernity's vertiginous peace. The passage does show his dissatisfaction with simple explanations of the cause of the war in terms of German aggression, and in the reference to "unsatisfactory democracy" we can see Pound trying to continue his artistic wars in this new context. Earlier, in a letter to H. L. Mencken, he had spoken of the war as "possibly a conflict between two forces almost equally detestable. Atavism, and the loathsome spirit of mediocrity cloaked in graft." The war may therefore be only "a stop gap . . . only a symptom of the real disease" (*SL* 46–47). His reluctance to make elaborate, explicit statements concerning the war, then, suggests his sense of a complex enormity with which he could not yet come to terms: as he confessed to Mencken, "one does not know; the thing is too involved" (*SL* 46). Pound does not attempt to confront the war directly, in part because he recognizes that it would probably defeat him.

Pound's poems, moreover, seem strikingly remote from the vertiginal agonistics of vorticism—in one poem he declares his intent to "cling to the spar" among the "insidious modern waves" of civilization, the vortex evidently being a turbulence to be undergone, not savored. And although he attacks those who would make him "a model of literary decorum," his protest must wrap its vulgarity in the decorum of French: "Merde!" (*Blast* 2, 22). Pound did attempt a Vorticist treatment of the war in *Blast* 2, in his "Dogmatic Statement on the Game and Play of Chess: Theme for a Series of Pictures." This poem marks a violent (if temporary) departure from his customary style. Its most striking feature, however, is its extreme refraction of the war. It distances itself from any direct contact first through chess, and then through painting. We are to imagine paintings (hanging in a safe gallery) of chess games, which in turn serve as rather traditional and reductive symbols of war. Pound uses short, disjointed phrasal units to convey movement and violence—

Whirl, centripetal, mate, King down in the vortex:
Clash, leaping of bands, straight strips of hard colour,
Blocked lights working in, escapes, renewing of contes[t]
(*Blast* 2, 19)

—but he does so within a framework that promises to keep that violence stylized and well controlled. In fact, the title of the poem (later altered) presents a further refraction, through William Caxton's 1475 *The Game and Playe of the Chesse*. Pound evidently required an extraordinary degree of insulation to approach the war at all.

The 1915 *Cathay*, too, though much more successful than "The Game of Chess," remains distant. As Henri Gaudier-Brzeska exclaimed from the trenches, and as critics have agreed, Pound's Chinese renditions "depict our situation in a wonderful way" (*GB* 58). Yet the poems reflect nothing of what is distinct about modern war, about World War I; they instead invoke eternal verities of war: the wives' loneliness, friends' sorrow at parting, the soldiers' feelings of displacement and loss. The poems do present a vague sense of individuals being caught up in the machinery of much larger sociopolitical events, but those events are shaped by individuals—powerful and distant, but still individuals. The "Song of the Bowmen of Shu," for example, laments the hardship and inequity of war, yet deploys an elegant, noble rhetoric to do so:

We have no rest, three battles a month.
By heaven, [the general's] horses are tired.
The generals are on them, the soldiers are by them.
The horses are well trained, the generals have ivory arrows and quivers
    ornamented with fish-skin.
The enemy is swift, we must be careful.
When we set out, the willows were drooping with spring,
We come back in the snow,
We go slowly, we are hungry and thirsty,
Our mind is full of sorrow, who will know of our grief?
(*P* 127)

Pound's vision of war is strikingly unaffected by the actualities of World War I, by the qualitative difference effected by modern technology. Sorrowful as his bowmen are, they are heroic actors, not "tiny, fragile human bod[ies]" merely placed "in a field of force of destructive torrents and explosions," as Walter Benjamin described the actuality of trench warfare. A number of works in *Blast* 2, such as Wadsworth's "War-Engine" and Lewis' cover design, did in fact present the impersonality of the vortical machinery of modern war. In Lewis' work, in particular, anonymous human figures seem constituted by the lines of force that make up the picture, and the battle. Pound, on the other hand, seems to remain committed to Paolo Uccello's vision of war: a ferocious angularity that still provides a background for striking, powerful individuals. Indeed, *Cathay*'s feudal settings evoke a rather romanticized image of the medieval period, an image that is protected from Pound's (and his readers') knowledge of the realities of medieval Europe by its displacement to the East. A good part of the poems' attraction stems not from their accuracy but from this nostalgic evocation of a vanished world, an evocation all the more poignant because a relic of precisely that world being destroyed by the "relentless, mechanical affair" of World War I (Jones ix).[3] Although the past may prove interesting, significant, and useful, even Pound must have recognized that it was unlikely to prove sufficient to solve the problems of the present.

These and other poems, then, show Pound wanting to deal with the war but tentative, unable as yet to develop a clear approach, and evidently without any clear sense of the war's scope or significance. Rather than be overcome by the war in direct confrontation, Pound engaged it at considerable remove, both through the refractions of *Cathay* and through his esthetic researches: although Pound's work on troubadours or "Elizabethan Classicists" may seem unrelated to the war, it was not entirely a refuge, for it comprised research into forms of social life he believed to be completely opposed to war—at the same time, of course, that his heroes, Bertrand de Born, Sigismundo Malatesta, and even Wyndham Lewis, were definitively men of war. While Lewis countered facile propaganda with his acerbic prose, deftly forging an appositive resistance, a negation of the negation, Pound sought a more socially acceptable (and perhaps more viable) response: he sought, in short, to secure a position of his own. This he attempted to realize by uncovering the deeper causes of, and intimate relation between, political and esthetic wars.

Eventually, of course, Pound was to settle on economics as the primary cause, hindering the progress of the arts and promoting war. What I am interested in here, however, is less Pound's eventual solution than the causes of his avidity and tenacity in championing that solution, causes that predate the economic obsession and that are more directly related to the war. Indeed, Pound's response to the war may conveniently be divided between a quasi-scientific analysis of causation, which centered on the Douglasite economics he discovered in 1918–19, and a more heuristic, mythological comprehension all the more powerful because never fully articulated or even acknowledged by Pound himself. In part Pound does not articulate that mythic background because it was embedded in the times: the wartime imagery of hell, of Armageddon, and of an eventual perpetual peace was powerful enough to exert considerable influence, yet common enough to do so without explicit formulation. Pound's artistic *milieu* was particularly rife with apocalyptic rhetoric: consider the Dadaists' destructive impulses, the Futurists' glorification of war, the Vorticists' own *Blast*. Pound's remarkable veneration of scientific method and his intense dislike of Christianity no doubt combine to blind him to these elements of a mythic narrative that, as we will see, clearly draws on the Christian apocalyptic.

Specific references to the apocalypse surface sporadically in Pound's prose of the period, but if individual instances seem occasional, that very casualness, coupled with the increasing urgency and purpose of the prose, indicates the pervasiveness of the apocalyptic narrative. Thus "Armageddon" itself is used of the war in a 1917 series of articles, "Provincialism the Enemy," where Pound laments the lack of attention paid to Henry James' "prevision" of German "general pervasiveness" in a piece that had been printed "in '83, thirty-one years before Armageddon" (*SP* 190). In an immediately postwar review of Joyce's *A Portrait of the Artist as a Young Man*, Pound defends Joyce from the charge of obscenity by arguing, "if Armageddon has taught us anything it should have taught us to abominate the half-truth, and the tellers of the half-truth, in literature" (*PJ* 139). Significant in both cases is precisely the lack of any dramatic gesturing: Pound is not raising his voice, not deploying exaggerated rhetoric to make some point about the magnitude of the war; rather, the war as Armageddon is simply a reference point, accepted as a given, in the course of another argument. The longed-for "millennium" also appears sporadically, for instance in the "Provincialism the Enemy" series (which we will shortly examine in more detail), and shortly thereafter in a letter to Williams ("the fuckin' millenium that we all idiotically look for and work for").[4] Throughout there is Pound's sense, religious if not Christian, that the war is not simply "detestable," "loathsome," or "diseased," but "evil and uncanny," a malevolence with supernatural overtones (*VA* 129).

The two modes, of reasoned analysis and apocalyptic narrative, enter into an uneasy alliance in Pound's thought and poetry, with the mythologic constituting an unstable but powerful "background" logic—a controlling logic—for Pound's specific historical and economic researches. Toward the end of the war, after Gaudier-Brzeska's death and Wyndham Lewis' enlistment, Pound's views became more clearly defined, and we can see the two modes developing side by side, even in what purports to be a discussion of the merits of stylistic clarity. In a February 1917 review of Joyce's *Portrait*, Pound relates the "Irish trouble" directly to a lack of clear, direct prose. Echoing Flaubert's claim that "if they had read my 'Education Sentimentale' these things would not have happened" (qtd. in *SP* 189), Pound declares that "if more people had read *The Portrait* and certain stories in Mr. Joyce's *Dubliners* there might have been less recent trouble in Ireland" (*PJ* 90). As he explains in some detail, bad prose is also one of the two main causes of the European war:

> It is very important that there should be good prose. The hell of contemporary Europe is caused by the lack of representative government in Germany, *and* by the non-existence of decent prose in the German language. Clear thought and sanity depend on clear prose. They cannot live apart. . . . The mush of the German sentence, the straddling of the verb out to the end, are just as much a part of the befoozlement of Kultur and the consequent hell, as was the rhetoric of later Rome the seed and the symptom of the Roman Empire's decadence and extinction. A nation that cannot write clearly cannot be trusted to govern, nor yet to think. . . . Only a nation accustomed to muzzy writing could have been led by the nose and bamboozled as the Germans have been by their controllers. (*PJ* 90)

The last sentence in fact implies that the lack of representative government is incidental to, or perhaps dependent on, the problem of poor prose: with good prose, the people would almost inadvertently become their own "controllers." The argument from linguistic structure is rather strained, however, since linguistic "mush" would seem characteristic of any inflected language, including Latin (which Pound perhaps intends to imply) and Greek (which seems an unlikely target). And the mention of representative government seems merely a concession to popular opinion: Pound is evidently far more interested in the necessity of good, clear prose. Indeed, the ideal of representative government to some extent conflicts with Pound's conviction that the arts are not democratic.

The reference to the political situation is nevertheless significant, for it establishes a parallelism that makes Pound's subsequent remarks on the problem of prose—which in fact betray the influence of the apocalyptic narrative—more readily acceptable. According to Pound, the problem is not caused by the innate difficulty of attaining clarity, but rather the active, willed malevolence of individuals: "The terror of clarity is not confined to any one people. The obstructionist and the provincial are everywhere, and in them alone is the permanent danger to civilization" (*PJ* 90–91). As the people are absolved of responsibility for their leaders' political acts because poor prose has muddied their thought, so are they absolved of responsibility for poor prose. This ascription of the problem to the will of particular individuals derives a specific, deliberate enemy from what is evidently a broader social problem, providing an early instance of Pound's general tendency to ascribe systemic problems to individual will. The obstructionist and the provincial do not, in fact, represent specific individuals, but an impersonal, universalized enemy—soon to become an invisible coterie, characterized by the use of subterfuge and sabotage. The hyperbole of the last clause gives a mythological sweep to what had begun in the guise of a reasoned analysis of causation. That we move from "the hell of contemporary Europe"—which became "Armageddon" in a later review of the novel—to the final "permanent danger to civilization" argues that the last phrase is not merely a rhetorical flourish, but affords a glimpse of the submerged apocalyptic animating the entire passage.

The conjunction of apocalyptic narrative and reasoned analysis continues to develop in "Provincialism the Enemy," an important series that ran in *The New Age* from July 11 to August 2, 1917, and which drew its epigraph and recurrent theme from the same statement by Flaubert paraphrased in the review of Joyce's *Portrait*. As the title indicates, the series focuses on the means of combatting the "enemy" already identified in the earlier review. Pound begins with a definition of his key term, in an analytic, almost scholastic manner: "PROVINCIALISM consists in: (a) An ignorance of the manners, customs and nature of people living outside one's own village, parish, or nation. (b) A desire to coerce others into uniformity" (*SP* 189). He now supplies the obstructionist with a motive, the control of others, and subsumes him to provincialism: who but a provincial would desire uniformity? Provincialism thus consists, rather confusedly, in both ignorance and the desire for power, for control, that enforces ignorance. This confusion, however, is undoubtedly useful, since it allows the deployment of invective against both malevolence and ignorance. In any case, the provincial is essentially destructive: consciously or unconsciously, he thwarts the development of culture in peace and works to destroy culture in war.

Pound goes on to specify the workings of Provincialism, its means of propagation. First is the Germanic university system, which compartmentalizes humanity and subjugates individuality: "entirely apart from any willingness to preach history according to the ideas of the Berlin party, or to turn the class room into a hall of propaganda, the whole method of this German and American higher education was, is, evil, a perversion" (*SP* 191). The analysis here is particularly important: first he discards the "surface" cause—specific individual or group—in favor of a "deeper" systemic cause, but then he describes the systemic problem as a "perversion," an "evil"—with the implication that individuals, themselves evil and inhuman, are responsible for this perversion. Pound identifies the ideas of man as slave of the state (which "has worked on the masses") and man as slave of learning (which "has worked on the 'intellectual' ") as two facets of the same failure, or the same willful refusal, to view man in his human totality (*SP* 192). These twin slaveries interestingly correspond to Jean-François Lyotard's analysis of the two major narratives of modernity: the cognitive subject as the hero of knowledge, or the practical subject as the hero of liberty (31). According to Lyotard, these are the two narratives that have been used to legitimate knowledge (and thereby restrict both knowledge and freedom), and the postmodern "condition" is characterized by "incredulity" toward such metanarratives. Pound's critique, then, would seem to mark his own postmodern skepticism—after all, the historical causes Lyotard suggests for such incredulity, the "blossoming of techniques and technologies" since World War II and the redeployment of "advanced liberal capitalism" since 1960, could already be seen in the years of and following World War I (37). But Pound's incredulity is only momentarily postmodern, for it is in reality but a phase in another narrative. It simultaneously motivates a search for a more fundamental, more totalizing narrative, an Ur-narrative, and is itself legitimated by the acceptance of such a narrative—in Pound's case, an apocalyptic narrative that could subsume all others.

Pound therefore seeks specific solutions to the dangers of Provincialism. A better educational system would presumably lead to clarity in writing, but Pound also identifies less abstruse problems and promotes more immediately tangible solutions. Provincialism is primarily marked by separation, by division, of which it is both product and producer. It signifies the simultaneous fragmentation of the world community, the individual state, and the individual human being. A primary cause of this fragmentation is the lack of commerce between countries, and particularly between their cultural centers, the cities: to Pound, "communication" and "transportation" are virtually synonymous. Hence Flaubert's statement on the necessity of good prose is displaced as favorite citation by a phrase from Rudyard Kipling, paraphrased by Pound as "intercommunication is civilisation" or "transportation is civilisation" (*SP* 198, 199). To counteract fragmentation, therefore, Pound argues in the last article of the "Provincialism" series for the construction of the Channel tunnel, which would double resources by linking Paris and London. This engineering solution is clearly a geographical manifestation of Pound's more general concern to open up the lines of communication between cultures and individuals.[5] It is especially significant that the apocalyptic resurfaces at just this moment, when Pound is trying to assert the importance of a "practical" enterprise: "There is something sinister in the way *the* tunnel disappears from discussion every now and again. I dare say it is not the supreme issue of the war. It may not be the millennium, but it is one, and, perhaps, *the* one firm step that can definitely be taken, if not toward a perpetual peace, at least toward a greater peace probability" (*SP* 199). The hesitations and qualifications here, like the shift from "millennium" to "perpetual peace" to "greater peace probability," indicate Pound's difficulty with this conjunction of mythological structure and practical enterprise. Pound wishes to connect the building of the tunnel to the millennium, but he is uncertain just what relation he wishes to claim. Is the tunnel a practical (realist) approximation of the millennium, or does it prepare the way for a later realization of a "true" millennium? This difficulty persists through Pound's career: indeed, his subsequent embrace of fascism, I would argue, derives to a great extent from this confused mix of the apocalyptic with the practical.

Whatever Pound's difficulty with the precise relation between these modes, we can see in this passage that his interpretation of contemporary events, his consequent aims, and the means by which he would achieve those aims are all informed by, and largely conform to, the narrative structure of the apocalypse. The three critical elements of that structure—a pervasive enemy, an Armageddon, and a millennium—combine to provide the dynamic for Pound's thought. In the background of the whole essay, of course, stands the common rhetoric of World War I as Armageddon. From that rhetoric of the apocalypse, however, Pound (along with others) slips into a logic of the apocalypse. The feeling that the Great War ought to be the last war, which Pound shared with H. G. Wells and others, is informed by an unarticulated narrative logic that predicts a perpetual peace following the cataclysm: "if Armageddon, then millennium." The absurdity of the proposition as logic does not affect the power of the narrative's hold over the imagination, a power that increases as the war and the enemy come to seem increasingly "evil and uncanny." Pound's reference to "something sinister" is thus neither incidental nor merely an instance of paranoia, but a necessary element of the apocalyptic structure. It is against that "something sinister" that Pound's struggle for a millennium will increasingly be defined.

Already at work here is a further slippage concerning the Armageddon. Although the Great War supplies the general atmosphere for the development of apocalyptic rhetoric, and although some no doubt believed the defeat of Germany might lead to a perpetual peace, Pound, in keeping with his dissatisfaction with England and America, extends the apocalyptic conflict into the future. Far from being the final battle, the Great War will resolve little: it is yet another instance, in fact the primary manifestation, of the sinister enemy. It is by this means, by subsuming it to an ongoing, more fundamental conflict, that Pound finally deals with the war. War as such therefore assumes a highly ambiguous function in Pound's work, as both a manifestation of the evil to be fought and, inevitably, the means of defeating that evil. As Douglas Robinson remarks, "without opposition the apocalypse is nothing" (10). Both individual revelation and a societal millennium—an earthly paradise—are possible only as products of war. Agonistics therefore become all-pervasive in Pound's life and work, defining and even constituting his thought and poetics. To understand this pervasiveness fully, however, we need to develop a more precise understanding of the millennium in his work, which actually interweaves three distinct versions of the apocalypse.

Image and Millennium

The main interpretations of the biblical apocalypse are relatively straightforward: the historical (or literal) and the allegorical.[6] Biblical scholars agree that the Book of Revelation was initially intended and read as a historical prediction of the very near future, of an imminent millennium—"the time is near," the author tells us, echoing other New Testament writers, as well as Jesus (Rev. 1:3).[7] Such an interpretation was particularly attractive to the early Christians, who, like all the dispossessed, the alienated, and the persecuted, had everything to gain by the destruction and reconstitution of the current social order (Cohn 21; Mackenzie 40–41). Such groups are likely to respond to any delay in the fulfillment of millennial hopes, at least at first, by a simple refiguring of the dates, for the continued imminence of the millennium at the very least makes present conditions more tolerable, and if sufficiently widespread may itself exert great pressure on the existing social order. From Old Testament times to the present, therefore, historical interpretations have been more popular among the lower classes, the poorly educated, and other groups excluded from power.

More direct and sustained contradictions of millennial expectations, however, lead to the adoption of various allegorical interpretations. The most straightforward such reading simply defers the literal millennium to a far distant future in order to focus on one's present spiritual state. This is particularly the case among those comfortable within the existing social order, who would have everything to lose if the current order were destroyed. The struggle between Good and Evil becomes internal, and thus does not threaten social structures at all—in fact, the ethical injunctions tend to reinforce those structures. This interpretation, initially developed by Origen in the third century and detailed by Augustine in *The City of God*, developed historically as the Christian community became more accepted and more powerful. As the actual millennium became less palpable, fading into ever greater distance, it went on to become the dominant interpretation (Cohn 29; Robinson 14).

Although both interpretations persist in the Christian context (and of course in other religions), we should bear in mind that these apocalyptics have also been considerably secularized. The first has become the utter transformation of the social order in a political revolution (ideally accompanied by the disappearance of the state), while the second has become a struggle with humanist ethical decisions, rather than a spiritual battle between the forces of Good and Evil. In this form their cultural influence is pervasive, extending well beyond the boundaries of Christianity, to shape both the rhetoric and aims of many groups and individuals, even those that are avowedly anti-religious. There remains, however, another important interpretation, a variant of the allegorical: the visionary apocalyptic of Romanticism.

In the Romantic version, the apocalypse consists in a perceptual revolution that can occur at any moment: the ordinary world dissolves in favor of a new, visionary reality, the equivalent of the millennium. In this view, it is only our perceptual inability that condemns us to live in a "fallen" world, for the (visionary) *real* world exists now, ahistorically. As Robinson points out, William Blake provides the prime exemplar of this view; in *The Marriage of Heaven and Hell* Blake also supplies its most concise and most famous formulation: "If the doors of perception were cleansed every thing would appear to man as it is, infinite. For man has closed himself up, till he sees all things thro' narrow chinks of his cavern" (Blake 154; Robinson 19). This version of the apocalypse has remained particularly attractive to post-Romantic poets and other artists, because in it the artist occupies a privileged position as, in Joyce's words, "a priest of eternal imagination"—the Author as God (*A Portrait* 221). He is closest to this visionary reality, which provides the basis of his art and insight—the two are in fact seen to be inseparable. Along with that privileged position, however, there usually comes a social responsibility: it is the poet's task to try to effect a similar vision in his audience (the rest of mankind), or at least to mediate that vision and its wisdom for humanity.

Each of these versions of the apocalyptic generates its own distinct organization of the whole field of human endeavor, reconstituting the field according to the logic of its own particular narrative. According to the literal interpretation, all present acts must directly aid or prepare for the imminent millennium; there is literally no time for extraneous pursuits. In its secular version, all acts are political, for or against the impending revolution. The ethical interpretation, in its weaker, secular form, tends to something of a relativist position, avoiding extremes—there is no single, immediate goal to subsume all acts. While an ethical struggle persists, the consequences are not so fraught with import, and the boundaries are vague or ambiguous. The visionary interpretation is less easy to characterize. It can be both democratic, since anyone can experience the vision, and elitist, since not all in fact have such an experience. And these conflicting tendencies can occur at the same time and in the same individual. Moreoever, because the epiphanic moment of insight is privileged both as the basis from which to act and as a significant goal of action, there is a constant potential for means-end confusion. What becomes particularly significant, then, is the social context of the individual moments: in effect, the relation between the visionary and the historical apocalyptics.

The relation between these versions of the apocalypse is particularly significant to the development of Pound's poetics. His career begins with a version of the Romantic, visionary apocalypse that finds early and rather debased expression in the "stale cream puffs" of *A Lume Spento* (1908), before developing into the famous manifestos and poems of the Imagist period immediately before the war. So conventional are the poems of this first book, it is difficult to ascribe attitudes to Pound as individual rather than to Pound assuming the persona of the poet. However, the introductory poem, "Grace Before Song," proclaims the relation between the whole collection and poetic inspiration. In doing so, it also reveals Pound's understanding of the relation between his poems and society:

> Lord God of heaven that with mercy dight
> Th'alternate prayer wheel of the night and light
> Eternal hath to thee, and in whose sight
> Our days as rain drops in the sea surge fall,
>
> As bright white drops upon a leaden sea
> Grant so my songs to this grey folk may be:
>
> As drops that dream and gleam and falling catch the sun,
> Evan'scent mirrors every opal one
> Of such his splendor as their compass is,
> So, bold My Songs, seek ye such death as this.
>   (CEP 7)

Pound, of course, was not a Christian poet: by appealing to "Lord God of heaven" he adapts the poet's conventional appeal to the muse in order to give it a general religious force—or return to it the religious significance it had for Homer. It is the poet's duty to begin with divine inspiration and then to help the products of that inspiration, the "heaven-sent" poems, to convey as much of the divine vision as possible to the "grey folk"—Pound already shows a tendency to assume superiority and treat others as an anonymous mass. Particularly interesting here is the threat—or rather, the hope—of death: although the folk as sea and god as the sun are opposed, both in fact promise extinction of the drops, the individual poems and individual lives. The sea as symbol thus tends to escape its narrow use as metaphor for the folk and becomes a complement, in a sense a mirror, to the divine sun, with both representing the infinite that threatens, or promises, to absorb the individual. In the Provençal lyrics Pound studied the envoi instructs the poem to represent the poet, to speak and act for him; in the final line of this poem we can read the poet's own desire for dissolution in a visionary, millennial union with humanity and the divine.

It may seem, then, that Pound seeks already in 1908 that postmodern dissolution of the stable ego recent critics have seen in the Pisan Cantos, after World War II and the collapse of Pound's political hopes for Mussolini. Yet that is clearly not the case: the poem is actually articulated from a firm, consistent position, and by a very stable voice. It is tempting, in fact, to see in the sea Pound's future fear and dislike of communism and in the sun his fascist aspiration. We can in any case glimpse Pound's superior position in the poem's single pun: the elision of the major accented syllable of "evanescent" in order to pun on "heaven-sent" and "heaven-scent," aside from being awkward, intrusive, and ineffective, betokens the assumption of an external, dominant position in relation to language, a willingness to twist it against itself to the author's (or Author's) purpose, rather than work with it and seize the opportunities it presents. This poem's proposed dissolution of the self, then, does not mark an abandonment of a secure position in favor of a tactical postmodernism, but is part of a larger strategy that becomes particularly evident in the shift from "my songs" in stanza two to "My Songs" in the final line, the sudden capitals elevating Pound to the status of the Joycean Author as God. Any dissolution Pound seeks is only a means to this final identification of the author with the divinity: the subject pretends subjection only to become the master.

This concept of the artwork accords with Pound's eager insistence on a "visionary interpretation" of Arnaut Daniel in his well-known essay, "Psychology and Troubadours," where he declares his belief in "a sort of permanent basis of humanity" comprised of "delightful psychic experience[s]" that form the basis of Greek mythology (*SR* 90, 92). In that essay the experience in question is sexual, but the inclusion of all Greek mythology argues a belief that contact with some form of the divine (or demonic) is achieved in most intense psychic experiences. As Pound wrote later, "a god is an eternal state of mind," manifested "when the states of mind take form" (*SP* 47). One thus achieves union with the divine, becomes divine, when one achieves such a state. Poets and artists, as he writes in "Psychology and Troubadours," are "close on the vital universe" of such divine states, and it is the function of their " 'germinal' consciousness[es]" to "affect mind about them, and transmute it as the seed the earth" (*SR* 92, 93). Hence Pound's claim in the first of his 1915 "Affirmations" essays that the music of Arnold Dolmetsch had made him see "the God Pan" in the person of Dolmetsch himself, who "by a pattern of notes" could "throw us back into the age of truth"—the golden age before the degradation of the Greek myths (*LE* 431–32). Pound sought an analogous effect with the "intellectual and emotional complex" of the Image (Pound's capital), created by the artist's "intense emotion" and producing a "sense of sudden liberation; [a] sense of freedom from time limits and space limits" (*LE* 4; *SP* 374). The aim is not to produce something to be "appreciated," but, and in keeping with the visionary tradition, to provide a sudden, apocalyptic liberation by changing the way people perceive: Pound was pleased to have convinced a Russian correspondent that he wished "to give people new eyes, not to make them see some new particular thing" (*GB* 85).

This emphasis on the visionary argues that the techniques of the Imagist movement were not ends in themselves but means: to revitalize the Romantic, visionary apocalyptic, to reestablish its possibility and validity in the modern age. Critical guides commonly point to Pound's stress on "objectivity and again objectivity," and on procedures that would simplify, streamline, and "cleanse" the language (*SL* 49). But the stress throughout is in fact on immediacy: direct treatment of the object, elimination of superfluous words, eschewal of abstractions and logical connectors, even composition in the sequence of the musical phrase (*LE* 3–4). The basis common to these technical injunctions is Pound's rejection of the poem as mediation in favor of its presence in itself and as itself: hence his various formulations of the *energy* of words and images in themselves, from words as hollow steel cones "charged with a force like electricity, or, rather, radiating a force from their apexes" in 1910, through the "radiant node or cluster" of the Image or Vortex in 1914, to the perfected word as the sun's lance in the Pisan Cantos (*SP* 34; *GB* 92; *C* 468). Pound's famous technical program is designed to eliminate precisely those discursive features of language indicating mediation, and to lessen the mediation necessarily still present by absorbing it into the immediacy of music. Ideally, the poem would enact the experience it is to convey, so that there would be no distinction between the poet's initial experience of an Image that is "real because [he] know[s] it directly" and the reader's experience of the Image in the poem (*GB* 88). Rather than represent, the poem should act.

The working of these techniques can be seen clearly in one of the three poems Pound singled out in a September 1914 article on Imagism that was later reprinted in *Gaudier-Brzeska: A Memoir* (a testimony to both the man and the Vorticist movement). Here is Pound's most famous Imagist work, "In a Station of the Metro":

The apparition of these faces in the crowd;
Petals on a wet, black, bough.
(P 109)

The poem provides a fine example of both direct treatment and economy of words, but crucial to its effect is its intricate sound pattern and carefully constructed cadence. Of the many overlapping and echoing patterns, the echo of "faces in the crowd" in "petals on a . . . bough" is most significant, since it unites the two objects not only in parallel clauses, but in the repeated cadence. The delay occasioned by "wet, black," with "wet" echoing "petals" and beginning a sequence of accented vowels that descend in pitch (overtones) to "bough" is particularly effective in creating a sense of finality and inevitability—to the poem and to the juxtaposition.

Considered from a logical, discursive point of view, of course, this poem merely presents a simile with "like" suppressed. It is just that point of view, however, that the poem seeks to avoid: Pound reported that he was "trying to record the precise instant when a thing outward and objective transforms itself, or darts into a thing inward and subjective" (GB 89). He was trying, that is, to present or achieve a state that can only exist outside, prior to or beyond, discursive language: "the image is the word beyond formulated language" (GB 88). As Herbert Schneidau points out, Pound later found a theoretical basis for this fusion of the objective and the subjective in the "way across the terrifying Cartesian gap between internal and external, between subjective and objective" offered by Ernest Fenollosa's *The Chinese Character as a Medium for Poetry* (Schneidau 61). There Pound discovered that the structure of the sentence, by miming *relations* in nature, could present, or reenact, the structure of nature, beyond discursive capabilities. He attempts to articulate such a state later in the "Imagism" essay, declaring that "the image is not an idea. It is a radiant node or cluster . . . a VORTEX, from which, and through which, and into which, ideas are constantly rushing" (GB 92). The image is not an idea because conceptual ideas occur in the domain of discourse, to Pound a lesser mode of language that, he implies, both stems from and aims toward the Image or vortex.[8] The suppression of simile in "In a Station of the Metro" is thus only one mark of its attempt to achieve a language outside discursive logic, wherein the faces and petals can combine in a visionary union, rather than be related in an interesting but ultimately inconsequential "figure of speech."

The visionary basis of Imagist poetics has received little attention, in part because many Imagist poems seem rather slight, or even mere technical exercises, and in part because Pound's critical emphasis appears to be almost exclusively on technique. Yet the other two poems Pound singled out in his 1914 essay are overtly visionary: "The Return," which Yeats felt gave him "better words than [his] own" as preface to his own *A Vision* (29), and "Heather," of which Pound noted that it "represents" or "implies" or "implicates" a "state of consciousness" (*GB* 85). He is unwilling to settle on "represents" because representation is inadequate to the poem's vision:

> The black panther treads at my side,
> And above my fingers
> There float the petal-like flames.
>
> The milk-white girls
> Unbend from the holly-trees,
> And their snow-white leopard
> Watches to follow our trace.
>
>   (*P* 109)

This visionary "state of consciousness," with Pound as a kind of Dionysian messiah, accompanied by a panther and surrounded by "petal-like flames," is clearly in the apocalyptic tradition. Similar states occur in later poems, notably in the 1918 "Phanopoeia" and "Cantus Planus." The title of "Phanopoeia" significantly links the "casting of images upon the visual imagination" to the poem's presentation of three highly sexual, visionary moments (*LE* 25). Also significant is Pound's choice of "Cantus Planus" to end the 1926 edition of *Personae*, indicating that there is nothing plain about Imagism's "plain song":

> The black panther lies under his rose tree
> And the fawns come to sniff at his sides:
>
>> Evoe, Evoe, Evoe Baccho, O
>> ZAGREUS, *Zagreus*, Zagreus,
>
> The black panther lies under his rose tree.
>
>> ‖ Hesper adest.   Hesper ‖ adest.
>>   Hesper ‖ adest. ‖
>
>   (*P* 231)

Many such moments also occur in the *Cantos*, where their importance has long been acknowledged. What I wish to stress here, though, is that even in the Imagist period this vision is neither peripheral nor occasional, but integral, providing the very basis of Imagist poetics: without the Vision, there can be no Image. It is the moment of Vision that effectively grounds Pound, providing his poetics with a transcendent basis that escapes, or lies beyond, the vorticist flux.

Just what Imagism was intended to accomplish—beyond cleansing the contemporary journals of drivel—Pound leaves rather vague. Presumably the enlightenment brought about by Imagist poetics would spread to other domains "not only in the arts, but in life, in politics, and in economics"—especially when magazine editors join the "Risorgimento"—but nowhere does Pound specify the connection (*SP* 112). However, we can see a more direct approach, in fact an explicitly moral approach to contemporary society, in the many epigrammatic poems Pound wrote beginning roughly in 1913 and culminating in the 1918 series, "Moeurs Contemporaines," and in a few of the poems in "Hugh Selwyn Mauberley." Although epigrams are not conducive to the subtleties of musical cadence, these poems are otherwise Imagist in technique. They extend to the social world the Fenollosan-Imagist technique of using a structural syntax to present rather than comment, often using simple juxtaposition to establish a contrast and thereby imply a comment. Yet these poems, which constitute a considerable portion of Pound's output in the actively Imagist and Vorticist periods, are quite distinct in content, and should be considered separate from both movements, a development not of the romantic, visionary apocalyptic, but of the secular, ethical version. Pound's satiric vignettes are peopled with individuals who have made some irrevocable choice—equivalent to that between Good and Evil—between life and mere existence, drifting along in accord with social expectations rather than truly living. He generally makes the distinction on a sexual basis: those who choose life choose sexual fulfillment, sometimes within and sometimes outside social norms, while those who merely exist are sexually repressed, deprived, or inadequate. Although the ethical poems are not explicitly integrated with Pound's more visionary work, this sexual basis of his ethics provides a clear means of doing so. For Pound a primary means of achieving a divine vision was through sexual intercourse—hence his interest in the Eleusinian mysteries and their continuance through the Middle Ages (as outlined in "Psychology and Troubadours"). The eroticism of some of the visionary poems, such as "Heather," scarcely needs stating. Pound's ethical poems record the effect on the individual of the failure to achieve, or even properly respect, that erotic, visionary, and essentially apocalyptic, moment.

It is important to bear in mind, however, that the poems themselves do not make this connection. The two versions of the allegorical apocalyptic, the visionary and the ethical, coexist in Pound's work in the 1910s, but despite their common basis they remain at this point unintegrated. Moreover, although the individual vision could supply a basis for judging individuals in specific social relations—a marriage or an affair—Pound seemingly could relate it to larger social patterns and issues only as a vague ideal, bordering on nostalgia for an earlier golden age. Given the Great War's pressure to develop an alter-

native, a solution, to the war—a means, that is, of preventing future wars—
vague nostalgia could no longer be enough. It would require the longer poems
and larger forms at which Pound labored during the war to achieve a greater
integration of these distinct modes.

What finally enabled the creation of those longer poems and that greater
integration was Pound's adoption of the historical or literal apocalyptic. The
apocalyptic basis common to the visionary and the ethical made the adoption
of the historical apocalyptic a relatively easy, almost unobtrusive step. For
Pound, the millennium vaguely implied by the Armageddon of World War I
soon shifted from a possibility to a necessity, a necessity that was being
thwarted, as we have seen, by ignorance and evil intent. The development of
a historical apocalyptic can be seen in the shift from his vague sense of a *Risorgimento* of 1913, through the specific, if sporadic, references to the millennium during the war, to Pound's explicit declaration that a New Era, a pagan
era, began at the stroke of midnight, October 29, 1921—October 30 being both
the date *Ulysses* was completed and his own thirty-sixth birthday. That his
"Calendar" of the New Era, published in the *Little Review* of Spring 1922, is
only half in jest is demonstrated by Pound's frequent references to *Ulysses* as
the harbinger of a new era.[9] Later he readily adopted the new fascist calendar
on his personal stationery—it could only have seemed a singular and highly
significant coincidence that Mussolini's March on Rome took place in 1922, the
first year of his own New Era. Indeed, the *directio voluntatis*, the "direction of
the will" so important to Pound's fascism, first came to him through the historical apocalyptic, which supplied Pound and his work with a *telos*, a direction, and thence a dynamic. It was this temporal dynamic that finally enabled
Pound to bring the ethical and the visionary into meaningful, explicit relation,
and to make sense of the war by making it a necessary step to a new world.

As we will see, the precise relations among these apocalyptics vary. Although Pound always assumes they are fully consistent, at times they are actually contradictory. Pound's ethics, for example, become significantly double:
where before individuals were judged according to how well attuned they
were to the divine vision (already problematic, since it is unavoidably the author's divine vision), large groups, such as the Jews, become judged in the
1930s according to whether they aid or inhibit progress toward the paradisal
telos of a new age (when, presumably, all would be attuned to the divine).[10]
Even the validity of other claims to visionary experience—of others' experience—came to be judged by its contribution toward the new age. Although
Pound's commitment to the historical apocalyptic seemingly allowed him to
retain his past work and values intact, it was in reality a tremendously significant step, providing the means to create longer forms and to integrate the

visionary and the ethical, but doing so largely by subsuming them to a much greater and more powerful dynamic.

The *Cantos*: History and Apocalypse

The effect of the historical apocalyptic on Pound's poetics is evident not only in the *Cantos*, but, less overtly, in the other longer works of the World War I period: the sequences "Homage to Sextus Propertius" and "Hugh Selwyn Mauberley," and the combined sequence of "Langue d'Oc" and "Moeurs Contemporaines." As these examples suggest, the apocalyptic narrative also influences the organization of collections, such as *Poems 1918–1921*. The catalyst, however—or, rather, the work in which the historical apocalyptic first catalyzed the visionary and the ethical—was Canto 4. The critical importance of that work, both chronologically (as the first completed canto) and stylistically (as the progenitor of many of the *Cantos*' devices), has long been recognized.[11] It initiated the transformation of the *Cantos* from the discursive, uncertain musings of the 1915 *Three Cantos* (published in 1917) to the tightly organized, dynamic unit of *A Draft of XVI Cantos* (1925). If the early *Three Cantos* are characterized by a search for an appropriate means of action, a poetic appropriate to the modern world, in Canto 4 the means is discovered, and the call to action issued. Massimo Bacigalupo, in fact, speaks of an "unmistakable breakthrough" from "discursive form" to an "apocalyptic presentation," which he unfortunately does not specify further (18). Certainly Pound himself thought that Canto 4 marked a new beginning. Where previously he had worked through a series of "masks of the self" in the short poems and in "Propertius" and "Mauberley," Cantos 4–7, he told John Quinn, "come out of the middle of me and are not a mask, are what I have to say" (*GB* 85; qtd. in Pearlman 301). Canto 4 was also the first Pound believed could stand on its own, and it could do so because it both set the basic problem for the *Cantos* and outlined in miniature the journey of the work as a whole.

In her recent edition of Pound's various drafts of the canto, Christine Froula observes that "Pound's first groping toward a Fourth Canto links the breakdown of the story [i.e., epic narrative] to the incomprehensible scale of destruction made possible by the technology of modern warfare" (6). The first draft, which Froula labels MS Ur 1 and which probably dates from fall 1915, shows clearly Pound's inability to deal successfully with the war. An English soldier gives a conversational account of his prewar adventures on the continent. In Poland, and despite Polish resistance to the Germans, he found that he liked, even "sopped up" German "kultur," and so he "moved up a peg" to Jena, where he received his doctorate (70).[12] Next came employment running an estate in Hungary, until shortly after the outbreak of hostilities, when, despite his local popularity, he left. He was then arrested and imprisoned in Salzburg, but escaped (or was allowed to escape), and made his way to Switzerland and then by train to Paris. His narrative ends with him enlisting and spending six months at the front in Flanders, of which we are told nothing. The remainder of the manuscript, some twenty lines, consists of the poet-narrator's reflections on the modern world, turning particularly to the Orient and "Sen-sei Pere Henri Jacques," the Western Jesuit whose attempt to commune with the Eastern spirits on "Mount Rok-ko" would be almost the only item retained in the final version (73).

This summary necessarily omits much of the detail by which Pound attempts to make his point. The soldier's German education and happiness with German "kultur" and people indicate the common bond between German and English (and by implication American) cultures and peoples—or perhaps a common corruption. In fact, he receives better treatment from Germans than from the English—a German consular official gives him £5, while an Englishman is "sniffy and cold" until the soldier mentions Cambridge (presumably the site of his earlier education), when he receives £2 (72). He enlists largely because the English on the train are somewhat less hostile to him when they hear of his imprisonment—military service is chiefly a means to gain respect and overcome class distinction. Pound apparently intends us to recognize that the English are no better than the Germans, and that there is no valid reason for them to be enemies.

In any case, the soldier's uncertainty and bewilderment scarcely give Pound a means to understand and thereby control the war. His confusions, shared no doubt with many caught up in the war, seem also to mirror Pound's. In the final section Pound attempts a larger perspective, stepping outside the war both geographically and culturally. But the relation between Henri Jacques' union of East and West and the problems of the modern world—specifically the Great War—remains vague and uncertain. Perhaps he promises a superior vision, but Pound also recognizes that the West is vulgarizing the spiritual traditions of the East, noting that "young bucks" in India now sacrilegiously place "beef bones at brahmin's doors" (73). Nor is it clear how an individual's superior vision may achieve translation into social reality. In the next draft (MS Ur 2), also discarded, Pound again attempts a larger vision by trying to relate the war to "the ineffable" (74). However, the ineffable remains the province of the individual artist rather than of society, and therefore the relation between individual vision and social reality remains vague and uncertain, while the draft of Canto 4 remains rambling and discursive.

In subsequent drafts and in the final version, Pound shifts from the actual

Great War to the archetypal Trojan war, thereby controlling and dominating World War I by mythologizing it, by assimilating it to a tradition of war and making it part of a larger, ongoing war. An important temporal shift reinforces this development: by using the cataclysm at Troy as a backdrop to subsequent events, Pound moves from an attempt to understand an ongoing war (by relating it to artistic and spiritual quests), to the question of what action to take in its aftermath. The opening itself develops through the drafts from an invocation of Troy—"Rise o thou smoky palace"—into the more immediate presentation of "Palace in smoky light," the ruins of Troy, or Europe, being by 1919 a part of the background, something to be assumed rather than created (MS A, 81; C 4:13). Other changes reinforce this temporal shift: for example, the parallel between the stories of Itys (killed by Procne and fed to Tereus) and Cabestan (killed by Raymond and fed to Soremonda) is eventually recast as a parallel between Procne (turned into a swallow) and Soremonda (turned into a swallow), as the focus changes from both stories' moments of destruction to the subsequent, miraculous effects of destruction. In rejecting the early drafts, then, Pound rejected a stance within the ongoing war in favor of an external, superior position. He turned, that is, from an uncertain search for a strategy that in fact produced only disjunct, ineffective tactics—rambling, dislocated monologues—to a successful strategy that carefully controls the impact and significance of the war by locating it within the possibility of a larger narrative structure.

The formal, epic opening of the final version presents the aftermath of Armageddon, the evil empires having more or less destroyed themselves in a final cataclysm. (One, of course, is victorious, but neither Mycenae after Troy nor England after the Great War would ever regain its splendor.) What is needed is a new Odysseus, or better an Aeneas, or even better a Christ or Dionysus, as Pound came to see himself, to help the people attain the promised Edenic world. Pound in fact chooses Cadmus, the Ovidian founder of Thebes, to represent this figure:

> Palace in smoky light,
> Troy but a heap of smouldering boundary stones,
> ANAXIFORMINGES! Aurunculeia!
> Hear me. Cadmus of golden prows!
>   (C 13)

Despite the obvious urgency, and despite a certain obscurity of reference, Pound's rhetorical intent is clear. "Hear me" is a crucial injunction: the speaker evidently has something urgent to say concerning the wreckage of the previous civilization and the founding of the new. The formality of the occasion and the

invocation of Pindar ("anaxiforminges") and Catullus ("Aurunculeia") invest
the speaker with sufficient authority to command the reader's attention, establishing for the poem both a public context and an expectation of considerable
social relevance.[13] There is, however, an interesting ambiguity concerning both
subject and object of "hear me." The phrase is obviously directed at the reader
(auditor), but also, since it follows their invocation, at the sources of art and
fertility (Pindar's "lords of the lyre"—but note the pun on "forming"—and
Catullus' Aurunculeia). Thus it at once invokes the source of the speaker's art
and power—his vision—and the reader to whom he would transmit that
vision.

More important, though, is the ambiguity concerning Cadmus: is he another object of "hear me," making the reader a potential Cadmus, or, as in
Pound's own reading of the canto, a gloss on "me," and thus identified with
the poet? This uncertainty of reference shows both the extraordinary importance Pound claimed for his poetry and his careful rhetorical manipulation of
the reader. As Cadmus himself, the poet Pound promises to lead us directly to
a new Thebes, while if the reader is potentially a founder of civilizations, the
position of the injunction indicates that to achieve that potential he must first
listen to the poet. In this ambiguity lies some confusion, or overlapping, between the reader and the speaker—a subtle means for Pound to establish his
dominant position as a master enjoining his pupil to attend well, while at the
same time inviting the pupil to identify with him, thereby assuring his agreement and, more important, commitment. Pound's ideal reader, in fact, would
already be an initiate, for only someone who has already had the vision can
properly receive his message. This paradox is also embodied in the cryptic nature of the opening: obscure in its references and difficult in its structure, it
speaks to an elite even as it claims broad social relevance.

The main idea of the poem is also implied, albeit elliptically, in these opening lines. Pound does not claim a critically important position for the poet
merely to be self-serving. In keeping with the visionary background of Imagism, the poet's function is to help publicly acknowledge and celebrate the necessarily private vision of the divine, and particularly the workings of the divine
in history. The poet thereby helps to unite the divine vision with the public
world, to Pound a necessary foundation for any successful civilization, and especially for the new society to which he aspires. It is for this reason that line
three conjoins the public rhetoric of Pindar to Catullus' more private celebra-
tions of sexuality: Pound may have disdained Pindar's rhetoric, but he recognized that Catullus alone could not achieve the social and political effect he
sought. The two poets represent opposite poles that must be fused in both the

poem and society, for only such a union will allow the city, the civilization, to be properly rebuilt and renewed.

The poet, then, should seek to uncover and praise manifestations of the divine, which for Pound, of course, are intimately connected to sexuality. Thus Carmen 61, in which Catullus praises Aurunculeia, not only celebrates the social aspect of sexuality, fertile marriage, but also asserts the necessity of the gods' presence, in the person of Hymen: society is fertile only under the auspices of the gods, only when they are properly invoked and praised. But the hymn to Hymen, in which Canto 4 later joins Carmen 61 (4:15), is necessarily also a celebration of metamorphosis (from girl to woman) and consequently of destruction (of the hymen), both to the greater good of society. It is the special function of the poet—Pound—to discover this fertile conjunction of destructive and creative powers in history also. While most see only the ruins of Troy's great palace, only the "smouldering boundary stones," the poet, as soon as we attend, uncovers new possibilities, new forms, as in the next line of the canto, when "the silver mirrors catch the bright stones and flare" (4:6).[14] It is the poet's task, finally, to discern in the smoky light not merely a ravaged palace, but Pallas (Athena) herself, to see that destruction is the work of the divine (the dread goddess, Κύθηρα δεινά, of later cantos), and to understand that it will be followed, eventually, by the creation of an Athens—providing, of course, he can help others to share his vision.

As many commentators have noted, Pound consequently becomes an Ovidian poet in Canto 4, a celebrator of change—natural, social, political—or of what he would later call simply (if somewhat simplistically) "the process." Following his recounting of various Ovidian and Provençal tales of metamorphoses, Pound supplies a more general statement of their significance:

> Thus the light rains, thus pours, *e lo soleills plovil*
> The liquid and rushing crystal
> beneath the knees of the gods.
>
> (C 15)

Or more simply: "No wind is the king's wind" (C 16). However, there is a very important distinction between Ovid and Pound in their relations to metamorphoses. While Ovid's thesis, that everything changes, may imply an instability in the present, this implication is largely countered by the apotheosis of Caesar, and the implied apotheosis of Rome itself, at the end of the book. Ovid, in any case, recounts history to "explain" the present, a conservative act. Pound, on the other hand, deploys a dual time frame, initiated by Troy's dual function as archetypal war, the type of World War I, and historical war, the

necessary precedent to Greek, and thence European, civilization. Canto 4's se-
lective history of manifestations of the divine from the time of Troy to the present (a contemporary religious procession by the Garonne) does not seek to
explain the present so much as to make the reader see what direction should
be pursued in order to create the next, millennial civilization on the ruins of
the latest Troy, Europe in the aftermath of World War I. Where Ovid writes a
history that will entertain his audience and to some extent rationalize the caprices of fortune, Pound seeks to produce a particular effect on the reader; he
seeks to spur the reader to action for a future goal. Canto 4 therefore possesses
an added public dimension, together with a marked sense of urgency, for the
millennial vision of a future city can only come about if the poem is sufficiently
effective, if it spurs readers to take appropriate action.

In seeking to produce this effect, Pound actually contradicts the overt conceptual content generally ascribed to "the process." The alliance of Pound's
process with Heraclitus' river and the erratic wanderings of Odysseus, encouraged of course by the Pisan Cantos and by Pound himself, has created among
commentators a vision of an ongoing, endless flow, orderly but not ordered,
of which Pound merely wishes to assert (perhaps demonstrate) the existence.
It is an abstract pattern in which all participate, consciously or unconsciously,
and which is therefore ahierarchical, a basis for neither desire nor judgment.
The "true" Pound, such a reading implies, was too much a mystic ever to become a *real* fascist and anti-semite.[15] Thus the author of a recent guidebook,
emphasizing "the process" in Canto 4, and consequently the moral dictum,
"no wind is the king's wind," asserts that the canto "contains almost no 'complete' sentence in the normal sense. Everything flows along on commas, co-
lons, semicolons, ellipses—syntax expressing content." In sum, and in keeping with this notion of process, "the liquid crystal energy [of Canto 4] cannot
be forced into a pattern of subject-verb-object" (Kearns 34).

Marvelous as it is, however, this use of syntax is surely only a surface fe-
licity, for the canto as a whole does indeed force that energy "into a pattern of
subject-verb-object." Far from being a constant flow, the canto is composed in
distinct scenes, carefully fitted together, through which the reader is purposefully, if subtly, guided. Immediately after the opening, for example, comes the
following transition:

> The silver mirrors catch the bright stones and flare,
> Dawn, *to our waking*, drifts in the green cool light
>
>   (4:13, emphasis added)

The first line, as we have noted, displays the poet's ability to conjure. The second invites us to join him in a landscape, positioning us at what appear to be

the beginnings of a narrative, and underscoring the importance of this historical moment's potential for a new awakening, a new renaissance (an idea retained from MS Ur 1, which ended with the assertion, "so the world wakes
and turns" [Froula 73]). It is from this vantage point, on the verge of a new
enlightenment, that we can catch glimpses of the divine in the next section:

> Dew-haze blurs, in the grass, pale ankles moving.
> Beat, beat, whirr, thud, in the soft turf
>   under the apple trees,
> Choros nympharum, goat-foot, with the pale foot alternate;
> Crescent of blue-shot waters, green-gold in the shallows,
> A black cock crows in the sea-foam;
>   (4:13)

This scene is held in front of us, but Pound keeps us at a distance. The allusion
to Whitman's "Drum Taps," in "beat, beat, whirr, thud," shows both the continuing presence of war and, in the substitution of "thud" for Whitman's
"pound," the poet's effort to maintain sufficient distance. The crow of the black
cock and the subsequent pause signal an impending, momentous shift to a
new scene, for which a formal context is next supplied:

> And by the curved, carved foot of the couch,
>   claw-foot and lion head, an old man seated
> Speaking in the low drone . . .
>   (4:13)

From here we move to the Ovidian and Provençal vignettes, which provide the
"data" on which Pound's more general statement, "thus the light rains, thus
pours," is based. In this section the poem also maintains distance by the use
of elaborate, formal repetitions and balances.

  This careful construction continues through the rest of the canto, Pound
as Author purposefully, and strategically, staging events and manipulating the
reader throughout the poem. Pound's syntax may not express logical propositions, and Pound may largely eschew direct comment, but the elaborate, carefully ordered formal structure clearly expresses propositions and implies comment. This more elaborate structure was no doubt what Pound had in mind in
1920 when he remarked, in the midst of a parody of Henry James, on the inadequacy of simple sentences: "the sentence [is] the mirror of man's mind, and
we [have] long since passed the stage when 'man sees horse' or 'farmer sows
rice,' can in simple ideographic record be said to display anything remotely
resembling our subjectivity . . . " (*PD* 3). Pound was himself moving beyond
an expressionist poetics (as his contemporaneous interest in Aeschylus sug-

gests), but this statement certainly provides an indication of his dissatisfaction, while working on Canto 4, with simpler versions of Imagism.[16] The larger structures of meaning characteristic of the James sentence provide a spur to his own more complex ordering of his material. Thus if the syntax in the canto is paratactic, simply additive, the overall structure is hypotactic, culminating in the clear contrast between present degradations and decadence, embodied in the images of the Garonne "thick like paint" and the procession of the Madonna, and past clarity and vigor, embodied in the Edenic image of the "Madonna in hortulo" "across the Adige" (4:16). Significantly, the sharp focus of this contrast was the result of Pound's last major revision, for the 1925 *A Draft of XVI Cantos*.

In Canto 4, then, the common notion of Pound's quasi-mystical process needs to be reconsidered. And Pound's 1921 praise of Brancusi indicates that the canto is not an anomaly: "with the ideal form in marble it is an approach to the infinite *by form*, by precisely the highest possible degree of consciousness of formal perfection; as free of accident as any of the philosophical demands of a 'Paradiso' can make it" (*LE* 444). This stress on formal perfection would seem incompatible with a sense of the process as something in which the author himself participates and in which he is therefore subject to accident. Moreover, the Confucian analogue for Pound's process also asserts a definite hierarchy and basis for judgment, the best citizens, those suited to rule, being those most attuned to the process.[17] In Pound, as I have suggested, these citizens are those who experience the visionary apocalyptic of the Image, or contribute to his millennial Idea of a future city. Indeed, it is precisely that vision that enables Pound (and thus, for the moment, his readers) to step outside the process. The liquid symbolizing the process in Canto 4 flows beneath the knees of the gods, implying the existence of a realm outside, above or beyond, the process: the king may not possess the wind, but the Author can at least direct it. And although the canto's use of "me," "we," "us," and "our" may suggest an intent to move away from the authority of Joyce's superior and indifferent Author, the pronouns in effect merely supply a persona as an additional means of manipulation. Pound is not indifferent, but he is superior. Neither the concept of the process nor the fragmentation characteristic of his poetics should obscure his position as *strategos* in Canto 4. Pound does not subscribe to the process, the process is scripted by Pound.

The final success of Canto 4 to a great extent stems from the series of revisions it underwent from 1919, just before its first publication, to 1925, when it appeared in *A Draft of XVI Cantos*. All are aimed at strengthening the effect of the poem, strengthening its ability to incite the reader to take *action* for the millennial city, rather than simply observe an abstract pattern, or settle for personal vision. One change, as noted above, was the addition of the modern procession by the Garonne. The addition follows immediately upon a statement of the eternal potential for the divine vision and fecundation:

> Upon the gilded tower in Ecbatan
> > Lay the god's bride, lay ever
> Waiting the golden rain.
>
> (*Poems* 76)

In the early printings—*The Fourth Canto* (1919) and *Poems 1918–21* (1922)—the succeeding contrast between past and present, though evident, is ineffective:

> > Et saave!
> But to-day, Garonne is thick like paint, beyond Dorada,
> The worm of the Procession bores in the soup of the crowd
> The blue thin voices against the crash of the crowd
> > Et "Salve regina."
> In trellises
> > Wound over with small flowers, beyond Adige
> In the but half-used room, thin film of images,
> > (by Stefano)
> Age of unbodied gods, the vitreous fragile images
> Thin as the locust's wing
> Haunting the mind . . as of Guido . . .
> Thin as the locust's wing.
>
> (*Poems* 76–77)

It seems that the speaker's vision, or memory, is beginning to fade, so fragile and vague are the images of the past (from "In trellises" on). Additionally, a good deal of explanation and commentary weakens the effectiveness. In the final version, however, the whole passage is greatly condensed and the contrast greatly intensified:

> By Garonne. "Saave!"
> The Garonne is thick like paint,
> Procession,—"Et sa'ave, sa'ave, sa'ave Regina!"
> Moves like a worm, in the crowd,
> Adige, thin film of images,
> Across the Adige, by Stefano, Madonna in hortulo,
> As Cavalcanti had seen her.
>
> (C 4:16)

Turning particularly on the separation marked by the Adige river, this revision, though still descriptive, very nearly transforms the passage into a challenge, impelling the reader to act in order to restore and regain a lost power, to see as Cavalcanti had seen.

Two other changes reinforce this impetus to action. The poem's final "landscape," in the passage beginning, "Smoke hangs on the stream," originally ended with "three steps in an open field / Gray stone-posts leading no-whither"—a sign of the destruction of the Provençal civilization, with its proximity to the divine (*Poems* 76). Inadvertently, however, "nowhither" implies that we have nowhere to go, that we can have no hope for the future. Not until the 1925 edition did Pound replace the word with ellipses, thereby continuing to stress the parallel between the destruction of medieval and modern civilizations but, more importantly, indicating that it is up to the reader to discover where the path leads, to complete the sentence himself by discovering, or more actively creating, a conclusion—by creating, that is, a new civilization. The canto's conclusion was also significantly altered. Pound's drafts of Spring 1919—before his trip to France and consequent addition of the "Garonne" passage—had concluded by conjoining the centaur and the jesuit, as in the last manuscript completed before his trip to France:

> The Centaur's heel
> Plants in the earth-loam.
> A Jesuit seeks the sennin upon the cusped peak of Rokku
>   (MS D, Froula 124n)

For Pound, the centaur is a figure for a pagan poetry—and, by extension, for himself—a poetry that would combine the animal and the human, the libidinal and the logical: "the thinking word-arranging, clarifying faculty must move and leap with the energizing, sentient, musical faculties."[18] The centaur's "planting" therefore implies a greater eventual effect than is at first apparent, a definitive breakthrough.[19] It remains, however, a very gradual effect, and the two lines together present the divine vision as a largely private affair, however universal its content may be. Before the poem's first publication, however, Pound deleted the final image of Père Henri Jacques, sacrificing the reminder of an abstract universality to emphasize the concrete and more social act of the Centaur.

Only in the 1925 printing, though, did Pound settle upon the final, dramatic ending. Having greatly improved the impact of the contrast between past and present, Pound used spaces to isolate and emphasize the line concerning the Centaur, stressing the importance and potential of the pagan and particularly of the (properly inspired) poem. In this sense, the line now functions as a comment on the poem we have just read. The poet, Pound, has done his job:

the tremendous potential for renewal, for rebuilding, is there, waiting. But the new ending no longer allows us to remain content with mere potential:

> The Centaur's heel plants in the earth loam.
> And we sit here . . .
>   there in the arena . . .
>   (4:16)

"Here . . . / there"—the gap could not have been stated more forcefully. Even as they embody the poet's superior, strategic perspective, these final lines maximize the tension between the actual and the possible, shift the contrast from past and present to present and future, and transfer the burden of action, by means of the ellipses, wholly onto the reader. By 1925 Pound had concluded that the meditational portrayal of the state of things was not in itself sufficient, and he was consequently entering a new, more activist phase. By that time, Pound had become infatuated with Italy and was in the process of moving to Rapallo. He had already completed Cantos 8–11, celebrating Sigismundo Malatesta, while Mussolini, who was to become the next Malatesta figure, had begun the new era in politics.[20]

Canto 4 is thus apocalyptic both in content, with revelatory moments of vision set against the Armageddon of the Great War, and, more significantly, in its structure. The apocalyptic structure is the result of the wartime shift, thematized in *Hugh Selwyn Mauberley*, in Pound's concept of poetry: from a primarily descriptive discourse, the "rag-bag" for the modern world of the early *Three Cantos*, to a focus on more prescriptive capabilities, on social efficacy more than "pure" esthetics (*SC* 1). Apparently unwilling to accept prescription as a function of poetry, critics have mistaken the poetics and point of Canto 4. Ronald Bush, for example, while recognizing that "the rhythms and repetitions of Canto 4 do not describe or suggest the reality of objects," ascribes this fact to an attempt to structure "a mental event by rendering the sequence and impact of perception upon consciousness"—still within the realm of description (203–04). Froula, for her part, attempts to argue against any authoritarian or fascist element in Pound's poetics. In a sense she is correct that the canto does not aspire to completion, that it renders "the texture of history more truly," for as the tension in the final lines attests, a great deal remains undone when the canto ends (14). But it should now be clear from those final lines that Pound does not "relinquish the story," that this incompletion is in fact a deliberate provocation of the reader to effect the canto's, the story's, completion in the world (13).[21] The reader should metamorphose from passive observer to active participant by stepping from "here" down into the arena of public action "there."

The canto thus aspires to completion through the reader's response and subsequent actions, and in fact expects its own ultimate efficacy in closing the gap so forcefully realized in the final lines. At this point, however, Pound's poetic begins to waver between radically distinct discursive modes—not merely between the descriptive and the prescriptive, but between the prescriptive and the performative. Since the performative utterance must depend on its material effectiveness for its validity, Pound's apocalyptic poetic in Canto 4 (and with it the reconceived *Cantos*) already implies a dependence on effective realization of the millennial city. The power of Canto 4, then, stems only in part from Pound's eschewal of a narrowly conceived estheticism in favor of a poetic intimately involved in social issues. More significant is the canto's mode of entering the field of social pragmatics: not in terms of a truly practical politics, but as the product of an apocalyptic, implicitly performative poetic, giving voice to a powerfully apocalyptic vision of both individual and collective experience—an apocalyptic epistemology conjoined to an apocalyptic history. Indeed, far from rendering more truly the texture of history, Pound's commitment to this apocalyptic, together with his extensive use of mythology to establish perspective, at least implies an ultimate surmounting of both politics and history: where the Image promises a personal "sudden liberation" from "time limits and space limits," the sweeping apocalyptic of Canto 4 strives toward an equally sudden liberation from the complex actualities of history itself.

The *Cantos*: Contradictions of War

Pound was fond of quoting T. E. Hulme's remark that "all a man ever *thought* would go onto a half sheet of notepaper. The rest is application and elaboration" (*SP* 328; *GK* 369). And certainly the remark applies well to his own work. Up to the end of World War II, the various sections of *The Cantos*, the work as a whole, and even Pound's prose of the thirties and forties consist largely in an elaboration, application, and even intensification of the apocalyptic first presented in Canto 4. As we have already noted, Pound ended his definitive selection of short poems for the 1926 *Personae* on an apocalyptic note with the poem "Cantus Planus." More significantly, the first substantial collection of cantos, the 1925 *A Draft of XVI Cantos*, is both built around Canto 4 and structured according to a strikingly similar dynamic. We begin with Odysseus' postwar search for home, then move through glimpses of the divine city and hints of a possible earthly realization (in the Malatesta and Confucius cantos). Countering this possibility, however, are the corruption and degradation of the contemporary world, as represented (and suitably mythologized) in the hell cantos. Canto 16 ends the sequence with a portrayal of the dismal realities of

World War I—precisely where the first drafts of Canto 4 had begun—stressing General Haig's ineffectiveness and implying that particular "interests" deliberately instituted and prolonged the war, in the process destroying the Vorticist Renaissance. The sequence draws a forceful contrast between potential and reality, between "here" and "there," and outlines the general (mythic) narrative that would lead to the realization of potential. *A Draft of XVI Cantos* leaves the reader with the actual task of that realization.

Cantos 17–30, published in *A Draft of XXX Cantos* (1930), replicate the pattern we have already observed. A passage in Canto 21, in fact, reprises Canto 4's dramatic close, contrasting past order and achievement to present chaos and slaughter:

> and we sit here . . .
> By the arena, *les gradins* . . .
> And the palazzo, baseless, hangs there in the dawn
> With low mist over the tide-mark;
> And floats there nel tramonto
> With gold mist over the tide-mark.
> The tesserae of the floor, and the patterns.

The culture that built this palazzo, hovering between the visionary and the actual, is still potential, but now we are surrounded by

> Fools making new shambles;
>   night over green ocean,
> And the dry black of the night
>   (C 98)

—a world of "sabotage" and "war, one war after another," as Canto 18 tells us, started by men "who couldn't put up a good hen-roost" (C 83). In keeping with the apocalyptic narrative, however, this utter blackness becomes the "night of the golden tiger," the scene of visionary breakthrough:

> Floating flame in the air, gonads in organdy,
> Dry flamelet, a petal borne in the wind.
> Gignetei kalon.
>   (C 99)

The shift to Greek for "beauty is born" should not prevent a recollection of Yeats' prophecy of the birth of a "terrible beauty"; indeed, Pound's use of disguised abstraction at this point seems symptomatic of the condition Yeats' poem predicts.

As a look at the first and last poems can demonstrate, the apocalyptic nar-

rative also forms the basis of the sequence as a whole. Thus Canto 17 begins
with a celebration of Dionysus:

> So that the vines burst from my fingers
> And the bees weighted with pollen
> Move heavily in the vine-shoots:
>   chirr—chirr—chir-rikk—a purring sound,
> And the birds sleepily in the branches.
>   ZAGREUS! IO ZAGREUS!
>   (C 76)

It is worth noting, in passing, that "IO" is Greek for "hail" but Italian for "I,"
the poet's praise of the god including at least an element of self-praise through
identification with the god. Pound manages to make this celebration function
as both the visionary source and the social goal, in part by means of the uncertain location of "so that" (a repetition of the device that ended Canto 1), in
part by the scene's duplication of Dante's "paradiso terrestre" and in part by
its inclusion of elements of past civilizations, such as the "baseless palazzo"
mentioned in Canto 21 (Terrell 73).[22] It is this vision that establishes Pound's
own authority, the authority that allows him to enter his poem directly and
"assure" the truth of a story: "That, I assure you, Happened. / Ego, scriptor
cantilenae" (24:112).[23] Like Dante's final vision in *Paradiso* XXXIII, Pound's vision functions as both goal and guarantee, providing the true base for the
"baseless palazzo" of the future, "beautiful" civilization, and the ground for
these cantos' anecdotal, somewhat rambling critique of the contemporary
world.[24]

    That critique necessarily presents a gloomy portrait of current conditions.
Even "tovarisch," representing the Russian revolution, is lost, with neither
direction nor leader, reduced to cursing and blessing "without aim"—Pound
perhaps critiqueing *Blast's* ebullient lists of "blasts" and "blesses." Hence the
reprisal of the visionary moment in Canto 29—this time highly sexualized—
stresses the great difficulty of its achievement.[25] Then Canto 30 begins with
Pound's complaint against pity, a major impediment to the social realization of
the Dionysian vision:

> Pity causeth the forests to fail,
> Pity slayeth my nymphs,
> Pity spareth so many an evil thing.
> Pity befouleth April,
> Pity is the root and the spring.
> Now if no fayre creature followeth me

It is on account of Pity,
It is on account that Pity forbideth them slaye
    (30:147)

Although some critics have argued that Pound means *excessive* pity here, nothing in the text provides adequate support for such a reading. And critics have generally sidestepped the human consequences of this view of pity.[26] While forests and animal herds (and even literary movements) may require pruning for their own welfare, the applicability of this concept to the human world is, to say the least, questionable: in 1933 Pound explained that the "hsin" ideogram, usually translated by the famous phrase, "make it new," showed "the fascist axe for the clearing away of rubbish" and "the tree, organic vegetable renewal" (*JM* 113); in 1939 he wrote that usury was "the cancer of the world, which only the surgeon's knife of Fascism can cut out of the life of nations" (*SP* 300). It would, of course, be unfair to read the passage entirely in terms of later Nazi racial policies—yet it seems a terrible lapse to celebrate its "beauty" without noting how readily it lends itself to a justification of such policies. Pound's esthetics are inseparable from his politics. And his ethics, originally based on a visionary apocalyptic, become increasingly distorted under the urgent pressures of the historical apocalyptic.

The final lines of Canto 30 approach the present by analogy with Renaissance Italy:

And in August that year died Pope Alessandro Borgia,
        Il Papa mori.

        Explicit canto
          XXX
    (30:149)

By ending abruptly with the Pope's death, which left a political vacuum and ended the Borgias' efforts to advance culture and unify Italy, Pound invites comparison to the similar vacuum that has afflicted Russia since the death of Lenin and Europe as a whole since the Great War. (He perhaps also implies that Renaissance civilization did not finally come to an end until August 1914.) The closing formula, unique in *The Cantos*, further strengthens this invitation into the present: rhyming Canto 30 with its year of publication, 1930, Pound suggests that this is our position in the thirtieth year of the century, needing and awaiting a new leader. In fact, Canto 28, with its story of "God the Father Eternal" himself deciding that "something was lacking" and therefore creating "the Romagnolo," had already prepared the way for the appearance of Mussolini, a native of Romagna.[27] *Il Duce* would in any case be introduced in person at the end of the next section, in Canto 41. And that canto, the eleventh of "Eleven New Cantos," rhymes with the year "XI of our era" (C 202).

Pound had already rhymed, almost incidentally, Canto 27 with the year 1927.[28] In the case of Canto 30, however, the rhyme between canto and year invokes almost a sympathetic magic, whereby this conjunction both exemplifies and helps to ensure the efficacy and validity of the poem. Yet a rhyme is but a paltry thing; it will not in itself make Pound's discourse performative. Indeed, the recourse to such a rhyme perhaps signals his own uncertainty at this point. For Cantos 17–30, despite some fine moments, seem uneven, more uncertain than the earlier group: significantly, neither Pound nor his publisher selected any material from this section for the 1970 *Selected Cantos*.[29] This uneven quality may of course be ascribed simply to flagging invention, but I think it stems more from the failure to achieve, or make sufficient progress toward, the millennial realization upon which Pound's new poetic and poem depend. The prescriptive can continue without objective confirmation, though in practice continued disconfirmation produces considerable strain and frustration, as is increasingly evident in Pound's prose of the thirties and forties. As noted above, however, the performative both expects and requires objective confirmation, external completion. Any delay threatens to invalidate the discourse itself, both in its "predictive" capability (though it is not really predictive, since it intends to effect what it states) and in its claim to truth—here Pound's entire historical analysis and even his epistemology. In response to this threat, Pound in Cantos 17–30 presents his economics more explicitly and in greater detail, and adduces much more historical material, but he is nevertheless unable to counter a diffusion, a distinct loss of focus and force.

The well-known rigidification of Pound's poetry and prose in the 1930s stems from the continuation of this threat to his enterprise: the continuing deferral of the millennial city and the increasing likelihood of war against Mussolini's Italy. Although the poem continued to be based on apocalyptics, Pound evidently saw that apocalyptic presentation in itself would not suffice, and would virtually self-destruct if prolonged *ad infinitum*. As a result, the poem became increasingly remote from the realm of esthetics as Pound sought to make it fulfill other, more specific functions. One of these was to provide a guide for the new ruler through the illustration of Douglasite economics and Confucian principles of government—hence Pound sent *A Draft of XXX Cantos* to Mussolini before their 1933 meeting, and was extraordinarily pleased when *Il Duce*'s pronouncement, "questo è divertente," indicated that he had both read the work and got "the point" (C 202). Another, simultaneous function was to provide a justification, or rationalization, for Mussolini and the fascist state. The rationalization is based first on the harmony achieved between the Confucian ruler and the natural order—the fascist state is "natural," not a perversion but an outgrowth of nature—and second on a kind of historical descent—though not in a line of filiation or even of direct influence, Mussolini is the last and the only contemporary in a line of great leaders, the rightful heir, as *Jefferson and/or Mussolini* (1935) indicates, to Jefferson's mantle. Increasingly, the *Cantos* became propaganda for Mussolini and the fascist state, the success of which alone could validate the poem.[30]

Pound's dilemma, then, was to discover a means of extending his apocalyptic presentation, of making the societal dimension more concrete and specific, without succumbing to the lie, however beautiful, of some system that would unavoidably obscure the visionary. Such systems, he clearly felt, were the cause of much of the contemporary problem: the last war, the economic situation, the increasingly evident preparation for another war. In 1928 he declared that "theoretical perfection in a government impels it ineluctably toward tyranny. . . . it is the theoretical justice or perfection of the organism, the to, for and by the plebs, that puts this more moral fervour and confidence in so dangerous a place, i.e., as powder in the cannon, and behind the projectile" (*SP* 220). Consequently Pound frequently attacked the very bases of systemic thought, reductive "Aristotelian logic," "Euclidian stasis," and the syllogism itself, "that old form of trickery" (*SP* 239, 304; *JM* 28). In the modern world, he claimed, "we no longer think or need to think in terms of mono-linear logic, the sentence structure, subject, predicate object etc." (*VA* 166). Linear thought is not only unnecessary, but is a kind of mental tyranny, unrelated to reality. It produces the "*idée fixe* . . . a dead, set, stiff, varnished 'idea' existing in a vacuum," and ultimately leads to political tyranny based on "theoretical perfection." In contrast, "the ideas of genius, or of 'men of intelligence' are organic and germinal" (*JM* 21). Pound claimed to have found the alternative—for his poem, for thought itself, and for the world as a whole—in his famous, or infamous, ideogrammic method. Since many commentators have discussed the ideogrammic method, and in considerable detail, I will not provide my own version of it. In their understandable desire to determine precisely what the concept means, however, commentators have tended to gloss over, as mere inconsistency, one of the most obvious facts about Pound's use of the term: that his meaning changes, not simply from year to year, but from context to context, and even within a single book.

In *Guide to Kulchur*, for example, Pound defines the method in terms of its revelatory intent: "The ideogrammic method consists of presenting one facet and then another until at some point one gets off the dead and desensitized surface of the reader's mind, onto a part that will register. . . . the writer's aim, at least this writer's aim being revelation, a just revelation irrespective of new-

ness or oldness" (*GK* 51). Hence "we shd. read for power," and a book based
on the ideogrammic method should become "a ball of light in one's hand" (*GK*
55). Later, though, Pound calls chapters seven and eight a single ideogram,
consisting in extended quotation of Gaudier-Brzeska's vorticist writings, an
outline of Pound's theory of the Great Bass, a brief discussion of Leibniz'
monad, and a single, short quotation from Erigena on right reason as the basis
of authority.[31] Here the ideogram evidently groups together diverse theories
that have in common the identification of a single principle as the basis for all
else in an art, a society, or entire world. That is, the seemingly disparate items
are combined according to a specific classification, but the class is left un-
named. In this case the ideogram is obviously neither revelatory nor opposed
to rational methods. Then in chapter 25 Pound sees Shakespeare's plays as
ideograms, dangerous because formless and rooted in nature, although "the
ideogram is in some way so much more definite, despite its root filaments,
than a shell-case definition" (*GK* 165–66). Here the ideogram is a complex, organic whole, as opposed to fragile, mechanistic (and militaristic) logical concepts.[32] Finally, in *Guide to Kulchur* and elsewhere Pound uses the term "ideogram" for Chinese characters, apparently believing his own ideogrammic
structures to be equivalent, despite the Chinese characters' utterly distinct
means and function. In Pound's polemical writings, and particularly in his correspondence, we can see that this inconsistency is not unfortunate and accidental, but necessary and substantial. The "ideogrammic method" is not so
much a concept denoting a specific poetic method (though it is related to juxtaposition) or a specific method of a-rational thought (it consists largely of a
principle and examples, or the examples alone), as it is simply a term that ful-
fills various *functions* necessary to Pound's enterprise. It provides Pound with
a positive term with which to oppose reason and the syllogism; it enables him
to avoid the charges of obscurity, confusion, contradiction and ignorance that
were leveled at him in the thirties (by allies as well as enemies); and, finally,
the use of a single term makes Pound's thought and poetics appear the pure,
natural outgrowths of an intuited or directly perceived reality—the visionary
basis.

Since the method applied to every level of composition, from the individual word to the entire text, Pound could constate "numinous details," distinct Images, to create a larger unit—an interpretation of history and the relation between culture and nature—without apparent recourse to any system
and without appearing even to offer an interpretation. Pound's increasing dis-
trust of systemic thought, of strategy, anticipates a good deal of postmodern
poetry and theory. Yet his response was never to celebrate or even accept fragmentation as such, but to create what amounts to a super-system: a transcendent, paradisal system that could enable the coordination of complex knowl-

edges without mediation. The ideogram as a catch-all took on properties of the Image writ large: by retaining the name of the Chinese character, Pound could invest the ideogram with all the immediacy and force of the Image, yet with the greater social consequence he saw in the Chinese character (Bernstein 47). In *Guide to Kulchur*, Richard of St. Victor's three modes of thought, "cogitation, meditation and contemplation," provide Pound with the closest Western analogue to the thought and discourse he has in mind: while in cogitation and meditation the mind moves around the object, in contemplation "it is unified with the object" (*GK* 77). Where the Image had achieved this state for a moment, Pound believes that the ideogrammic method could extend the unification characteristic of contemplation to an entire discourse. The history of Confucian rule in China gave Pound evidence of the practical effects of this extension of the Image to discourse as a whole, and certainly the Confucian example lies behind his 1935 advice to Basil Bunting: "the poet's job is to define and yet again define till the detail of surface is in accord with the root in justice" (*L* 277). Yet it is clear both from Pound's fervor and particularly from his frequent recourse to light imagery that his "totalitarian synthesis," based on the ideogrammic method, promises at least in imagination to do more than establish an adequate (accurate) discourse. For if it truly enables unification with its object, the method evidently does not simply transform, but actually transcends discourse. It would ideally—and it is the apocalyptic ideal that drives Pound—it would ideally provide an entirely nonconventional, immediate, and *natural* means of conducting social practices. In this vision, the world is a seamless whole, where language unites subject and object, where definition produces clarity, clarity produces justice, and justice produces the perfect state, by definition perfectly attuned to the natural (or divine) order. The apocalyptic Image would at last be fully realized in the millennial city.

Just as fascism achieved popularity by presenting itself as virtually the only alternative to social chaos or communism, so Pound saw his method as the sole alternative to discursive chaos. A major theme of *Guide to Kulchur* is the ability to reduce large fields to a single principle, and the ideogrammic method is in a sense the principle of principles: if it were followed, "right reason" could be achieved and all other principles—economic, social, artistic— would be revealed. Since Pound saw the ability to reduce complex fields to a single principle, a single monad, as the final, the sole defence against being set adrift "among mere nomenclatures," the ideogrammic method came increasingly to represent a last defense against all that was decrepit and deceitful, against both the distortions of reason and the weakness of diffusion (*GK* 74). So powerful and so beneficial is the ideogram that Pound can conceive of only one reason for the failure of Fenollosa's discovery to take hold, deliberate sabotage (*SP* 281): "we know that there is one enemy, ever-busy obscuring our

terms" (*GK* 31). This devious, satanic enemy—postmodern intertextuality—
would have to be dealt with in the strongest terms. As we have seen, Pound
saw the fascist axe in the "hsin" ideogram; in another favorite, "cheng," "to
focus," he saw the "sun's lance" (*Confucius* 20). During World War II the military analogy became more explicit. In 1941, in an article entitled "L'Ebreo,
patalogia incarnata," he wrote: "The ideogram is a bulwark against those who
destroy language. The ideogram is a sort of *rebus* . . . it has become a treasury
of stable wisdom, an arsenal of live thought" (qtd. in Nicholls 153). That a man
so concerned with the misuse of money and the use of war should see his great
contribution to method, to clarity, as at once a treasury and an arsenal shows
how little Pound now analyzed his own ideas. "Live thought," in any case, no
longer means independent thought, but thought subsumed to a blind faith in
Mussolini's fascism. And faith, as Pound wrote in 1942, is necessarily totalitarian, and therefore only weakened by debates, by logic and the syllogism (qtd.
in Nicholls 158).

In reality, of course, the ideogrammic method could neither achieve
Pound's ideal nor, as we have seen in the "great bass-right reason" ideogram
in *Guide to Kulchur*, present a true alternative to rationality. As George Santayana wrote to Pound in 1940, "When you ask for jumps and other particulars,
you don't mean (I suppose) *any* other particulars, although your tendency to
jumps is so irresistible that the bond between the particulars jumped to is not
always apparent? It is a mental grab-bag. A *latent* classification or a *latent* ge-
netic connection would seem to be required, if utter miscellaneousness is to be
avoided" (qtd. in Stock 477). (Later Santayana declined to collaborate with Eliot
and Pound because he did not share their "prophetic zeal and faith in the Ad-
vent of the Lord" [qtd. in Stock 478].) Pound's ideograms usually exhibit, and
perhaps more important seem to have been composed in accord with, a basis
capable of rational analysis and classification. The "great bass-right reason"
ideogram provides a concise example, but the Middle Cantos as a whole are
based on revealing the strengths of Confucian rule and the degree to which
one intelligent man, by following Confucian precepts, can accomplish the ideal
state. By denying rationality any validity, however, Pound makes criticism of
his work impossible. The ideogrammic method allowed its author to believe he
had escaped all rational criticism and to avoid self-criticism. Because his
method supersedes rational thought, there is no means to critique his extraordinary faith in Mussolini: "Any thorough judgment of MUSSOLINI will be in
a measure an act of faith, it will depend on what you *believe* the man means,
what you believe that he wants to accomplish" (*JM* 33). Having refused the
terror of reductive reason, Pound could only embrace the terror of fascist ideology.

The key, in fact the sole criterion for the validity of Pound's method (and with it the fascist state), is once again its realization, its immediate effectiveness. More and more, Pound's utterance had to take effect; it had to be as practically effective as Lenin's or Mussolini's (or, later, Hitler's). Both Lenin and Mussolini, in fact, were valued as much for their style as for any particular act. Pound compared Mussolini's Milan speech to Brancusi's sculpture, "the stone blocks from which no error emerges, from whatever angle one looks at them" (*JM* ix). As early as 1928, in his own *Exile*, Pound praised Lenin above all for his means of expression: "LENIN is more interesting than any surviving stylist [!]. He probably never wrote a single brilliant sentence . . . but he invented or very nearly invented a new medium, something between speech and action (language as cathode ray) which is worth any writer's study" ("Data" 116).[33] The last sentence goes some way toward accounting for the more propagandistic and less overtly poetic nature of the Chinese and Adams Cantos: because they aspire toward this in-between condition of a new, revolutionary medium, of writing becoming action, esthetic value becomes a function of practical effect. But in denying that "*real* intelligence exists until it comes into action," Pound seemed willing largely to eschew intelligence for the sake of action (*JM* 18). Concern for truth could also be jettisoned: "The truth is that Jefferson used verbal formulations as tools. He was not afflicted by fixations. . . . Jefferson as a lawyer and as a law scholar used legalities and legal phrases as IMPLEMENTS, Mussolini as an ex-editor uses oratory. . . . And if one takes it from the spoken news-reel, one sees that it differs from town to town. For the guy knows his eggs and his Italy" (*JM* 62, 65). As the last sentence indicates, Pound's zeal would scarcely permit him to stop to consider the possible ramifications of this extreme pragmatism.

Of course, discourse is always and immediately involved with pragmatics. Pound, however, eschewed all means of judgment. Because of the urgency of the situation and because of his aspiration toward a performative discourse, Pound increasingly distorted his own words to suit particular audiences, eventually ignoring or glossing over immense distinctions. *Jefferson and/or Mussolini*, for example, ends climactically with Pound's equation of beauty with order:

> I assert again my own firm belief that the Duce will stand not with despots
> and the lovers of power but with the lovers of
> ORDER
> τὸ καλόν

(*JM* 128)

Despite the explicit denial, this capitalized and centered order, heavily stressed, seems inseparable from despotism and the exercise of power—a terrible beauty indeed. Although he continued to stress the intimate connection between accurate definition and justice, Pound wrote that "another form" of his (reasonable and humane) statement that the purpose of an economic system is "to make sure that the whole people shall be able to eat (in a healthy manner), to be housed (decently) and be clothed (in a way adequate to the climate)," was Mussolini's "DISCIPLINE THE ECONOMIC FORCES AND EQUATE THEM TO THE NEEDS OF THE NATION" (*SP* 298). First "beauty," then "order," now "discipline" and "equate": one would scarcely think this sentence involved actual human beings at all. Here, for the sake of performance—of "ideas going into action"—Pound willingly, eagerly accepts precisely that political tyranny he had always sought to avoid (*GK* 44).[34]

Inseparable from this desire for a fully performative discourse was an acute intensification of Pound's already developed apocalyptic. His friends and correspondents of the thirties were quick to note his increasingly messianic tone, his shift from practicalities to absolutes. Zukofsky, for example, remarked on it to Pound on several occasions ("You seem to think you are the Messiah"), adding that he seemed "sunk in an absolute which has no useful relation to the present, or a bettering of the present" (*PZ* 172, 183). And Pound himself repeated McNair Wilson's observation that his trip to America was the product of a messianic urge.[35]

Certainly Pound's frenzied writings of the thirties and forties show a marked increase in overtly apocalyptic rhetoric. Evocations of Utopia and of his importance for its achievement become ubiquitous, albeit presented in a tone at once sincere and ironic, acknowledging the extravagance of what was nevertheless an informing rhetoric. He saw the war as a product of the millennial struggle between good and evil: "This war was not caused by a caprice of Mussolini, or of Hitler. This war is part of the millennial war between usurers and peasants, between usury, or rather the usurocracy and those who spend the day in honest labor with their hands and intelligence."[36] Usury, of course, was "age-old": by this point Pound was reading the biblical fall as a usury parable (*P* 190).[37] The very term, "usurocracy," served to transform particular cases of usury and particular usurers into instances and agents of a "never-dying" maleficent force, an eternal, palpable evil (*America* 18). Hence Roosevelt is "not autonomous, not self-created [as Satan claimed], but an unclean exponent of something less circumscribed than his own evil personal existence" (*America* 18). The financiers and their allies are evil incarnate, "the spawm [*sic*] of hell. These are the men who fear the light, and who pervert the whole of human education in order to preserved [*sic*] a darkness which shelters them."[38] Pound believed that he was continuing the Revolutionary War, attempting to correct the "great betrayal of 1863"—the echoes of Satan's original "great betrayal" and of the Pope's "gran rifiuto" in Dante are unmistakable—when the American people were condemned to debt slavery by the financiers (*Radio* 392–

93). Europe was united in defence of the "heritage," "the treasures of CIVILI-ZATION," while "allied with its enemies are two governments ONLY, and both of them are subject to the black influence of men who make war for money, to men who restrict human output, who [like Satan] hate every gift of god."[39] That Mussolini's blackshirts contradicted this imagery of light and dark no doubt contributed to the increasing strain evident in Pound's rhetoric. Overt fascist violence, however, could always be excused as the outcome of other governments' attacks, or as the act of "some black sheep" having "succeeded in getting in among the Black Shirts," as Luigi Villari had explained in his 1926 account of *The Fascist Experiment* for a British public (viii).

But World War II was not simply another in an unending series of wars. As in World War I, Pound embraced a confused mixture of historical and alle-gorical apocalyptics, at times creating rather bizarre fusions of apocalyptic im-agery and practicality: "American editors and newspaper men hav[e] a per-fectly well grounded terror of the power that rules by night, and strikes mercilessly at the pocket" (*Radio* 394). He does not articulate his ultimate aims, but his extraordinary, even fanatic intensity indicates an underlying belief that a united Europe would at last defeat and eradicate the forces of evil, thereby leading to something like a world government—based on Confucian percep-tions, "a nation that should never do wrong must necessarily govern the world."[40] If the usurers were eliminated, there would no longer be any serious hindrance to such a government, or to the general prosperity that "WAS just round the corner" (*Radio* 86). It was the old mythologic narrative, but the pre-sence of Mussolini and the nearness of the final battle, Armageddon, now com-bined to render all else superfluous.[41]

The two factors together—the drive for a fully performative discourse in the context of apocalypse—produce another significant effect: an utter depen-dence on speed. The increasing urgency (and corresponding rancor) of Pound's prose and poetry in the thirties no doubt reflects in part the rising tension of the political climate, but it also and more importantly stems from a need to accelerate writing itself. Speed, after all, was essential to good government: in *Jefferson and/or Mussolini* Pound wrote that "the best government is that which translates the best thought most speedily into action" (*JM* 91). During the war he declared that "le beau monde governs because it has the most rapid means of communication," a means that closely resembles Pound's practice in the *Cantos*: "it communicates by the detached phrase, variable in length, but timely" (*SP* 313).[42] Also, Pound's conspiracy theories included, as we have seen with respect to the ideogrammic method, the real possibility of sabo-tage—war itself being "the highest . . . and most atrocious form of sabotage"—and sabotage is perhaps best avoided by preemptive speed (*America* 15).[43]

More significant is the direct connection between speed and the immediacy of revelation characteristic of the visionary apocalyptic—hence Pound's long-standing adoption of Aristotle's definition of genius as the "swift perception of relations," and his praise of Mussolini's "swiftness of mind, . . . the speed with which his real emotion is shown in his face, so that only a crooked man cd. misinterpret his meaning" (*GK* 105; the last phrase also shows his continuing fear of sabotage). Finally, speed becomes an absolute necessity for the perfection, which is to say the transcension, of discourse. For Pound's emphasis on speed is markedly distinct from Vorticist speed, from the explosive speed of *Blast*'s laughter. Speed here is a means to an end, a means toward the establishment of a specific, superior position. Pound's work does not create a "vortical occupation of a space," constituting "the absolute movement of the weapon," but rather seeks to abolish movement altogether: not the freedom of speed, but the totality of immediacy (Deleuze and Guattari 397). Indeed, the word "vortex" itself now becomes associated with evil: in Canto 41, Jefferson refers to the rising price of real estate "in a vortex of paper"—money cut off from its ground and therefore subject to artificial manipulation (41:206). Like "HIEN TSONG the idolater," celebrated in Canto 56 for honoring Confucius, Pound sought "a word to make change" (*C* 313). Although Pound deplored the "Taozers' " claim to have "a medicine that gives immortality," this emphasis on the perfect word—the "precise definition" taken to an absolute—indicates his actual affinity with such claims. With its reference to elixirs and alchemy, the passage from Canto 56 even seems to acknowledge the extravagance of his own aims: Hien Tsong is

> another Lord seeking elixir
> seeking the transmutation of metals
> seeking a word to make change
>   (*C* 313)

The "rays idiogram" that prefaces the Chinese History Cantos also alludes to the possibility of a transmutational word (*C* 254). Pound's would ideally become the incarnate word, abolishing any need of interpretation and all possibility of mistake. It would thus circumvent, or rather preempt, what was to become the "always already" of postmodernism, the loss of the origin—or the loss of faith in the origin—that necessitates the adoption of tactics rather than the production of strategy.

Speed, then, is both a means to transcend conventional discourse and a sign that it has been transcended, that an insight or discourse or government constitutes a direct extension of nature and the divine. Without sufficient speed, the people, especially the leaders, would not learn from Pound's work; without sufficient speed, the smooth, seamless whole of the work itself, from root to surface, would break apart into disjunct fragments of mere convention, mirroring the fragmented culture it sought to surmount (*SP* 309). This relation between speed and discourse is figured most clearly in Pound's light imagery, where light both figures and exemplifies a kind of continuous instantaneity. Hence Pound's remark during the war that "in our intellectual life—or 'struggle', if you prefer it—we need facts that illuminate like a flash of lightning, and authors who set their subjects in a steady light" (*SP* 327). Such facts and such authors would presumably combine to create a "steady flash," a permanent visionary immediacy. The pressure of the apocalyptic finally pushes Pound's discourse into what D. J. O'Connor terms a "pragmatic paradox," a state in which "the effective truth of a proposition appears to depend on the precipitation or haste with which it is discursively produced" (Klein and Warner 3). Speed becomes so important, in fact, that in Canto 62 Pound has John Adams make the general statement, "Immediacy: in order to be of any effect," when Adams had actually regretted that circumstances compelled him to write his *Defence of the Constitution of the United States of America* too quickly (C 347).[44] Pound's entire enterprise, which increasingly became, as he put it later, a "continual polemic in two languages," thus came to depend on speed: if he could only go fast enough, the work would be whole and the *Cantos* could still achieve confirmation, embodiment, in the ideal state (*Selected Poems*, "Biography").[45]

It is in light of this "pragmatic paradox," this absolute necessity of speed (and very nearly of speed alone) that we should understand both the remarkable rate of production and the content of the 170 pages comprising Cantos 52–71, the last sequence to be completed before the war. Though begun in 1938, the sequence was substantially written and completed within the first three months of 1939 (*SL* 322; Nicholls 112). Pound's increasing frustration at his readers' inability to get the point is evident in the first lines of Canto 52, when he declares that the reader already knows the truth:

> And I have told you of how things were under Duke Leopold in Siena
> And of the true base of credit, that is the abundance of nature
> with the whole folk behind it.
> (C 257)

Later, over Rome Radio, this frustration becomes more acute: "I have been twenty years on this job, but you will not read" (*Radio* 382). Despite his efforts and despite the simplicity of the solution, the world's problems continue. In Canto 52 Pound at first locates the responsibility in a mythic evil, "neschek . . . the serpent," but the serpent is quickly identified with a specific group:

> better keep out the jews
>   or yr/ grand children will curse you
> jews, real jews, chazims, and *neschek*
> also super-neschek or the international racket
>   (C 257)

Faber and Faber's insistence that the next five lines be blacked out to avoid libel suits could only have strengthened Pound's conviction that these evil forces were out to sabotage his efforts. (The lines have now been restored; they refer to "Stinkschuld.") But since the material already presented, despite its self-evident clarity, "no longer holds against *neschek*," the poem could only "make the song firm and well given" again by intensifying the mode of attack it had already deployed (C 52:258).

Cantos 52–71 therefore seek to secure and strengthen the basis of the poem by expanding both the geographical area (to China) and the time frame (from "2837 ante Christum" [C 53:262]). This enlarged base would also and by no means incidentally supply greater leverage for influencing the reader. Not only the poem, however, but the poet, too, needed to strengthen the claim to authority by establishing a greater temporal perspective. Pound came to refer frequently, in and out of the *Cantos*, both to the length of his own struggle and to his grandfather's earlier participation in the ongoing battle: "even my own observations date largely before the opening of the present hostilities, as do those of my grandfather expressed in the U.S. Congress in 1878" (*Radio* 393). This need to buttress his personal authority also indicates the increasing strain on Pound himself.

The poem's co-option of China also has striking geostrategic implications, as if Pound were actually thinking of the *Cantos* as a kind of guide to military strategy. Pound several times refers to the allies' "encirclement" of the axis powers and in particular of Germany (*Radio* 30, 305). He is especially scornful of the alliance between the United States and Communist Russia, since it is clearly based on convenience, rather than principle—such allies could only continue the "general indefinite wobble" already noted in Canto 35; they could not create the "unwobbling pivot," the true unity, of Kung and Eleusis, or of Jefferson and Mussolini (C 173). Pound's 1945 translation of Confucius' "Chung Yung" as *L'asse che non vacilla*, the "unwobbling axis," clearly attempts to have the sage speak directly on behalf of the axis powers.[46] Already in Cantos 52–71, however, Pound uses China as if to counter the allies' treacherous encirclement with his own, grander encirclement of the reader, who would thus find it impossible to escape the force of the poem's argument. This would seem to be the point of the historical rhymes and puns in a passage of Canto 53:

'Peace and abundance bring virtue.' I am
    'pro-Tcheou' said Confucius five centuries later.
With his mind on this age.

周

Chou

(C 268)

"This age," of course, can refer to both the age of Tcheou and that of Mussolini, another believer in peace and abundance. And the ideogram "chou" means "to encircle"—and so to control and order.

Perhaps above all, however, these Cantos bombard the reader with a great deal more information, and at a faster rate, in an apparent attempt to obliterate all resistance. "Know then" is Canto 52's dramatic, forceful, and in retrospect almost ominous transition from despair at the present situation in Europe to the great mass of Chinese history. Besides making his own speed possible, Pound's means of composition—mostly a reductive transcription and selection of his sources on Chinese history and John Adams—was also intended to accelerate the spread of this information to the proper authorities. As Canto 54 declares, "History is a school book for princes," a sentiment echoed later by John Adams (C 280). Indeed, these cantos look, read, and function much like a textbook, if a rather chaotic one, including a table of contents, marginal lines to emphasize crucial points (usually concerned with economics), and even suggestions for further study: the pupil, for example, should "look up his [Yong Tching's] verses" (C 340). This textbook would presumably provide the "catechumen" with the basis for proper thought, proper action, and proper judgment: the unwobbling pivot, of course, of "Kung and Eleusis" (C 258, 272). In this sense, there is little difference between these instructional cantos and Pound's other writings on economics and politics; they are but different modes of the same enterprise, a continuation of Pound's war by other means. The straightforward juxtaposition of quotations that constitutes his 1938 "Introductory Textbook" on the economic history of the United States, for example, could easily have been placed in the poem—the Adams quotation that begins the textbook is in fact central to this sequence of the poem (SP 159). Some specific devices, in fact, seem intended to point out the similarity: the use of "SO THAT" in one speech echoes Cantos 1 and 17 (309), while the varied repetitions of "Pound speaking" echo the poem's "ego scriptor." Moreover, some of these cantos were first published in journals devoted to social and economic issues, while one became the text of a radio broadcast.

Pound nevertheless told several correspondents that Cantos 52–71 constituted his "best book" (Norman 375; Stock 479); he sent the volume to Mussolini with a note claiming that the book was "far from neutral" and expressing the hope that he had "done a useful job" (qtd. in Bacigalupo 98). Indeed, the famous phrase, "make it new, day by day, make it new" clearly rhymes with the fascist "continual revolution" (C 53:265; 54:278). In *Jefferson and/or Mussolini* Pound himself connects the Confucian ideograms to the symbol of fascism (taken from Roman soldiers) by reading the Hsin ideogram for "renovate" or "renew" as showing "the fascist axe for the clearing away of rubbish" (113).[47] And the last two cantos, which present an indictment of England, together with Adams' arguments against going to war with France, are aimed directly at the United States' relations with Mussolini's Italy—according to Canto 70, Adams had been in favor of "eternal neutrality in all wars of Europe," Pound taking care to omit, without indication, Adams' qualifying "if possible" (C 410). At one point in the sequence Pound directly addresses Mussolini: "TSONG of TANG put up granaries / somewhat like those you wish to establish" (55:298). Canto 40, immediately before Mussolini's entrance into the poem, had ended with a declaration of intent:

> seeking an exit
> To the high air, to the stratosphere, to the imperial
> calm, to the empyrean, to the baily of the four towers
> the NOUS, the ineffable crystal
>   (C 201)

In retrospect, this passage seems ambivalently situated between desire for the poem's *paradiso* and desire for an actual *paradiso terrestre*. Pound's inscription in his wife's copy of the published volume—"To build up the city of Dioce / (Tan Wu Tsze) / whose terraces are the colour of stars"—makes the purpose of his haste and the rationale for the sequence clear: the securing and perfecting of *Il Duce's* regime, identified with the millennial city.[48] The sequence ends by juxtaposing the essential problem, "ignorance of coin, credit and circulation," with a hymn to Zeus, reminding the reader that correct rule should be by civil law in harmony with natural law. Once again, the juxtaposition functions as a call to action. Cantos 52–71 were originally to be followed by the poem's *paradiso* because their timely contribution, "ideological and propagandist," would help to create the paradisal state on earth (*America* 14).[49]

Paradise, however, had once again to be deferred. Cantos 72 and 73 were not written until 1944, when the war was virtually lost, and they mark a return to Hell. However, the continuing desire for greater speed, for immediacy, is evident in Pound's abandonment of English for these cantos, which were written in Italian and partially published in January and February 1945. The two Cantos are explicitly and single-mindedly propagandist, pressing Marinetti and even Cavalcanti into service for the war effort. Canto 72 begins in a Dantesque mode, commenting à propos this "guerra di merda" [shit war] that God after creating the world "cacò il gran' usuraio Satana-Gerione" [shat the great usurer Satan-Geryon], who in turn was the prototype of Churchill's "fathers" or "bosses." In Dantesque fashion Pound encounters the shades of Marinetti—who at first wants Pound's body in order to continue fighting—and other dead heroes, all enthusiastic supporters of Mussolini's war. Marinetti even tells the bizarre story of a skull (of a fallen Italian) in the Gobi Desert that sings of Italy's future resurgence, despite major setbacks (C 425–31). In Canto 73 the spirit of Cavalcanti relates, in military rhythms, the story of a patriotic Rimanese girl who achieves martyrdom by leading a group of Canadian soldiers into a mine field. Now, Cavalcanti tells us, her ghost can be seen singing "Gloria della patria" as she walks through Paradise with a German on either arm (C 432–35). Tales of popular support and of heroic self-sacrifice among the common people are of course the stock-in-trade of the propagandist, whatever the war and on whatever side; Pound was especially interested in this story because it concerned the fall of Rimini to the allied forces—a fall that had resulted in damage to Sigismundo Malatesta's Church of San Francesco, the Tempio Pound so much admired.[50] Yet here the use of "shades" of the dead, like the switch to Italian, seems a clear measure of Pound's increasing despair of any real resurgence. Placing this tale in the mouth of the author of that great definition of love, "Donna mi Priegha," seems an utterly grotesque irony. With progress in English delayed and even, owing to the disruption of mail, completely blocked, Pound shifted to the only language—propagandistic Italian—that might still be capable of sufficient speed. In this respect, the Italian Cantos, while not especially successful, are critical to a full understanding of Pound's project—of its trajectory, as it were. The recent inclusion of these poems in the collected *Cantos* makes it difficult to estheticize or ignore Pound's politics; instead, they force us to grasp the political dimensions of his esthetics.[51]

In fact, the Rome Radio broadcasts, for which Pound was indicted for treason, should also be seen as a continuation of the *Cantos* by other means. If, as he frequently asserted, "dichten = condensare," to write poetry is to condense, radio offered such condensation as to effect a virtual effacement of the means of transmission. Pound's radio broadcasts attempt to make electronic immediacy compensate for printed delay.[52] With the turn to radio, however, suppressed contradictions came to the fore—"the air," as Pound acknowledged, "isn't the habitual place for bedrock" (*Radio* 152). It was no medium for the incarnate word, for vision. The people needed to *see* the ideogram, to *see* the truth. While radio came closer to supplying the necessary immediacy, it did so only at the cost of contributing to the fragmentation Pound was struggling to counter. A letter to Ronald Duncan makes the dilemma clear. The radio was "a God damn destructive and dispersive devil of an invention," and Pound "was able to do 52/71 [only] because I was the last survivin' monolith who did not have a bloody radio in the 'ome." However, it had "got to be faced," and while the "mass of apes and worms will be further reduced to passivity," "if anyone is a purrfekk HERRRkules, he may survive, and *may* clarify his style in *resistance* to the devil box. I mean if he ain't druv to melancolia crepitans before he recovers" (*SL* 343). Much earlier, Pound had compared the style of Cantos 18–19 to radio broadcasts, in part because "there ain't no key."[53] But now he was attempting to provide the key in a medium that even he acknowledged would make him stumble about: "I lose my thread some times. So much that I can't count on anyone's knowing. Thread, as they call it, of discourse" (57). When he did keep to the thread, it was often completely illogical: the very fact that the Protocols of Zion were a forgery, for example, was cited as "the one proof we have of their authenticity."[54] Even the speed of radio seemed speed in a vacuum: a rather plaintive Pound wished that someone out there would "pick up a point here and there, over some faint lonely wave-length, and apply it right in the home" (*Radio* 105). The loneliness Pound ascribed to the medium was doubtless his own; having little knowledge of any audience, he came to feel even more isolated.

Both the shift to Italian and the abandonment, however temporary, of print for electronic aurality reveal, and no doubt at the time increased, the tremendous strain on the very basis of Pound's contradictory enterprise. After all, it was the usurer who was "always in a hurry" for quick profit, and whose "accelerated grimace" Pound had rejected long before; for true prosperity, based on agriculture, "slowness is beauty" (*Radio* 251; *P* 188; *C* 586). And even if speed were necessary, sufficient speed—to attain the "root in justice," to ensure its direct connection to "detail of surface," to reveal the truth to all, and finally to effect its material realization—could never be attained.

Paradise Postponed

Given this drive toward immediacy, performativity, and transparency, all ultimately dependent on the realization of the millennial city, the *Cantos* could have achieved only a false paradise, even if Mussolini had been successful. But in any case, the defeat of Mussolini and the arrest and incarceration of Pound himself shattered his and the *Cantos'* world, destroying any hope of an impending realization of the ideal state. In the face of this extreme disconfirmation of his enterprise, the Pisan Cantos, written while Pound was incarcerated at the Detention Training Center near Pisa, necessarily abandoned the persuasive, propagandistic discourse of the Middle Cantos. Although some readers of the sequence have attributed to Pound a new humility, a new willingness to admit to error—evidently meant to "redeem" Pound for his support of Mussolini and Hitler—Pound in fact neither abandoned his beliefs nor retracted his support of fascism. While such passages as "I surrender neither the empire nor the temples / plural / nor the constitution nor yet the city of Dioce" from the beginning of the sequence are often cited as evidence that Pound retained his ideals, the many passages wherein Pound celebrates or laments various fascist leaders are seldom given as evidence of his retention of more practical beliefs (C 74:448). Yet on the first page Pound does not merely note Mussolini's death, but very nearly deifies him, and insists that his death leaves an unfillable void, comparable to that left by the death of Confucius.[55] And only one page from the end of the sequence Pound honors a string of fallen fascist leaders for their "humanitas," translated as "manhood": "Xaire Alessandro / Xaire Fernando, e il Capo, / Pierre, Vidkun, / Henriot": Alessandro Pavolini, secretary of the Fascist Republican party; Fernando Mezzasoma, minister of popular culture; Mussolini himself; Pierre Laval, premier of Vichy France; Vidkun Quisling, collaborator and head of Norway under occupation; and Philippe Henriot, journalist, radio propagandist, and minister in Vichy France (C 84:553). Yet the impossibility of embodying the ideal state in anything like the near future—together with the very real possibility of Pound's execution—made persuasion futile and the achievement of a socially performative discourse impossible. Rather than present a false paradise, then, the Pisan Cantos, because of the necessary decentering of persuasion, resort to a difficult, fragmented paradise that has been much admired by both critics and poets.

Indeed, this sense of a necessarily scattered paradise, together with the often playful fragmentation evident in the sequence, has made it an important source for postwar American poetics. It is not that Pound's perception of the world was radically altered by the war: in 1942 he had remarked that "our culture lies shattered in fragments" (SP 309). But where the earlier cantos strategically exhort readers to strive for attunement to "the process" in order to achieve the ideal state and surmount this fragmentation, the Pisan sequence seems to embody the process in its poetics, with propositions and structures arising out of and dissolving into the ongoing poem like ad hoc tactics. The poem is inventive rather than systematic: the shattering of the dream, as Pound would later refer to it, shattered strategy also (C 816). It is for this reason that the Pisan Cantos are particularly important for us. Even though Pound refused to concede that his earlier strategy was wrong, the Pisan Cantos in many respects exhibit an abandonment of strategy in favor of tactics that has come to typify postmodern, postwar poetics. They embody a highly developed, yet hybrid poetic that displays the postmodern while retaining the modern.

As Anthony Woodward has remarked, confident summations of the Pisan Cantos tend to elide the basic, indeed obvious fact of their extreme fragmentation, so extreme as to produce considerable uncertainty concerning both the local meanings and, as a result, the overall significance of these cantos (36). Where earlier cantos attempt to thwart systemic, rational thought by choosing fragmentation and juxtaposition, in the Pisan Cantos Pound seems cast adrift among the shards of various systems, various discourses, and to be rather desperately, if in the end adroitly, swimming from one to another. The sequence's more famous affirmations—"now in the mind [or heart] indestructible," "nothing counts save the quality of the affection," "Amo ergo sum," etc.—may well be judged valid, but they first appear as shards, tenuous, unstable, and subject to the considerable pressures of Pound's experience (C 74:456; 77:480; 80:507). As Pound famously puts it, his is "by no means an orderly Dantescan rising / But as the winds veer" (C 74:457). The integrity of the sequence, then, does not derive from its structuring around or in accord with a set of propositions, for propositions, being provisional, cannot support a final structure: their "suave air" may "give way to scirocco" (C 74:439).

The provisional nature of such statements can be illustrated by many passages in the Pisan Cantos, and especially by larger contrasts, but here one passage, from Canto 77, must suffice:

> As Arcturus passes over my smoke-hole
>   the excess electric illumination
>   is now focussed
> on the bloke who stole a safe he cdn't open
>   (interlude entitled: periplum by camion)
>   and Awoi's *hennia*   plays hob in the tent flaps
>   k-lakk. . . . .thuuuuuu
>   making rain
>   uuuh
> 2,   7,   hooo
>   der im Baluba
>
>   Faasa !   4 times was the city remade,
> now in the heart indestructible
>   4 gates, the 4 towers

(Il Scirocco è geloso)
     men rose out of Χθόνος
     Agada, Ganna, Silla,
  and Mt Taishan is faint as the wraith of my first friend
  who comes talking ceramics;
    mist glaze over mountain

  "How is it far, if you think of it?"

Came Boreas and his kylin
to brreak the corporal's heart
 (C 479)

Out of context, "now in the heart indestructible" (echoing the earlier "now in the mind indestructible" [C 456]) appears a striking affirmation of the indomitability of the individual.[56] In context, however, the statement is much more tenuous. The parenthetical scirocco can only be jealous of this city: wind and rain may be part of the process that creates fertility, but they are also part of the process that gradually wears down material cities. And Pound's current "city" is his tent, itself threatened by the wind: in the Noh play, "Awe no Uye," Awoi's *hennia* is her demon, the demon of jealousy. Pound explains in his introduction to the play that it is a manifestation of her own "mind or troubled spirit," rather than a separate creature: "the whole play is a dramatization, or externalization, of Awoi's jealousy" (T 325). In this passage, then, the wind is both an external and an internal threat: the material wind attacking Pound's tent (which represents all that now opposes him), the material forces that destroyed Mussolini's Italy (many of which, Pound will suggest, were internal), and the corresponding internal turbulence that threatens Pound's mental and emotional stability. The faintness of Pound's Mt. Taishan, "mist glaze over mountain," and his query, "how is it far, if you think of it," therefore gain poignancy from their assertion of a tenuous stability in the face of the surrounding, overwhelming reality, for the real Mt. Taishan is as impossible to see as Mussolini's Italy. Finally, the scirocco is transformed into the north wind, the ferocity of which—"kylin," perhaps a Chinese fabulous animal, may be rhymed with "killin' "—ends the passage on a particularly bleak note: far from being indestructible, hearts, like minds, may be broken.

  The passage is not, however, as serious as this analysis would suggest, for Pound is perhaps above all else playing. The trilled "r" of "brreak" indicates that he is mimicking an accent, while earlier he presents a Chaplinesque "periplum by camion," a Japanese demon playing hob, and a rather madcap rain dance. Not incidentally, the rain dance is initiated by the demon and itself results in the city that the rain threatens to destroy. Both the constructive and the destructive aspects of the process are acknowledged here, and the whole process is celebrated by Pound's activity rather than by any set proposition. The entire passage, in fact, develops from the preceding lines:

things have ends (or scopes) and beginnings. To

know what precedes and what follows

will assist yr/ comprehension of process

(C 479)

To understand the process is to acknowledge both construction and destruction, and to take joy in the activity.[57] The poetic of the Pisan Cantos therefore implies a writing that is particularly attentive to its own activity, and which tends toward a fugal interplay of themes and discourses rather than a structural synthesis and resolution within one discourse.[58]

This avoidance of synthesis also stems from factors other than fragmentation and particularly from the sequence's famous obscurity. Pound's accumulation of disjunct, paratactic phrases produces such ambiguity and indeterminancy that it is often difficult for the reader to be certain just what claims are being made in any given passage. As Peter Nicholls observes, even the context of a seemingly straightforward line, such as "To build the city of Dioce whose terraces are the colour of stars" on the first page of the sequence, is uncertain: the city here could be Mussolini's project, Pound's earlier project, or the visionary city of the Pisan Cantos (164). This indeterminacy allows the reader to maintain at least the appearance of a critical distance from some of the sequence's more unpalatable statements. The remarkable multiplication of discourses and brief references—historical, literary, personal, and local—is also significant, for the consequent obscurity effectively thwarts any immediate resolution of the meanings of even brief passages. Even the short quotation above from Canto 77 uses four foreign languages and makes some half dozen references, not all of which have as yet been explained.[59] The consequent, extraordinary difficulty of the Pisan sequence implies an abandonment of the great synthesis, the great strategy, Pound had for so long sought to develop.

Moreover, the extensive use of Chinese ideograms—which at times form a distinct, parallel text—could well be taken as the intrusion, rather than representation and absorption, of the "other" of the Western world. Where in Canto 4 the East is included by means of the story of Père Henri Jacques and in the Chinese Cantos it is translated en masse, as if its entire history could be absorbed, the ideograms in the Pisan Cantos appear to be simply, materially, *there*: the other as such, incapable of absorption. Christine Froula correctly points out that the ideograms' "most powerful import remains, even after one learns their significations, the unassimilable difference with which their obscure and silent presence confronts the Western reader" (154). This is particularly the case in Canto 77, where on one page eight ideograms form a sentence that visually parallels and perhaps comments on an alphabetic text that makes no reference whatsoever to the Chinese (C 481; cf. 512). Pound's new and highly praised attention to the minutiae of nature, to his fellow prisoners, and to the details of daily life around him would seem to corroborate this reading: all are acknowledgments of the "other," and thus of the impossibility of achieving his totalitarian synthesis.[60]

And yet, while the Pisan Cantos undeniably produce this effect of an abandonment of strategy, there is another explanation of their distinctive features entirely consonant with Pound's previous work. The text's obscurity, for example, can be seen in a quite different perspective: not so much thwarting meaning as deferring it to a time when the references will be explained and the fragmented syntax resolved. The references encourage readers to make their own contributions to a resolution, while the markedly propulsive, paratactic syntax pushes readers onward, toward some future synthesis. Moreover, Pound had always celebrated the "other"—not as a limitation of self and strategy, but as their basis, as the apocalyptic insight beyond discourse that guarantees the image, the word, and the world. Thus the Chinese ideograms, while acknowledging the limits of Pound's alphabetic language, also embody in his text that "simple" wisdom, "past metaphor," that formed the basis of both Imagism and the right reason of the Confucian ruler (C 82:540). The ideogram is not present as an emblem of a social "other," but as the foundation of Pound's synthesis. Pound's attention to nature also continues his earlier project. Nature's plenitude, itself an expression of the divine, not only saves Pound's sanity in the Detention Training Center—through grass, birds, a lizard, an ant's forefoot, and so on—but had long before provided the agricultural basis for his economic and social vision of the thirties: the Sienese bank, Monte dei Paschi, had been based on harvest, while proper concern for agriculture is an important and consistent theme of the Chinese Cantos, and Mussolini's agrarian policies are frequently noted admiringly. Nor does the Pisan Cantos' assimilation of human destructiveness to the process, symbolized throughout by the wind and rain, instance a new humility. For by ultimately ascribing Mussolini's defeat to the process, Pound reaffirms the basis of his support for Mussolini—the error must lie in fascist Italy's inadequate embodiment of the process, not in the enterprise as such. What is in fact new about nature and the ideogram in the sequence is not so much their presence as their primary relation, which is to Pound as individual rather than to the state in the abstract.

Indeed, the sequence's most famous statement of humility, the "pull down thy vanity" passage ending Canto 81, does not on inspection reveal any humility in Pound's relation to others:

> The ant's a centaur in his dragon world.
> Pull down thy vanity, it is not man
> made courage, or made order, or made grace.
>   (C 535)

Pound has already identified himself "as a lone ant from a broken ant-hill / from the wreckage of Europe, ego scriptor" (C 74:472). The ant also exemplified the "perfect and complete intelligence" of men like Mussolini, while the three ants that in Canto 48 kill a "great worm" probably represent the fascist leaders, together with Pound, destroying usury (*JM* 18; C 243). And much earlier, in Canto 4, he had identified the centaur with the special position and power of the poet. Here it is not the poet, Pound, who is vain, for he has always believed in a divine basis for human order, in a doctrine that "is one, indivisible, a nature extending to every detail" (*SP* 82). It is rather the dragons, the warmongers around him, who thwart the divine order he so clearly sees.[61] Far from questioning and qualifying his enterprise, the "other" in the Pisan Cantos is the divine "beyond" to which Pound is most attuned, and which therefore continues to guarantee his own integrity and his project's validity.

What I am suggesting, then, is that the Pisan Cantos in effect abandon strategy at the social and historical level in order to recuperate it by precisely the means early Christians used in the face of the disconfirmation of their millennial hopes: internalization and deferral. To some extent reversing the process of externalization Pound's apocalyptic underwent in response to World War I, the sequence continues Pound's war by other means. Deferral and internalization enable him to acknowledge the defeat of fascist Italy without conceding the failure of his own discourse. In fact, Pound blames the defeat largely on the ignorance and corruption of those around Mussolini,

> half-baked and amateur
>   or mere scoundrels
> To sell their country for half a million
>   hoping to cheat more out of the people
>   (C 80:510)[62]

The renewed intensity with which Pound invokes a synthesis of Kung and Eleusis in the sequence—particularly at the close of Canto 77—marks his need to develop a firm yet distant perspective on the war, a position outside the present chaos, in which he can recoup his synthesis and from which he can again deploy his strategy. The danger of this new strategy lies in the ease with which Pound's project could become idealized, completely eschewing any material correlative. That Pound himself was acutely aware of this problem is evident in the frequent refrain, "Le paradis n'est pas artificiel," a direct refutation of Baudelaire's "artificial paradise" (C 74:452; 76:474; 77:482; 83:542). A passage from a 1938 article should clarify Pound's meaning: "*When* the idea is complete, it goes into action. The defective (unripe) idea stays in the shell of the 'private world.' The great mind will not create an 'artificial paradise' but a world which will come, which will objectify itself more or less quickly" (qtd. in Nicholls 100). Haphazard fragments of paradise, such as "unexpected excellent sausage" and "the smell of mint," may be a sufficient temporary substitute, but there must finally be some more direct, causal relation between Pound's discourse and the paradisal. Hope can legitimately continue only because the deferral of the ideal city or state, although indefinite, is yet finite.

The internalization of the apocalyptic—in a sense merely a return to its Imagist roots—provides the opportunity for more immediate evidence of the validity of Pound's discourse. There may be no hope for its immediate social performativity, but it can be personally performative. Such passages as the following, which abruptly ends the first section of Canto 74, are not so much propositional statements as performative acts:

> I believe in the resurrection of Italy   quia
> impossibile est
>   4 times to the song of Gassir
>   now in the mind indestructible
>   (C 456)

Both this belief in an eventual resurrection and the statement's indeterminacy are characteristic strategies of deferral and internalization. But it is the sheer aggressiveness with which this faith is asserted, stressing rather than eliding its paradox—"I believe in the resurrection . . . *because* it is impossible"—that makes "now in the mind indestructible" a valid statement. (It is noteworthy, though, that the acknowledgment of the impossibility is relegated to a scholastic gloss in a dead language.) The fact that it is not generalizable, that minds, like hearts, are scarcely indestructible, does not affect its current applicability—precisely because he has uttered it—to Pound as an individual. Pound's visionary moments also seem to some extent conjured by the intense, hypnotic language in which they are manifest, as if the experience itself comes only when linguistically invoked and embodied, whether in the incantatory repetition of the Χθόνος passage in Canto 83 or the more formal stanzas of Canto 79's climax (C 547, 504–06). The assertion in Canto 83 that "when the mind swings by a grass blade / an ant's forefoot shall save you" perhaps acknowledges this relation, given his earlier identification with the ant (C 547). In any case, Pound's affirmations of faith in effect create and sustain the reality of that faith: an immediate performativity that embodies precisely Pound's ideal "word . . . made perfect," the word become act (C 76:468).

Despite the threat (and appearance) of dissolution, the climactic vision that closes Canto 79—precisely in the center of the sequence—guarantees the legitimacy and stability of the self by securely grounding it in the divine. While the abandonment of strategy in the sociopolitical or historical sphere results in a tactical fragmentation and indeterminacy, that very fragmentation is simultaneously deployed by the self as strategy: it is recuperated as the expression of the emotional dynamic of the self. In other words, the self coheres as a unified whole in the very fragments that signal the present destruction of a correspondingly unified culture. Indeed, the shattering and fragmentation of discursive strategy make the Chinese ideograms, the natural world, the divine, and thus finally the self, all the more powerful images of wholeness and totality.[63] Yet since the self can be whole and possess its own proper place only on the assumption of a corresponding culture, only the eventual but deferred realization of that ideal culture saves Pound from ultimate contradiction, and the possibility of contradiction remains very much present. The resurrection of Mussolini's actual Italy may be impossible, but the eventual realization of some such state remains a necessity. It is of course unwise to make too close a connection between Pound's writing and his mental condition, but it seems evident that this situation of near contradiction would result in considerable mental strain. With no social structure to rely on, Pound would bear the full weight of maintaining the wholeness and integrity necessary to the self and to the eventual realization of a corresponding state.

Certainly this sense of an embattled self struggling to survive despite threatened dissolution is the cause of much of the Pisan Cantos' power and pathos. And it is from this drama of the self, struggling to reestablish a center in the face of material, mental, and physical dissolution, that the sequence derives its emotional or experiential structure. Freed from the constraints of a particular didactic point, Pound can now include a vast range of material, yet this vast range expresses, finally, a single, unitary point of view. In this sense, the sequence exhibits a fairly traditional unity as a dramatic soliloquy. Because

Pound sought to establish a unity encompassing self, discourse, and world, however, his dramatic soliloquy does not take a traditional form. Although there are frequent references to his own struggle, they do not dominate the sequence. Instead, Pound's struggle is largely implicit: even passages seemingly concerned with "objective" topics—economics, politics, history—should in the first instance be referred back to the self, as expressions of Pound's mental and emotional state. The rain dance in Canto 77, for example, is significant for its overt, thematic context, but perhaps even more significant for its comic tone, Pound's means of surmounting despair.

Tone is in fact crucial to understanding many passages in the Pisan Cantos, since Pound's cryptic syntax often requires a knowledge of his tone to determine the meaning of a given passage. The relation between author and reader is thus considerably different from that established in earlier cantos. There Pound interposed the argumentative structure of the poem between himself and the reader, while in the Pisan sequence the reader must identify with Pound in order to understand the dramatic soliloquy. This identification is encouraged from the very beginning of the sequence:

> The enormous tragedy of the dream in the peasant's bent shoulders
> Manes! Manes was tanned and stuffed,
> Thus Ben and la Clara *u Milano*
> > by the heels at Milano
> That maggots shd/ eat the dead bullock
> DIGONOS, Δίγονος, but the twice crucified
> > where in history will you find it?
> yet say this to the Possum: a bang, not a whimper,
> > with a bang not with a whimper,
> To build the city of Dioce whose terraces are the colour of stars.
>
> (C 74:439)

The first six lines could continue the method of earlier cantos, yet even here references are somewhat more casual and private, suggesting a soliloquy. Then the process of identification begins: "You" in line seven can refer to both Pound and the reader, making the line both a directive to the reader (to search history) and a purely rhetorical question. In either case—in a sense the two readings fuse—the reader does not merely eavesdrop, but is invited to duplicate Pound's attitude and activity. The identification extends into the next line, where the directive may be aimed at the reader, but is enacted by Pound as he gives it. This doubling of "you" continues as Pound generalizes and mythologizes his own journey:

> The suave eyes, quiet, not scornful,
>   rain also is of the process.
> What you depart from is not the way
> and olive tree blown white in the wind
> washed in the Kiang and Han
> what whiteness will you add to this whiteness,
>   what candor?
> "the great periplum brings in the stars to our shore."
> You who have passed the pillars and outward from Herakles
> when Lucifer fell in N. Carolina
> if the suave air give way to scirocco
> ΟΥ̓ ΤΙΣ, ΟΥ̓ ΤΙΣ? Odysseus
>   the name of my family.
>   (C 439)

If the reader has been responding to "you"—and there is no other way for a reader to enter the poem—this final conjunction of "no-man" and "my family" should complete the identification. And if the reader can identify with Pound, his tone, and therefore much of his meaning, should become relatively clear.

The use of many distinct forms in the sequence, while it may at first seem an instance of a postmodern skepticism regarding form, also stems from Pound's dramatic struggle, with shifts in form most often corresponding to shifts in emotion. He continues to believe in "an 'absolute rhythm' . . . which corresponds exactly to the emotion or shade of emotion to be expressed" (*LE* 9). More formal structures, for example, often mark increased intensity, as in the lynx-Cythera passage that closes Canto 79. There the poet's intensity of expectation gradually increases in a series of formal stanzas and formulaic repetitions, until the coming of the goddess at the sexually charged climax. The recourse to Latin for "the grove needs [wants] an altar" further intensifies the climactic moment, which is immediately followed by a final, long line that enacts the sudden release of tension:

>   aram
>   nemus
>   vult
>   O puma, sacred to Hermes, Cimbica servant of Helios.
>   (C 506)

Later, in the midst of the "rambling, prosy interior monologue" of Canto 81 (Kearns 159)—a passage embodying considerable tiredness and despondency—even the recollection of that earlier moment spurs Pound's flight into Elizabethan song:

and my ole man went on hoein' corn
    while George was a-tellin' him,
come across a vacant lot
        where you'd occasionally see a wild rabbit
or mebbe only a loose one
    AOI!
    a leaf in the current
            at my grates no Althea

libretto   Yet
    Ere the season died a-cold
    Borne upon a Zephyr's shoulder
    I rose through the aureate sky
          Lawes and Jenkyns guard thy rest
          Dolmetsch ever be thy guest

    (C 533)

In the midst of a despondent, rambling passage, "AOI" seems a cry of acute distress, yet it is also a call to order and renewed effort.[64] "A leaf in the current," too, describes Pound's aimless drifting, both formal and substantial, while also recalling the goddess, Cythera, from earlier passages in the sequence.[65] "Yet" thus marks the simultaneous transition from distress to celebration and from rambling monologue to formal song. Shortly thereafter Pound characteristically uses an Imagist mode to render a quieter intuition of the divine through nature:

sky's clear
night's sea
green of the mountain pool
shone from the unmasked eyes in half-mask's space
    (C 534)

Imagism is used to similar effect elsewhere (see, for example, 83:535). More formal, declamatory rhetoric marks public declarations on the basis of this private vision: immediately after the passage quoted above, Pound shifts into the famous section beginning, "What thou lovest well remains," which in intensity resembles the angry rhetoric of Canto 45's denunciation of usura (C 534).

As this brief consideration of formal variety would suggest, the overall structure of each canto is also primarily emotional: if there are only intermittent indications of an explicit narrative in the Pisan Cantos, Pound's situation creates a distinct implicit narrative, with style and form corresponding directly to his emotional responses, as in Canto 81's transition from prosy monologue to song. These cantos are not structured so as to achieve adequate coverage of some material or to make some point. This is particularly evident in the conclusions, which, with no possibility of structural closure, must resort to some other device to create a feeling of closure independent of structure, much as a fugue ends with a pedal point rather than an elaborate cadence.[66] Several cantos therefore end with a two-line unit resembling a couplet, which enables Pound to bring the canto to a close virtually whenever he likes. Cantos 74, 76, and 83 use two-line units, while Cantos 77 and 78 use more elaborate variants. Appropriately, Canto 84 brings the entire sequence to a close with the only true couplet: "If the hoar frost grip thy tent / Thou wilt give thanks when night is spent" (C 554). We may take this ad hoc, personal ending to the sequence as the final indication, the final instance, of the Pisan Cantos' nearly simultaneous surrender of strategy in the sociopolitical sphere and recuperation of strategy in the individual. The self, seemingly forced to admit its subjection, would yet emerge in a position of mastery.

The Pisan Cantos thus embody a remarkable, postmodern reliance on tactics that is yet predicated upon—made tolerable by—a modern ideal of totality and therefore of strategy. Pound's syntactic and discursive disjunctions reflect the real shattering of the dream of totality at the social and historical levels, yet at the same time these tactics enable him to avoid the full consequences of this shattering by allowing him to reaffirm a divine ground in his own present experience and in the state's distant future. The multiplication of disjunct discourses proceeds on the assumption, the assurance, that one, ultimate discourse will strategically encompass the whole.

Afterwords and Deferral

It is not surprising, then, that later sections of the *Cantos* turn from the Pisan sequence's focus on the personal to renewed efforts toward the deferred, ideal state. To be sure, the weakness of Pound's position—incarcerated in St. Elizabeths—and the bleakness of the world situation—he saw no new Mussolini on the horizon—rendered the urgency of the prewar work useless. *Section: Rock-Drill* (1955) and *Thrones* (1959) consequently present the reader with difficulties even greater than those of the Pisan Cantos: annotation and scholarship become prerequisites for even a cursory understanding of some of these late cantos. Yet this obscurity, even hostility, in no way marks a retreat to an apolitical, quiescent contemplation of transcendence. Pound's discourse does not become apolitical; its political efficacy is merely deferred to an indefinite future (Bernstein 154). Nor does Pound now believe in a gradual process of amelioration: enlightenment may take time, but its arrival will yet be apocalyptic. If in these later sections Pound seems to be thwarting unification and communication, deliberately fragmenting and delaying, it is a fragmentation to ensure unification, a delay paradoxically dependent on an eventual "sudden liberation."[67]

Committed to his apocalyptic perspective, Pound could only intensify his efforts to unify the fragmented postwar world. The increased reliance on ideograms, the increased obscurity, the turn to Egypt—all these features of the later sections show Pound attempting to gain greater distance—greater leverage, as it were—in the face of the immense task of seeing the world whole, of knowing it and affecting it as a totality. Acknowledging the difficulty to Donald Hall in 1962, he used terms that make the continuity of his imaginative perspective clear: "it is difficult to write a paradiso when all the superficial indications are that you ought to write an apocalypse" (Hall 47). Nor do the confessions of error in the late Drafts and Fragments (1969) constitute a renunciation of Pound's strategic intent. They admit to errors in execution—he resembles "Muss., wrecked for an error" (C 809)—and lament his own inability, given the postwar world, to make "it"—the poem, the world—cohere (C 810). That failure weighed all the more heavily on Pound because, as we have seen, the integrity and wholeness of the self ultimately depended on the wholeness of the state and the world. He told Hall that "the whole fight is for the conservation of the individual soul" against "this awful maelstrom," but that he feared the fight would fail: "it is doubtful whether the individual soul is going to be allowed to survive at all" (43, 42). It was that fear, and all it entailed, that prompted his admission in the Cantos, "that I lost my center / fighting the world." Unable to impose a center on a recalcitrant world, his own could not hold (C 816). Yet even Pound's acknowledgment of failure in these last fragments (in the passage previously placed at the end of the volume, as Canto 120) retains the dream of totality:

> I have tried to write Paradise
>
> Do not move
>   Let the wind speak
>   that is paradise.
> (C 816)

When Dante confesses his inability to record the great vision at the end of the *Paradiso*, the confession itself reveals the ultimate power of that vision, which grounds and so justifies the *Commedia*. The passage remains ambivalent, confessing Pound's failure, yet continuing to affirm the validity of his originary vision. Of course, Pound is confessing a real failure here, and he has actually "tried to write Paradise"—perhaps committing the sin of pride, Dante's sin. Yet this wind, speaking an untranslatable language—perhaps the divine word—and expressing an unknowable power, is the same wind that blows relentlessly through the Pisan Cantos, now "suave air," now scirroco, and it is the same wind "out of Rhodez" that in Canto 4 caught in Soremonda's sleeve just before she plunged to join it: the wind that Canto 4 announced could belong to no man, but which even then spoke clearly to Ezra Pound.

It is also—and here we may supplement Pound's text—the wind that sweeps through scenarios of the world after nuclear Armageddon, ambiguously symbolizing both impersonal fate and divine justice, as man's tremendous creation turns against him in an act of retribution. In the Pisan Cantos, Pound had simply dismissed the fission bombs dropped on Hiroshima and Nagasaki with a sarcastic acknowledgment of their purely destructive power:

seven words to a bomb

dum capitolium scandet
        the rest is explodable
Very potent, can they again put one together
as the two halves of a seal, or a tally stick?
    (C 77:481)

The west's monument to itself, the fission bomb can only sunder and shatter, while Pound sought a higher perspective from which to surmount and unify this fragmentation. But by 1952 "they" had indeed "put one together": the first hydrogen bomb, using a process of fusion rather than fission, was detonated on November 6 at Eniwetok Atoll, midway—as it happened—between East and West. And fusion—as it happened—produced even greater destruction than fission. The alchemical "word to make change" had been spoken. Pound, however, had little interest in such armaments, as they merely continued the process of militarization he had diagnosed long before, while his interest in scientific analogies for his paradise was satisfied by the electromagnetic field, by the rose in the steel dust.[68] He could acknowledge that "the dreams clash / and are shattered," but he could not renounce the struggle for a strategy to surmount this strife, for a Dream of dreams (C 816). Nor could he acknowledge the complicity of his own dream of totality, of his own strategy, in the massive destruction of World War II. He continued the project through the fifties and sixties, hoping to discover "a verbal formula to combat the rise of brutality—the principle of order versus the split atom," something that would enable others to take up his "great ball of crystal" (Hall 47; C 809). And throughout, Pound continued to image his paradisal whole as an intense, blinding light: even as the Bomb was preparing a material realization, a consummation, of the immediacy and the totality, the power and the glory, of precisely that "great acorn of light" that his poem, finally, could only dream (C 809).

3

Dr. Williams' Position

Beginning After

"ANTAGONISTIC COOPERATION," Williams declares in *Paterson* IV, is "the key," the solution to the postwar dilemmas of modern man and of Williams' own poetics (*P* 176). Yet if *Paterson*, with the recent war, provided the immediate occasion for this declaration, its roots lay much earlier in Williams' career. Indeed, he could as well have been thinking of the history of his friendship with Ezra Pound. In a series of articles and letters, each poet had struggled to articulate the other's "position," praising it while yet making it clear that his own was superior—and of course, even the ability to define, to encompass, the other was a mark of superiority. The relation became markedly more antagonistic during World War II, as Williams struggled to articulate his distance from Pound's poetics and politics. In a 1940 letter to James Laughlin, Williams complained of Pound's patronizing, insulting letters, in which he was treated, he said, like an eighth grade student in relation to Pound's "catastrophic knowledge of affairs, his blinding judgments of contemporary values" (*SL* 192). Williams' critique of Pound is at times remarkably perceptive, and his attempts to distinguish himself from Pound provoked many of his clearest articulations of his own poetics.[1] For my present purpose, though, one simple assertion, made to Laughlin and repeated elsewhere, is especially pertinent: "My own perceptions overtook him twenty years ago—not however my accomplishments" (*SL* 192). Williams' self-confessed lack of "accomplishment" does not stem from a deficient technique, though he always acknowledged that Pound was the better maker. Rather, his more advanced perceptions reject all the recognizable forms, the polished structures, the strategies, of the traditionally accomplished poet. Williams did not want to be, particularly did not want to have been, *accomplished*. Where Pound strove, with varying urgency, to accomplish an apocalyptic consummation—socially in the millennial or heavenly city and personally in a union with the divine—Williams, refusing to succumb to the lures of fusion, struggled to move beyond these consummations: in a sense, he struggled through much of his career to become a *post*-apocalyptic poet.

88

Williams' claim that his breakthrough had occurred twenty years earlier
would place it in the period immediately after World War I, the period of *Kora
in Hell* (1917–18) and *Spring and All* (1923). Indeed, these works have for some
time been recognized as marking both Williams' first great breakthrough and
his first great achievements. Even earlier works, however, show considerable
divergence from Pound's developing poetics. In a 1914–15 article on Vorticism
(published only recently), Williams significantly differs from Pound's and
Gaudier-Brzeska's Vorticism even as he adopts its expressions. He does not
seek a true basis on which to erect his own system in opposition to (and eventually supplanting) current social structures, but asserts the existence of the
individual only as constituted within an agonistic social field. It is this other-
related existence, in fact, that justifies his use of Vorticist terms: "I affirm my
existence by accepting other forces to be in juxtaposition to my own either in
agreement or disagreement. Thus . . . I have no compunction in borrowing
phrases from Brzeska's 'Vortex,' on the contrary I accept his show of force as
an affirmation of my own" (*RI* 57). Williams goes on to develop a tactical approach—albeit tinged with Romanticism—wherein he occupies no position of
his own, no depth, but expresses himself and asserts his existence by temporarily appropriating the appearances, the surfaces, that surround him, whether
they be physical or discursive: "By taking whatever character my environment
has presented and turning it to my purpose, I have expressed my independence of it" (58). This stance strikingly prefigures his later formulation in "An
Essay on Virginia" of "multiplicity, infinite fracture, the intercrossing of opposed forces establishing any number of opposed centres of stillness" (*I* 323).
In his *Autobiography*, too, Williams distinguished his early stance from Pound's
on the basis of his relation to the other: where Williams assumed humility and
caution, Pound, "scorning the other made himself ridiculous by imitating that
which he despised" (*A* 58). In his early response to the Vorticists, then,
Williams acknowledges that the self is constructed, known, only through its
relations to a plurality of social "others." The independence he asserts—from
"all emotions," from "any one technique and so from all technique," and from
any specific place, geographical or discursive—also indicates an acceptance of
what can only be a fragmented, multiple self (*RI* 58, 59).

It is in "The Wanderer," however, that Williams diverges most markedly
from Pound. First written in 1914 and slightly revised in 1917, the poem neatly
spans the Great War, the same period in which Pound developed his apocalyptic perspective. While the poem presents a critique of the romantic tradition
in general, it in many respects seems a direct refutation of Pound's apocalyptic
yearnings, and particularly of his yearning for a consummation with the goddess. Briefly, the narrator of the poem, while ferrying to Manhattan one day,

glimpses a lady who embodies "all the persons of godhead." He immediately decides to chase her and at least in his mind flies off in pursuit. After she presents him with various sights—crowds in the modern city, a strike in Paterson, and even a pastoral scene—she brings him to the filthy Passaic river, with which he undergoes something like a mystical union. Since J. Hillis Miller's *Poets of Reality* (1965), critics have taken this poem to represent Williams' "homecoming," with the narrator's experience representing the consummation of Williams' "marriage to all that is," when he "possesses all time and space and has complete knowledge of everything" (287, 292). The difficulty with this reading is that, far from showing Williams' move "beyond romanticism," as Miller claims, it connects Williams firmly to the romantic quest: this marriage to the world, this union with the Passaic river, is only another version of Pound's marriage to the goddess. Carl Rapp, for example, uses essentially the same reading of the poem to argue that the narrator, Williams, "*is* purged of his yearning for transcendence, but only because he achieves it" (13). In this view, Williams struggled to reject romantic idealism, but succeeded only in embracing it. Yet Williams himself, a few years later, explained that the appearance of a poem like "The Wanderer" may be deceiving: "Rich as are the gifts of the imagination bitterness of world's loss is not replaced thereby. On the contrary it is intensified, resembling thus possession itself" (*I* 18). Just so, critics have mistaken intensity of loss for possession. Williams' poem does not celebrate a homecoming; its title, after all, is "The Wanderer." Rather, it presents a critique of the quest as such, and particularly of the submersion, the extinction of the self in some "other" that, whether it be Pound's goddess or "all that is," is thereby possessed.

The narrator's desire throughout the poem is for a union, not with the river, but with the lady herself. Thinking that he sees her at the end of section two—ironically beside the river—he swerves "clamorously downward" and exclaims, "I will take my peace in her henceforth!" (*CP1* 109). In the next section he actually proposes to her, but she merely laughs in response—surely not an indication that his desire will be fulfilled. In the final section of the poem, when she brings the narrator to the Passaic, he seems remarkably peripheral to her interests, which center rather on her relation to the river, the object of her desire:

> Old friend, here I have brought you
> The young soul you long asked of me.
> Stand forth, river, and give me
> The old friend of my revels!
>   (*CP1* 115)

She then invokes the union of river and narrator, a union that seems an utter surprise to him, and in which his only role is as victim, sacrificed to a relation of which he has no knowledge.

The union itself occurs at an ironic distance. All the typical features of a union with the divine, whether transcendent or immanent, are present: the narrator moves toward the "crystal beginning," the origin or source, until time is abolished, "washed finally under," and then, at the still center, he shares in the divine omniscience and omnipresence: "And its last motion had ceased / And I knew all—it became me" (*CP1* 116). At just this moment, however, comes a remarkable, and highly significant, shift in tonality:

> And I knew this for double certain
> For there, whitely, I saw myself
> Being borne off under the water!
> I could have shouted out in my agony
> At the sight of myself departing
> Forever—but I bit back my despair
> For she had averted her eyes
> By which I knew well what she was thinking—
> And so the last of me was taken.
>   (*CP1* 116)

It is difficult to share the narrator's knowledge of her thoughts, though in context the averted eyes suggest some shame at her betrayal of him. What is of particular importance, though, is the shift from the narrator's formal claim to omniscience—"And I knew all"—to the colloquial, "And I knew this for double certain." Not only does the tonal shift undermine the earlier claim, but "knowing all" suddenly depends on being "double certain," which undermines this omniscience even further. The subsequent doubling of the narrator also marks an ironic distance surfacing under the guise of his ecstatic union. And finally, he seems to take the notion of a religious ecstasy, a standing outside oneself—a death of the self—rather too literally when he sees his own pale, drowned corpse floating off in the river, submerged in the "all."

The narrator's quest, then, results only in the knowledge that the quest itself is useless, in many respects a fraud: the apocalyptic vision is inadequate or even irrelevant. At the end of the poem, the "marvelous old queen" bids goodbye to the river in terms that stress its existence in a fantastic realm—fertile, rich in vegetation and life, "a bird's paradise"—a realm wholly apart from human lives and for that matter from the real Passaic. And so the narrator is finally left with nothing but "the new wandering," which is "new" in only two respects: first, this wandering is not linear, it proceeds to no fixed goal, and second, there is no possibility of escape from it, either through transcendence or immanence. "The Wanderer," then, is on the surface a quintessential strategic poem: not only does it recount a past experience from a secure, eternal position, rendering a preconceived narrative in verse (which is to say, using language transparently, instrumentally), but it recounts the very experience that should have given the poet a secure basis from which to deploy his strategies, his discourse. In fact, however, the related experience negates the possibility of such a basis and projects the poet-narrator forward into a world of loss, where there can be no secure self, anchored in a vision of the divine—a world where there can only be tactics. Where Pound was at this time developing a poetics of fragmentation, seemingly tactical but actually displaying an underlying, strategic basis, Williams makes tactical use of a traditional strategy. "The Wanderer" does not achieve an apocalypse; it uses the form of revelation to point to a condition where such forms, such desires, will be abandoned. In a sense, the poem says goodbye to all that, but has not itself left. Because the poet-wanderer can find no place in the present, he can only project a future poetics of tactics that will eschew his own current reliance on a traditional strategy.

Williams works toward that tactical, post-apocalyptic poetics in *Kora in Hell*, with its fragmentary, disjunct sentences, multiple voices, and explicitly apocalyptic imagery. Later Williams recalled that the war, by destroying all that he valued, including a renaissance in letters, was the determining context of the work: "it was Persephone gone into Hades, into hell. Kora was the springtime of the year; my year, my self was being slaughtered. What was the use of denying it? For relief, to keep myself from planning and thinking at all, I began to write in earnest" (*A* 158). To survive, then, he "had recourse to the expedient of letting life go completely," even at the cost of that "dislocation of sense, often complete" for which he later faulted the work, and which has continued to make *Kora* a remarkably recalcitrant text (*I* 116, 117). For *Kora*'s dislocation or obscurity stems from this fundamental intensity of loss and consequent struggle to "cross to the other side" at whatever level: literal, personal, social, natural, mythic, and so on (*I* 32). And that struggle strews the work with apocalyptic images—of madness, death, sunset and sunrise, and of course the world's end—from Jacob Louslinger's corpse in I.2 through "death's canticle" in IV.3 and the "beautiful white corpse of night" in V.1, to the dead leaves of the final section, XXVII.3.

Section V.3 provides a particularly good instance of Williams' tendency to combine various apocalyptic perspectives, as the "narrator," driven around the city by a syphilitic friend, ponders the sights in the context of his friend's encroaching madness:

Here the harps have a short cadenza. It's sunset back of the new cathedral and the purple river scum has set seaward. The car's at the door. I'd not like to go alone tonight. I'll pay you well. It's the king's-evil. Speed! Speed! The sun's self's a chancre low in the west. Ha, how the great houses shine—for old time's sake! For sale! For sale! The town's gone another way. But I'm not fooled that easily. *Fort sale! Fort sale!* if you read it aright. And Beauty's own head on the pillow, *à la Maja Desnuda! O Duquesa de Alba! Duquesa de Alba!* Never was there such a lewd wonder in the streets of Newark! Open the windows—but all's boarded up here. Out with you, you sleepy doctors and lawyers you,—the sky's afire and Calvary Church with its snail's horns up, sniffing the dawn—o' the wrong side! Let the trumpets blare! *Tutti i instrumenti!* The world's bound homeward. (*I* 40)

Williams does not structure his discourse according to a submerged apocalyptic: unlike Pound, he invokes speed not to achieve apocalyptic consummation, but to be done with it. Rather than seek a millennium as necessary end, or final cause, Williams uses multiple, explicit images of the apocalypse to shatter the linearity of apocalyptic thought and of history itself. For history's "attempt to make the past seem stable" is "a lie" because its own linearity is teleological, subsuming actual diversity and alterity to an apocalyptic consummation— however that end be conceived (*I* 41). Williams variously images the end in order to shatter that linearity, much as madness shatters rationality. Indeed, his subsequent "interpretation" of V.3 combines madness and apocalypse while explicitly linking them to a critical perspective on the "ordinary" reality, the dull rationality, of the city's daily life: "It being evening he witnesses a dawn of great beauty striking backward upon the world in a reverse direction to the sun's course and not knowing of what else to think discovers it to be the same power which has led his companion to destruction. At this he is inclined to scoff derisively at the city's prone stupidity and to make light indeed of his friend's misfortune" (*I* 40). But in reality even this struggle for the "other side" is problematic. While it may temporarily provide a useful, tactical response to linear apocalyptics, when prolonged, and despite Williams' refusal of a millennial goal, it would itself become ambiguously linear, teleological, and hence apocalyptic. In the passage just cited, for example, the diverse apocalyptic images seem subsumed by the greater image of the world's end. *Kora in Hell* therefore provides other, tactical means to avoid or thwart the linearity that had led inexorably to the war, and from which "planning and thinking" could offer no escape.

One alternative, to which Williams returns late in his career, is to oppose speed with delay, to refuse to embrace telic linearity by dawdling along the way. Section II.1 presents this alternative as an explicit tactic: "Why go further?

One might conceivably rectify the rhythm, study all out and arrive at the perfection of a tiger lily or a china doorknob. One might lift all out of the ruck, be a worthy successor to—the man in the moon. Instead of breaking the back of a willing phrase why not try to follow the wheel through—approach death at a walk, take in all the scenery. There's as much reason one way as the other and then—one never knows—perhaps we'll bring back Eurydice—this time!" (*I* 32). Williams makes his point by mapping apocalyptic linearity onto a human life, whereupon the goal, the apocalyptic consummation, becomes literal death. Since the "scenery" includes all that linear apocalyptics omit as insignificant to the goal, devotion to such an end impoverishes life by transforming it into an obsession with death, a kind of living death.

Williams' use of the Kora myth in this section also suggests another alternative. A cyclical myth, of course, defeats any sense of a *telos*, since one end always leads on to another. *Kora in Hell*, moreover, seems to go a step further, conflating the stages of the cycle into one multiplicity. Like the sunrise and sunset in V.2, ends and beginnings frequently transform into one another. (Williams' Prologue provides an example of a similar transformation, since it was actually, as he notes, an epilogue.) Elsewhere the text asserts an even more jumbled approach: "there is neither beginning nor end to the imagination but it delights in its own seasons reversing the usual order at will" (*I* 35). This particular conflation recurs in the work's final sentence, which presents a striking view of human and natural seasons: "The true seasons blossom or wilt not in fixed order but so that many of them may pass in a few weeks or hours whereas sometimes a whole life passes and the season remains of a piece from one end to the other" (*I* 82). Kora is in hell, winter is in spring, and vice versa—there can be no escape from one to the other. The two realms, then, on this side and "the other" are not independent but interpenetrant. And we, like Williams and like Kora, with whom he identified, inhabit both realms simultaneously, which is to say that we are constrained by neither.

These various attitudes toward apocalyptics should not be construed as contradictory models of the real, as incompatible attempts at "truth," but as actions, as tactical means of disrupting linear, telic stability. In his Prologue, in fact, Williams makes it clear that his writing is directed against the fixed point of view Wallace Stevens had urged him to seize: he writes "to loosen the attention, my attention since I occupy part of the field" (*I* 14). And where Stevens, in Williams' view, wants to make himself a home from which to survey the field, Williams sees himself as part of the field—like the boll weevil, his refrain will be "that'll be ma HOME! That'll be ma HOOME!" wherever circumstances place him (*I* 7). Tactics, then, are the necessary means: the preference in II.1 for "follow[ing] the wheel through" rather than "breaking the back of a willing phrase" is precisely a preference for tactical improvisation over strategic organization (*I* 32). As Williams writes in the Prologue: "By the brokenness of his composition the poet makes himself master of a certain weapon which he could possess himself of in no other way" (*I* 16). His writing is conceived primarily as an act, a tactic, even a means of survival, as he says of *Kora* in the *Autobiography* (158). Williams' disjunct sentences and discourses, then, demonstrate his refusal to settle into one fixed, external point of view. So, too, do his interpolated "interpretations" and the Prologue itself, which really provide continuations and displacements rather than some superior perspective—in *Kora in Hell*, no one discourse is superior to any other.

Still, the move to interpretation, while demonstrating the remarkable flexibility of Williams' practice, also indicates his ambivalence, the felt need to develop some rationalization of—some fixed perspective on—a practice hostile to all evident orders. Where "The Wanderer" 's ambivalence stems from its adherence to a strategic narrative it can only reject, *Kora*'s ambivalence stems from an initial and continued rejection of all strategic orders, which does not, however, enable it to escape the impulse toward some new order. In this context, the reference to Eurydice in II.1 is particularly interesting because it invokes a linear, telic version of the Kora myth, and because it shifts Williams' own role from victim (Kora) to hero (Orpheus). Williams proposes the possibility of at last achieving the goal by abandoning its pursuit. Critical to our understanding, however, is the tone here, at once sincere and ironic. For Williams' stance produces an unavoidable, all-pervading ambivalence. Even as he rejects the apocalyptic consummation, he is immensely attracted to it as an image of power and presence. As a result, *Kora* is traversed by these contradictory impulses. Moreover, a further paradox arises, for the rejection of apocalypse is itself apocalyptic—or, as Derrida has recently put it, it constitutes an "apocalypse *without* apocalypse," where the *without* "marks an internal and external catastrophe of the apocalypse, an overturning of sense that does not merge with the catastrophe announced or described in the apocalyptic writings without however being foreign to them" ("Of an Apocalyptic Tone" 95). This, too, is a source of Williams' predilection for madness and disorientation. Henry Corbin, in fact, identifies such disorientation as the condition of history itself once it has overtaken the *eschaton* that previously directed it (7). Williams' position, then, is a *non*-position, and is therefore fundamentally paradoxical. Hence his apparent alternatives—to be victim *or* rescuer, to embrace *or* reject—are impossible because inseparable. He must act, must write, in a field where any action, any writing, necessarily remains ambivalent.

Spring and All

This ambivalence recurs, to produce a particularly fruitful "antagonistic co-operation," in *Spring and All*. Even the title is rather ambivalent, suggesting great importance, but in an offhand, casual idiom. The work's importance, though, has been widely recognized: Zukofsky felt *Spring and All* could inaugurate a century of American writing, while J. Hillis Miller has more recently called it "perhaps the most important single work by Williams" (*"A"* 378; *Linguistic Moment* 366–67). Certainly it is Williams' greatest early achievement, and since it also presents the most vividly imaged apocalypse, the loudest "bellow of the BLAST" in Williams' work, it is particularly important in the present context (*I* 171).

Williams begins the book with an introductory section in which he establishes the difficulty of achieving true contact with the world as his central concern, a concern at once phenomenal, social and esthetic. For "there is a constant barrier between the reader and his consciousness of immediate contact with the world," a barrier that Williams wishes to break through, both for himself and for the reader. It is created by those habits of thought, those habitual systems or strategies, that prevent the reader from attending to the present by focusing attention on the past, the origin, or on the future, the "vision of what he would be, some day. Oh, some day!" (*I* 89). But the barrier, Williams writes, is also "here," in the written word, the work of art itself, which "has been especially designed to keep up the barrier between sense and the vaporous fringe which distracts the attention from its agonized approaches to the moment" (*I* 89). Williams will therefore reject "the beautiful illusion" of art, despite the possibility that this rejection may in turn lead to public rejection of his work. It is in the context of this problematic that Williams' subsequent "monster project of the moment," the annihilation of "every human creature on the face of the earth," should be understood (*I* 90, 91). Even Miller, one of *Spring and All*'s most perceptive critics, misreads this section as an instance of the imagination's necessary destruction of nature, with man taken as nature's most important representative. Consequently, Miller decides that Williams shares with Rimbaud and other modernists a "wish to be himself the cause of the apocalypse" and a belief that "genuine art brings the apocalypse rather than describing its imminence" (*Linguistic Moment* 372). However, Williams in fact destroys *only* mankind; afterward, he says, "a marvelous serenity" will reign, "broken only by bird and wild beast calls" (*I* 91). Williams' real target is not nature but the strategies that bind humanity, strategies that had most recently led to the Great War, and which are here subsumed in that ultimate strategy, the Christian apocalypse. That is why we should kill "because we love them," and why only this slaughter will provide abounding "order and peace" (*I* 90, 91). Williams' imagined destruction should first be understood, then, as a parody of the Christian apocalypse. If we truly believe that life's rewards are deferred to the millennium, he implies, we should act now to hasten its arrival:

> This final and self inflicted holocaust has been all for love, for sweetest love, that together the human race, yellow, black, brown, red and white, agglutinated into one enormous soul may be gratified with the sight and retire to the heaven of heavens content to rest on its laurels. There, soul of souls, watching its own horrid unity, it boils and digests itself within the tissues of the great Being of Eternity that we shall then have become. With what magnificent explosions and odors will not the day be accomplished as we, the Great One among all creatures, shall go about contemplating our self-prohibited desires . . . (*I* 91)

By leading conventional lives, by reading conventional art, we assent to a protracted emptiness made tolerable only by the vision of eventual, but in fact forever deferred, fulfillment. Williams' mockery uncovers both that vision's negation of present life—the self-prohibition of desire—and its actual distastefulness: we exist as individuals only to annihilate ourselves in the "Being of Eternity."

But Williams' imagined act does not end here, in parody. After the destruction of humanity, he tells us, evolution repeats itself from the beginning, following precisely the pattern of "ages past" (*I* 94). At last—and Williams slows down our approach to stress its importance—we come to the present moment, *this* moment, which is the "exact moment when in the ages past the destruction of the species *Homo sapiens* occurred" (*I* 94). While leaving everything "the same," this exact duplication of the world, including humanity, yet means that everything is new, reborn: "A perfect plagiarism results. Everything is and is new. Only the imagination is undeceived" (*I* 93). The imagination is undeceived because, having destroyed the old world, it knows that the world is new and that we are therefore free of past preconceptions, conventions, repressions—free to make a new beginning. Williams imagines the apocalypse not in order to hasten an actual apocalypse, but to disrupt and so free us from apocalyptic, or strategic, patterns of thought and culture—those patterns that had already led to World War I and that, with continued technological progress, could clearly lead to an actual, man-made apocalypse, a "self-inflicted holocaust." Already in the 1920s, Williams sensed that he was living in a world where such an end could come all too true.

But the question then arises, what should follow this apocalyptically imaged breakthrough to the non-apocalyptic? More specifically, what can Williams write that will not reestablish strategy and apocalyptics? It is at this climactic moment, the moment of rebirth, that Williams presents the book's first
poem, "By the road to the contagious hospital," also known as "Spring and
All." Poetry, seemingly, will provide the answer, the fulfillment of Williams'—
and the reader's—desire to achieve contact. This is precisely the claim Miller
makes for Williams' art: where the prose of *Spring and All* remains caught
within inescapable "conceptual circles," in his poetic practice "Williams at last
takes possession of the presence of the present, of that eternal moment in
which we alone live. It is a present, however, that is not perceptual but linguistic, a present not present except in words" (*Linguistic Moment* 381). And Miller
in fact cites a few stanzas of "By the road" as evidence of what he rather
vaguely calls the "curious immediacy" Williams achieves "in or between the
words of his poems" (387, 384). Indeed, both "By the road" and the immediately following poem, "Pink confused with white," insist on their own presence by enacting a disruption of habit in its own way as violent as the previous
apocalypse. To the reader who, like a driver on a road, has been comfortably
skimming along lines of prose, not attending to what is there because intent
on getting elsewhere, the first lines must come as something of a shock:

> By the road to the contagious hospital
> under the surge of the blue
> mottled clouds driven from the
> northeast—a cold wind. Beyond, the
> waste of broad, muddy fields
> brown with dried weeds, standing and fallen
>   (*I* 95)

The first line ends with a comfortable (almost "natural") break at the end of a
phrase. The second line first delays the expected subject (we must read slightly
more attentively to retain control) and then ends abruptly and confusingly—if
we assume the line coincides with the phrasal unit and take "blue" as a noun,
presumably synecdochic for "sky," we are left with the expressive but nearly
nonsensical "surge of the sky." Instead, we plunge on, assuming "blue" to be
an adjective, an assumption that is quickly confirmed. A line ending with an
adjective, if unusual, is still explicable (done for emphasis), so the disruption
remains minor. It is, though, naggingly persistent: blue clouds are not what
realistic literature usually gives us. We can, of course, refer to the poem's miming of the author's experience: he notices the "surge" while not looking
directly, looks and sees "blue," and then, before the mind can supply "sky"

(for he is still searching for the "surge"), sees the mottling and identifies the clouds as the source of the surge. But that reading could only come later; it requires time, a leisure that the poem refuses to provide. If our attention is now stimulated by these unexpected breaks, our curiosity mildly aroused, the third line, still delaying the subject and ending with "the," engages us in an active struggle to maintain control, to make sense, compelling our attention onward to line four. In that line, interestingly, "northeast" presents a significant shift from perceptual particulars to a conceptual response—no doubt the difficult line break records this sudden distancing. But "northeast" remains a particular, and the line goes on to provide only the banality of "a cold wind" as climax, the cause of disruption and therefore focus of attention. And we still do not have a sentence. The lack of a verb, while not interfering with the sense of these lines, increases the feeling of being thrown in among perceptual particulars, refusing to allow us the comfort and distance afforded by a "complete thought." There is, to be sure, a certain feeling of closure, of completion at this point. Counteracting this effect, however, "Beyond, the" combines semantic and syntactic forces to push us onward even more forcefully than what has preceded. Perception will not now linger. Once broken out of convention, once freed of habit, it pushes on immediately, or "instanter," as Charles Olson has it, leaving reason off balance and therefore unable to assemble, to summarize—and so return to conventional patterns of inattention (*Human Universe* 53).

The poem continues to immerse the reader in accumulating particulars for the next two stanzas, providing no verb and thus no "complete thought." Throughout, the isolation of words and the disruption of syntax produce a sense of immediacy and force the reader to confront the presence of the poem. But then, precisely halfway through the poem, a significant shift occurs, as Williams supplies one verb, one "complete thought," after another. Here is the last half of the poem:

Lifeless in appearance, sluggish
dazed spring approaches—

They enter the new world naked,
cold, uncertain of all
save that they enter. All about them
the cold, familiar wind—

Now the grass, tomorrow
the stiff curl of wildcarrot leaf

One by one objects are defined—
It quickens: clarity, outline of leaf

But now the stark dignity of
entrance—Still, the profound change
has come upon them: rooted, they
grip down and begin to awaken
        (*I* 95–96)

Clearly, this poem begins to build anew: just as the explosive activity of birth
is followed by more settled growth, so the poem returns to the stable forms
requisite to conceptual understanding, to strategic control. Note, too, the return of narrative order and predictive ability in "Now the grass, tomorrow the
stiff curl," and the way objects settle into clear definitions and outlines—structures that return the observer to distanced objectivity.

Struggling against this return, Williams in the final stanza tries to insist
again on the rebirth itself, but the moment can be neither prolonged nor re-
trieved. A "profound change" may have occurred, but the intensity of that moment cannot be sustained; Miller's "presence of the present" may be entered,
but it cannot be possessed. The reversion to expected syntax and semantics,
then, mimes Williams' own distance while also distancing the reader—words
begin to lose their newly acquired immediacy as we in effect return to the ossifications of habit. And so the poem ends, enacting precisely the same dilemma as the preceding prose, and in language closer to prose than it at first
had used. The poetry of *Spring and All* can no more sustain immediacy, can no
more offer a solution, than the prose.

Immediately after the first two poems, therefore, the prose takes up this
question: "A terrific confusion has taken place. No man knows whither to turn.
There is nothing! Emptiness stares us once more in the face. Whither? To what
end?" (*I* 96–97). This confusion, of course, is precisely the disorientation
Corbin speaks of, a characteristic of life without a *telos*, of history after the *eschaton*. Williams can supply no end; he can only assert the rebirth of life and
hope. Subsequently he draws on the recent war, the *Odyssey*, and perhaps also
Moby Dick to create a particularly striking image of the new condition: "Wilson
has taken an army of advisers and sailed for England. The ship has sunk. But
the men are all good swimmers. They take the women on their shoulders and
buoyed on by the inspiration of the moment they churn the free seas with their
sinewy arms, like Ulysses, landing all along the European seaboard" (*I* 97).
Williams not only images the end of the West, the end of history, but also presents a means of survival. This image replays the apocalypse and aftermath—
or rather, it portrays the destruction of apocalyptic striving—precisely in terms
of the end of strategy, the end of objectivity, and the subsequent immersion in
the field and tactical dispersal. No longer is there a direction, a plan to achieve

a *telos*, but only the "inspiration of the moment," the evanescent moment of the tactic.

Tactical dispersion affects not only the society as a whole, in the "modern individualistic dispersion" Williams spoke of in *Contact*, but also the individual as such (*SE* 37). Williams places considerable emphasis on the individual, at times partially embracing a rather Romantic sense of the individual ego struggling to achieve control, to dominate the environment. Yet he was acutely aware of the impossibility of such control, of the helplessness of the self as a self-contained entity. Immediately after poem six, he writes that "the inevitable flux of the seeing eye toward measuring itself by the world it inhabits can only result in himself crushing humiliation," though the solution he offers may at first seem more akin to Beethoven than to postmodern tactics: "unless the individual raise to some approximate co-extension with the universe" (*I* 105). "Coextension," however, does not mean "separate but equal." Rather, it denotes something like an interpenetration of self and world, a tactical dispersion through the field that is made possible by the imagination, which thereby shows the individual "that his life is valuable" (*I* 107). The nature of this dispersion can be better seen in the preceding poem, "No that is not it," which in fact occasions the prose remarks. The poem begins with an admission of inadequacy that quickly threatens to become despair, if not "crushing humiliation":

> No that is not it
> nothing that I have done
> nothing
> I have done
>   (*I* 103–04)

Nothing is ever "it," is ever sufficient: nothing can ever constitute an object adequate to our desires. In what follows, though, this threatening sentence is literally, grammatically, disassembled, broken down and dispersed into the general system of language. But Williams goes a step further to deal with the threatened ego, breaking the grammatical "I" down into its phonetic structure, "the diphthong // ae" (104). Isolated in a separate stanza, these two letters manifest Williams' "deconstruction" of the linguistically, strategically constructed and imposed "I" of the ego—though the "I" appears single and self-contained, it is in reality multiple and even internally dependent on relation. But Williams does not endorse here what would later become the much-proclaimed death of the author; the "I" is not so much eradicated as relocated, translated from the realm of strategic *langue*, within which it can only be inadequate, to that of tactical *parole*, wherein the question of adequacy dissolves into its relational activity. The poem finally develops the argument that inadequacy is a necessary condition of all action and that only complete inaction—nonexistence—could be perfect. More important than this argument, however, is the series of puns through which it is conducted, for the pun, by disrupting this whole process of rationalization, establishes action rather than a static sufficiency as the basis of the "I." Once again, then, Williams combines the modern and the postmodern, establishing a counterargument, a counterstrategy, even as he works against all strategy.

Spring and All, then, like *Kora in Hell*, is traversed by contradictory impulses, modern and postmodern, strategic and tactical, that create an extraordinarily dynamic and richly textured work.[2] Both the prose and the poetry struggle to move beyond apocalyptics, to accept fully the contemporary world that Williams felt was beyond strategy, beyond apocalyptics, beyond history, but which he could only image apocalyptically. And both the prose and the poetry, while gesturing toward—without making a commitment to—conceptual and formal "answers" that could only be strategic, are yet characterized by fragmentation and by abrupt juxtapositions that disrupt generic, conceptual, syntactic, and grammatical expectations in a tactical practice. Many of the less anthologized poems, like "Nothing I have done," clearly exhibit postmodern characteristics. But even "chestnuts" like "The Pure Products of America" and "The Red Wheel Barrow" are distinctly tactical. The former even thematizes a world of tactics, with no one "to witness / and adjust," no one in a position of strategic control, while "The Red Wheel Barrow" plays extraordinarily disruptive line breaks against a balanced, elegant, strategic form (*I* 133). In fact, the poem is surprising not so much for its observation of a wheelbarrow—obviously a much more useful object than, say, a Grecian urn—but because it refuses to dwell on and elaborate the significance of that object, climaxing instead with white chickens as insignificant to its "argument" as a wheelbarrow may seem to esthetics. Our familiarity with these poems, together with their frequent abstraction from the surrounding prose, has tended to obscure their disruptive impulses.

As he declares repeatedly in *Spring and All*, Williams sees the imagination as the primary means toward a tactical practice in both the poem and the world. Williams' concept of the imagination has of course received a good deal of attention, but I think it needs to be approached from a quite distinct direction: not as a development of Romantic theories (though it is clearly related to them) but in terms of its function in Williams' prose. For his insistence on imagination and "place" has led to a general misunderstanding of both: a geographical conception of "place"—as, say, America or Paterson—and a conception of imagination as the "sphere" to which Williams aspires on the basis of this "place." Yet Williams' various feints at a definition of these concepts prove as varied and elusive as Pound's definitions of the ideogrammic method. Both serve him as terms for a practice that enables him to escape, at least momentarily and at least partially, the predictability, the desuetude, into which his work—and life—would otherwise lapse. In this context we might also consider two critical terms in "By the road to the contagious hospital" and "The rose is obsolete." In the first poem, after the initial observation of the sky and before the final turn to more conceptual articulations, the speaker's focus shifts to the vegetation alongside the road. A remarkable moment occurs in this section, a moment in which the entire poem—the entire process of perception, together with its linguistic elaboration—comes to depend upon a single and remarkably vague word as a series of adjectives climaxes in the stressed "stuff" (*CP1*). "Stuff" grounds the poem on all that escapes specific determinations, on a substance that is, as it were, only posited. Similarly, "The rose is obsolete" comes to a focus on an isolated, stressed "What," on a critical something that is also nothing, a place that can only be located negatively.

Williams' various characterizations of "place" and imagination, then, are rhetorical tactics, not placements within a conceptual system. This is precisely the point he stresses toward the close of *Spring and All*: "Sometimes I speak of imagination as a force, an electricity or a medium, a place. It is immaterial which: for whether it is the condition of a place or a dynamization its effect is the same: to free the world of fact from the impositions of 'art' . . . and to liberate the man to act in whatever direction his disposition leads" (*I* 150). The impositions of art are synecdochic for the impositions of all strategic domination—hence freedom from art's impositions also frees us to act. As this passage indicates, "imagination," like "contact" earlier and "place" in *The Embodiment of Knowledge* and elsewhere, functions as a force that disrupts strategies and thereby liberates us. What enables this freedom, therefore, is not elevation to the sphere of the imagination or the achievement of a secure "place" or "position," but the activity of Williams' work, prose and poetry. Even Williams' conceptualizing, though seemingly trapped within an insoluble dilemma, itself escapes that dilemma in its tactical refusal to settle into any one solution, into what he elsewhere called, with perhaps a deliberate pun, "a hole into which we sink decoratively to rest" (*I* 351).

At this point "liberation" may still seem a permanent condition, a condition we can unequivocally and permanently attain. But in the next paragraph, the last prose passage in *Spring and All*, we return to a sense of ongoing struggle, and "liberation" becomes a condition that can never be entirely, perfectly achieved: "The word is not liberated, therefore able to communicate release from the fixities which destroy it until it is accurately tuned to the fact which

giving it reality, by its own reality establishes its own freedom from the necessity of a word, thus freeing it and dynamizing it at the same time" (*I* 150). By
"fixities" Williams clearly means strategic sedimentations, the ossifications of
habit. The meaning of the critical term, "fact," however, is more difficult to
establish. "Thing" or "referent" may present obvious possibilities, but neither
seems particularly appropriate. For "the fact" seems much broader in scope,
rather like "the case" in Wittgenstein's "the world is all that is the case"—it
seems to include both the content and the whole context of an utterance, an
event, a situation (7). In any case, the relation between "the word" and "the
fact," as Williams describes it, repeats the relation between tactics and strategy—a relation in which words are not "dissociated from natural objects and
specified meanings" in some spurious, ideal state of liberation, but remain
bound by—attuned to—those objects and meanings, while yet being "liberated from the usual quality of that meaning" (*I* 150). "The place of a tactic," as
de Certeau says, "belongs to the other" (xix). Williams would have his words
and works attain a tactical ambivalence with respect to the apocalyptics of strategy—no more and no less.

The end to which *Spring and All* moves, then, is neither an apocalypse nor
a millennium. Beginning with a recognition of the inadequacies and dangers
of strategy, Williams as much as possible opposes strategy with his own tactical
activity. The ambivalence he achieves is both a result of his own tendency toward a modernist, Poundian poetics and a necessary characteristic of the tactic
itself. The book begins with a vivid image of public danger; it ends, in the last
poem, with what seems an image of private inadequacy:

> Black eyed susan
> rich orange
> round the purple core
>
> the white daisy
> is not
> enough
>
> Crowds are white
> as farmers
> who live poorly
>
> But you
> are rich
> in savagery—
>
> Arab
> Indian
> dark woman
>   (*I* 151)

"Dark," as Marjorie Perloff has pointed out, is one of the most repeated words in the book, almost always associated with nature or femininity (135–36). Here, with the other images of "savagery," it appears to present both the fecund origin and blissful goal: simply put, our ground. Thus the poem—and the book—closes with a gesture toward an unachieved and perhaps unachievable consummation. Despite this gesture, however, Williams continues to thwart such completion whenever it appears possible. This final poem does not present the black-eyed susan as an alternative to the conventional white daisy but as an ever-present supplement. And the "ground" here functions precisely like contact, not as a basis but as a disruptive insistence. The poem does not, therefore, simply gesture beyond convention toward an unachievable consummation; instead it presents both convention and disruption as necessary components of the contemporary world. Just as destruction and creation were earlier said to be simultaneous, so *Spring and All* ends with the coexistence of closure and incompletion (*I* 127). Williams' black-eyed susan images both the desire that impels us and the force that enables us to escape constraint, however temporarily. Moreover, the poem itself enacts that escape in the carefully stressed tactility of its words, in its semantic and syntactic play within a system of rigid constraints. Only the play of tactics can allow us to slip from white daisy to white crowds, can allow "living poorly" both material and emotional referents, and, finally, can translate the black flower into the dark woman. Contact is achieved in the poetics of *Spring and All*, but, in keeping with the nature of the tactic, it must remain ambivalent—imaged earlier as an evanescent moment, imaged here as a disruptive surplus beyond any end.[3]

The Bomb: Ambivalence and Power

Given Williams' early and sustained predilection for a variety of apocalyptic images, the spectacular blasts of August 1945 were bound to be of particular interest. Williams' initial enthusiasm, however, is quite surprising. Despite his ambivalence toward England and his early misgivings about the war—like Pound, Williams felt that international finance was behind it—by the end of the war he had developed a strong commitment to the American cause.[4] This commitment stemmed in part from simple loyalty and in part from his own sons' involvement overseas. And no doubt he also shared in the general exhilaration over the war's end, especially with such a decisive victory. But Williams also felt that the war against fascism was analogous to, a version of, his own ongoing battle against the tyrannies of rationality and convention. The war would not only defeat fascism abroad but would lead to the rebirth of American art and culture he had long been seeking (Mariani 432, 488).

In his 1944 "Author's Introduction" to *The Wedge*, first given as a talk at the New York Public Library in October 1943, Williams begins almost apologetically, acknowledging that "the war is the first and only thing in the world today." He soon becomes insistent, however, that the arts are not a "diversion," not a "turning away"—specifically, his writing "is the war or part of it, merely a different sector of the field" (*CP2* 53). Williams' famous subsequent assertions that "there is nothing sentimental about a machine" and that "a poem is a small (or large) machine made of words" should be read in light of the importance of efficient machinery to the war effort—a poem is not sentimental in the same way that well-made guns and bombs are not sentimental (*CP2* 54). As Williams makes clear at the end of the introduction, the war that characterizes art is a battle for formal invention: "There is no poetry of distinction without formal invention, for it is in the intimate form that works of art achieve their exact meaning, in which they most resemble the machine, to give language its highest dignity, its illumination in the environment to which it is native. Such war, as the arts live and breathe by, is continuous" (*CP2* 55). Particularly significant here is the implied reversal of the importance of military and artistic wars: at the beginning of the piece, Williams justifies art as an extension of the war; here the war is but one manifestation of the arts' continuous battle against stagnant forms, against tradition. This primary "continuous war" is implicitly contrasted to the (false) fascist *rivoluzione continua* championed by Pound. In an unpublished manuscript from this time, Williams even linked the construction of the poem to the construction of the state, concluding that, to avoid fascism, the state "had better look to the str[u]cture of a modern poem for its plan" ("A Cry in the Night").

Williams' own struggle toward a new poetic form, at this time centering on *Paterson*, was thus the primary struggle on behalf of democracy against forces of tyranny. In another prose piece, entitled "Let Us Order Our World" and at one time intended for *Paterson* III, Williams detailed poetry's war against tradition and its relation to World War II.[5] "The war is everywhere," Williams says, "and its participants are taking the same sides as the armies in the field" (19). Indeed since generals need imagination in order "to take new liberties with the traditions of arms," "a poet might well . . . be made a part of any board of strategy" (19). Closely allied to the war effort, Williams' struggle may well be more important, since he aims to prevent the supporters of tradition and traditional institutions from returning "to the defects of those establishments of yesterday, which forced [the war] on by their failures, which the war has shown to be calamities" (21). Against these men and against a restrictive "order [that] has meant too often no more than to maim," Williams asserts that "our attack must be in force, with every new weapon and utmost violence. I am not speaking of soldiering" (22). The poet, then, is the unacknowledged general, his poem the greatest secret weapon.

Of course, Williams' response to the war is in some respects fairly typical of literary responses, even to the first war. Yet Williams nowhere specifies the codification of a new order, only that such an order should allow the greatest freedom, should be open to "man's wildest thoughts," with no attempt "to limit the imagination" ("A Cry in the Night"). Williams' statements in fact imply that no new, definitive order can come into being, that the strategy of peace should be abandoned in favor of ongoing, tactical agonistics. There is no indication that the continuous war Williams speaks of in *The Wedge* will end with some permanent victory. Instead, the poem will continue to be a weapon, a violent act initiated by means of and for the sake of a freedom from tyranny that will remain a constant struggle.

The means, too, will be tactical: as Williams says in *The Wedge*, the poet-tactician will use "words as he finds them interrelated about him," words partaking of other, restrictive orders, and "compose them—without distortion which would mar their exact significances—into an intense expression of his perceptions and ardors that they may constitute a revelation in the speech that he uses" (*CP2* 54). Williams even spoke of *Paterson* as an "infiltration into the dry mass . . . of knowledge and culture" (qtd. in Mariani 479). In "Let Us Order Our World," Williams also distinguishes between tactical and strategic approaches, stressing that imagination, not entrenched wisdom, is needed for "a change of tactics, to go in among the trees and battle those who live there on their own terms" (20). The traditionalists want to maintain a position of strategic superiority, unaffected by change: "They wish to use America now for their purposes . . . regardless of the character of *the mass itself*, the thing they encounter and upon which they work, whose new character, whose back stroke upon them is denied and avoided. They do not want to acknowledge the imaginative force which would modify them, in their tradition, and give the field its new dignity. . . . They want to tell it what to do, they do not want to marry, they want to eat" (21). Williams, of course, wants just the opposite, a marriage, a tactical involvement, wherein "we shall all be modified by our victories or lack of them in the field. Not by them but because of them—new combinations in that furnace" (22). Williams' struggle with order, then—both in general and specifically in *Paterson*—was precisely to achieve a tactical relation to order, not to destroy order but to refuse it strategic domination.

In another, brief article, "The Poem as a Scene of Action," Williams turned from the poem as an act to the poem as a scene of action, or more specifically a scene of agonistics: "the poem as a scene of action calls up a battle field, the disorder of a battlefield, as it appears, which evidences an action with at least the intention of [o]rder." Evidently the formulation Williams works around is of an order existing in the poem's struggle itself—in its struggle to deal adequately with those various "surrounding" materials of which it is made. The poem as an uneasy combination of order and disorder, struggling against an order without which it cannot exist, embodies precisely Williams' view of the poem and of society as the scene of continuing agonistics, never to lapse into the stasis of any specific order.

The atomic bomb, then, marked the successful conclusion to one aspect of Williams' ongoing battle. The tremendous power, the unleashed energy of the bomb also made it an extraordinary accomplishment—both an instance of the imagination's almost miraculous ability to transform nature and a dramatic, material embodiment of its power. In "To All Gentleness," one of the poems in *The Wedge*, Williams had already compared "the packed word," the poetically charged word, to a bomb—the poem as equivalent in impact to area bombing (*CP2* 71). There Williams sought to discover whether violence or gentleness was "the core," but had to settle for a recursive alternation, the two inseparably united. The impact of the Hiroshima bombing on Williams may be gauged by two letters written on August 7, 1945, the day after the bombing—"letter day for some galactic reason." To Byron Vazakas he could do little more than exclaim: "The day following the atomic bomb blast! —the poor Jews who accomplished it. Now we'll hate them worse than ever." To James Laughlin he was more expansive: "But when we talk of explosions! the latest is mind quelling, touches more than the imagination—a blast out of the history of the Milky Way. It's got to end something but quick."[6] If ordinary poems are like ordinary bombs, the Bomb is like a super poem, a product of the imagination's ability to release cosmic forces that will produce vast effects—ending not simply the war, but "something," perhaps a whole phase or era of human history, transforming the world as only the imagination could manage. Already in 1940 Williams had reported to Vazakas that scientists had succeeded in producing gold in a cyclotron, radiation fulfilling the alchemists' dream (Mariani 438). Now the transformation Williams had imagined in *Spring and All* seemed about to occur, or even to have occurred.[7] One joyful, unpublished poem provides a striking example of Williams' enthusiasm:

I am the atomic
    bamb
      Bamb!
I make a grand
    Slamb.[8]

Playful as it may be, this poem clearly presents the Bomb as the embodiment of that sheer energy Williams had been defending and celebrating for many years. Even in a calmer time, in a 1948 talk entitled "The Poem as a Field of Action," Williams pointed to the Bomb's transformative potential: "For one great thing about 'the bomb' is the awakened sense it gives us that catastrophic (but why?) alterations are also possible in the human *mind*, in art, in the arts. . . . We are too cowed by our fear to realize it fully. But it is *possible*. That is what we mean. This isn't optimism, it is chemistry: Or better, physics" (*SE* 287). Similarly, in "The Old House," the desire and necessity that are the "aftermath of 'the bomb' " will lead to our rescue from the cultural decline that followed the Civil War (*CP2* 167). The Bomb, in sum, could awaken all to the radioactive light that is "too fiery for logical statement" (*SL* 240). The difficulty, however, was to detach the positive potential from the Bomb's fearsome destructive power.

For the Bomb, Williams knew, was also an enormous intensification of war's destructive violence—he already felt, as he told Zukofsky, that the ability to devastate civilian populations had transformed the country and by implication the world (Mariani 501). He knew, too, that the Bomb marked a culmination of the violence of rationality: in a letter to Kenneth Burke he linked philosophy and the Bomb in a glance at an empty future, in which there would be no distracting babies, no literature, and no culture, "only philosophers and bombs" (qtd. in Mariani 517). In poems like "To All Gentleness," "Catastrophic Birth," "War the Destroyer," and "The Birth of Venus," Williams attempted to resolve the problem of war and its relation to creativity but found it extremely difficult. "War the Destroyer," published in *Harper's Bazaar* in 1942, simply proclaims that war is an "appurtenance" to "the dance" and ends with an image of the dancer, like Shiva, combining elegance of motion with a "blood red" flush "in its place / beside the face." As that last couplet would suggest, however, this poem is not convincing. War is subsumed in the dance too easily, and by means of a too facile use of Shiva. It is not surprising that the poem was omitted in subsequent collections. "Catastrophic Birth" focuses on violence, yet takes an optimistic view and stresses the subsequent rebirth—no doubt with reference to Williams' catastrophic struggles with *Paterson*. Even this poem, though, concludes rather ominously with a look forward from present rebirth to another cycle (and with perhaps a glance at Yeats' "Second Coming"): "The broken cone breathes softly on / the edge of the sky, violence revives and regathers" (*CP2* 57). Like "To All Gentleness," this poem solves the dilemma by transforming it into a cycle. Both poems also acknowledge the thrill of violence, particularly the moment of release when the bombs are jettisoned.

"The Birth of Venus," however, takes a more distanced view. Violence offers no thrill, only destruction, and although Williams acknowledges that art and nature—even "the quietness of flowers"—may depend on violence, he refuses to settle for cyclical resolution:

> But why must we suffer
> ourselves to be so torn to sense our world? Or believe we must so
> suffer to be born again?
>
> (CP2 113)

Williams can provide no other resolution, only a wish that we might learn some other way, a way to experience rebirth by means of the imagination rather than violence. Yet, as Williams acknowledges, this distanced, strategic wish is itself implicated in the violence he would avoid:

> Governments are defeats, distor-
> tions. I wish (and so I fail). Notwithstanding, I wish we might
> learn of an April of small waves—deadly as all slaughter, that we
> shall die soon enough, to dream of April, not knowing why we have been
> struck down, heedless of what greater violence.
>
> (CP2 114)

Williams' wish is a mark of his own desire to control, to govern, and it therefore cannot succeed. It is not clear what "greater violence" Williams has in mind; the phrase seems to function, though—especially given its terminal position in the poem—as an insistence on the limits of human violence, on the fact that, however violence might offer mastery, it can never be mastered. It insists, that is, on the Bomb's ultimate control of the field.

The different forms of the three poems Williams retained, all of which employ a single voice, also show his varying responses to the dilemma of the Bomb and strategic order. "To All Gentleness" resorts to fragmentation and openness to achieve some freedom from the terror of violence, even while acknowledging the cyclical order. "Catastrophic Birth," in keeping with its optimism, its celebration of creative violence, is the most regular, with ten sestets of roughly equal lines and many lines ending at fairly natural breaks. "The Birth of Venus," however, presents the most interesting use of form, combining an orderly stanzaic structure (but comprised of five-line stanzas) with lines so long they have the feel of prose and with line-ends that seem about as arbitrary as prose lines. The effect is of a peculiar combination of order and freedom, or rather of an entrapment within a wholly other order, within which, however, that very entrapment allows (or perhaps compels) a measure of freedom. Like the human condition it addresses, Williams' poem is both tortuous and surprisingly graceful, an unstable and uneasy mix of conflicting drives to order and to spontaneity. A similar conflict can be seen in Williams' evident pleasure in the language's violent contortions—a pleasure that perhaps manifests a resurfacing of his own enthusiasm (here denied) for violence. On a smaller scale and with different means, "The Birth of Venus" addresses the same formal and thematic dilemmas Williams was confronting in *Paterson*.

Paterson's Catastrophes

Despite its long gestation—"the longest labor at which I was ever the attendant," he wrote Zukofsky—*Paterson*, too, was intimately involved in the war effort, as Williams confessed to Laughlin in 1943: "The main thing is that I'm in the war effort to the hilt—actually, physically and mentally. In other words the form of the poem stems also from that. It is one, inescapable, intrinsic" (qtd. in "*A*" 381; qtd. in Mariani 486). Not only would the completed poem be a blow struck for freedom, against tyranny, but Williams' struggles within the poem mimed the social struggles now in progress: "I am conscious of the surrealists, of the back to the home shit-house mentality, the church of England apostacy, the stepped-on, dragging his dead latter half Pound mentality—with the good and the new and the empty and the false all fighting a battle in my veins: unresolved" (qtd. in Mariani 486). As with war, violence, and the Bomb, discovering a satisfactory resolution, a form, was Williams' major difficulty with *Paterson*. His accounts of his progress are strewn, as Mariani notes, with military metaphors, from his 1939 call for a "machine gun style" for the epic, through to his "final onslaught" on Book I in 1945 (433, 501; *SL* 234–35). Mariani summarizes: "almost from the beginning of America's entry into the war, Williams had matched his own progress on his American epic with the progress of Allied troop movements, especially in Europe. When he spoke of *Paterson* it was in terms of pushes, assaults, retreats (strategic and otherwise), of being bogged down, mired, overrun, of making advances and breakthroughs" (477). At times Williams' progress even mirrored, albeit darkly, that of the war. After repeated stallings and arduous halts, a "major breakthrough" occurred at the same time as the Russian and American advances of late 1944, to be followed, of course, by the "final onslaught," with the completion of *Paterson* I roughly coinciding with the end of the war. By September 1945, a month after Hiroshima, Williams even had a firm plan for the four Books, although he still felt that *Paterson* I was too rough, looking "as tho' an atomic bomb had hit it before it was born" (qtd. in Mariani 509). For the poem as for the country, the Bomb marked a moment of triumphant yet troubled completion. Williams hoped it would also produce an eventual, if difficult, rebirth.

Paterson is filled with catastrophes, or apocalypses, but its major apocalypse occurs in Book III, with the burning of the library and subsequent flood. Williams turns to the library in response to the accusatory letter from Cress that ends the previous book—a letter that attacks Williams for being too literary, for making too radical a distinction between literature and life, and for dealing with others, specifically women, and more specifically Cress, by dominating them: "My attitude toward woman's wretched position in society and my ideas about all the changes necessary there, were interesting to you, weren't they, in so far as they made for *literature*?" (P 87). The letter necessarily accuses *Paterson* of the same damning faults, particularly since Cress anticipates Williams' inclusion of the letter in the poem and criticizes that inclusion as but one more instance of Williams' (and thus the poem's) stance toward others: strategic domination. With this letter, the poem in effect bifurcates into two polarized discourses—one that would control and one that refuses all control—that seem impossible to reconcile. The dilemma, for *Paterson*, is to find a means of including other voices without subsuming them to one, authorial voice, of granting each its own place without allowing the poem to fall apart— in sum, to write a poem that would not simply extend a tradition of strategic poems, as Pound's poem extended the tradition by attempting to consummate it. The "marriage riddle" Williams propounds in Book III (P 106), which echoes his statements in "Let Us Order Our World," provides another version of this dilemma: How can we live alongside another in mutual interaction, without either dominating or being dominated?

In the library, then, Williams confronts the essential emptiness of the literary tradition. As section one makes clear, it can provide no answers. The "cool of books" may offer a retreat for the mind, but the library still oppresses: "The Library is desolation, it has a smell of its own / of stagnation and death" (P 96, 101). In fact, the paradox of the library is that the books that promote life warn against books—which is also, of course, the paradox of *Paterson*. As Williams warned in "Let Us Order Our World," excessive reading leads to rigidity, to men being "too old before they are wise" (20). Whatever value books may hold, the critical "stain of sense" can never be separated "from the inert mass": like the "radiant gist" Madame Curie had discovered, this stain "resists the final crystallization," which is to say that it remains always apart, always outside any system, as a sort of unattainable surplus (P 108, 109). At the same time that he isolates this "gist" as an unattainable "cure," however, Williams is conscious of the implications of his act. For "the words that never get said," or what words cannot ever say, constitutes a promise of strategic totality precisely equivalent to death:

> Death lies in wait,
> a kindly brother—
> full of the missing words,
> the words that never get said—
> a kindly brother to the poor.
> The radiant gist that
> resists the final crystallization
>   (*P* 109)

Thus in "A Note on Paterson: Book III," Williams speaks of *Paterson* (man and poem) "plummet[ing] to his conclusions," "to his death" in the falls. The "answer" to the dilemma is but another turn, another dimension to the dilemma.

Williams' note, published on the dust jacket of the original edition, deserves to be quoted at length, for it encapsulates the difficulties and paradoxes of Book III and indeed of *Paterson* as a whole. Here are the first two paragraphs:

> *Paterson* is a man (since I am a man) who dives from cliffs and the edges of waterfalls, to his death—finally. But for all that he is a woman (since I am not a woman) who *is* the cliff and the waterfall. She spreads protecting fingers about him as he plummets to his conclusions to keep the winds from blowing him out of his path. But he escapes, in the end, as I have said.
>
> As he dies the rocks fission gradually into wild flowers the better to voice their sorrow, a language that would have liberated them both from their distresses had they but known it in time to prevent catastrophe. (*P* 279)

Given this description, it is difficult to see why we must wait for Book IV to find "the perverse confusions that come of a failure to untangle the language." But the perversity in this note, as in Book III, is accurate: *Paterson* is both man and woman because it embodies the "marriage riddle" of Book III, struggling within itself and with itself against dominating, strategic orders, whether its own or another's. Paterson's "escape" from the structure of his conclusions or from the protecting fingers is also perverse and paradoxical, for it seems predicated on his death—that is, escape from the spiritual death brought about by an overly controlled, overly rationalized life depends on physical death. I will have more to say about this condition of life and language in the next section; for the moment it will suffice to note that the "catastrophe" itself offers escape and should therefore be encouraged rather than prevented. If *Paterson* searches for "the redeeming language by which [to prevent] a man's premature death," that language is only to be found at the edge of catastrophe—it is founded upon the catastrophe, of the man and of the poem, that causes the rocks to fission into flowers and so voice the new language. Hence the poem, *Paterson*, is founded on its own catastrophe—a continuous "dive," or series of dives, that manifests a constant refusal and destruction of any strategic, redemptory scaffolding—and it is this refusal and consequent ongoing catastrophe that, Williams hopes, will paradoxically "redeem" the poem, redeem it from ultimate catastrophe and even from the necessity of redemption.[9]

The burning of the library, then, because of its diverse and even contradictory causes and effects, presents an apocalypse far more complex than that of *Spring and All*. The fire cannot simply be identified with any one meaning, since it begins in the "radiant gist"—it is in, or creates, a cyclotron (*P* 115)—that resists all attempts to crystallize it. At various times, or according to various voices, it possesses diverse implications. It is the fire of passionate life, or the poet's imagination, and so a positive force, but it is also the "destroying fire" that stems from a writer's surrounding conditions and is intended to "scotch . . . at the root" any new writing (*P* 113)—it is both the fire that burned in Sappho's veins and the fire authority used to destroy her poems and other "dangerous" books. As it destroys the library, even the poet—who earlier had been feeding on it—joins with others to squirt "little hoses of / objection" (*P* 120). Michael André Bernstein observes that *Paterson*'s images, including the fire, "collect ever-increasing clusters of signification" until they become overburdened with contradictory meanings (207). But comparison to Pound's consistent image of the book as a ball of light points not to a failure but to the integrity of Williams' attention to what he saw as a fundamental problem of the modern poem. It is precisely this complexity, this "overburdening," that enables the poem to escape a too superficial coherence, to avoid submission to strategic totality. Much the way anti-narratives escape what Jerome McGann calls "the imperialism of narrativity" by creating "imaginative localities and incommensurate particulars," Williams in Book III works against the narrative of *Paterson* he had established in Books I and II (633).

The apocalyptic fire in fact produces much the same ambivalence as the Bomb itself: it embodies a tremendous creative energy—which, unfortunately, we cannot or can only rarely achieve while reading (*P* 123)—that is also destructive, and destructive not merely of past, moribund structures, but of the poet himself and even of strong, "living" poems. Like gentleness and violence in "To All Gentleness," Book III's "beautiful thing" and fire are "intertwined," forming "an identity" at the core of the world (*P* 120). Indeed, it is the fire that transforms the impalpable "radiant gist" into the concrete "beautiful thing"— which is itself, of course, not an image of traditional, pure beauty, but of beauty as a "defiance of authority," as present, actual life: "scarred, fire swept / . . . nameless, / drunk," yet possessing, like garden rocks, "an attractive brokenness" (*P* 119, 121, 140).

Radiation accumulates similar meanings, though with a more positive tone, in Book IV, section two. Williams begins the section with an apocalyptic wish to "smash the wide world" for his son, and then turns to a consideration of fission and Madame Curie's discovery of radium. The initial discovery is linked to the library-destroying fire:

> an unhatched sun corroding
> her mind, eating away a rind
> of impermanences, through books
> remorseless   .
>
>   (*P* 171)

Prefiguring both the soon-to-be-discovered radiant gist and the atomic bomb, this unhatched, corrosive sun embodies the simultaneously wondrous and terrible power both of this particular discovery and of discovery, or imagination, in general. For just as "beauty is / a defiance of authority," so "dissonance," Williams asserts, "leads to discovery" (*P* 119, 175). In the more optimistic context of Book IV, however, Williams declares a clear separation between gentleness and violence, here between love and violence: "Love, the sledge that smashes the atom? No, No! antagonistic / cooperation is the key, says Levy" (*P* 176). Of course, the attribution to Levy (author of a relativistic *Philosophy for a Modern Man*) serves to keep Williams at some distance from the claim. But "antagonistic cooperation" does provide an active mediation between violence and love, between fission and fusion, remarkably like that adumbrated in Williams' World War I piece on Vorticism—a view of society and of the poem not governed by any one strategy, but constituted as self-regulating fields of diverse, disjunct tactics. Book IV also figures such a view in a striking image of uranium as

> the complex atom, breaking
> down, a city in itself, that complex
> atom, always breaking down   .
> to lead.
>   But giving off that, to an
> exposed plate, will reveal   .
>
>   (*P* 177)

Considered spatially, the city (also the poem and the man) fragments into antagonism, into insignificant, leaden parts, devoid of value. In the context of its temporality, however—which is to say in the context of tactics—the very fissioning that destroys the structure produces precisely what is most important, but which even when acknowledged, as here, cannot properly be named (and so controlled): the "radiant gist." This is the "plus" that may "cure the cancer" of "order, perfect and controlled / on which empires, alas, are built" (*P* 178). In the plus, the excess, lies the cure to strategic domination. As we will shortly see, this "plus" becomes more emphatically interstitial in the later works, an excess that arises from relations, not from some point beyond. Even at this time, however, Williams was thinking along these lines.[10]

Thus in Book III, section three, in the aftermath of the apocalyptic fire, Williams proposes no new strategy, for there are only texts that

> mount and complicate them-
> selves, lead to further texts and those
> to synopses, digests and emendations. So be it.
> Until the words break loose or—sadly
> hold, unshaken.
>
>   (*P* 130)

There can be no end, as Gertrude Stein said, to writing as explanation. Hence the apocalyptic fire is followed by a flood of distinct voices, sometimes contextualized but often not, which thwart any stability, just as the flood undermines "the railroad embankment" (*P* 136). Disparate prose fragments, sudden, hostile intrusions ("American poetry is a very easy subject to discuss for the simple reason that it does not exist" [*P* 140]), haphazard typography that shows multiple voices fracturing the very material of the book, a letter assigning more reading (from a poet confined to a mental hospital!), and even a substratum report revealing no basis of life-giving water—all these bespeak the catastrophe of the poem and of the postwar world. Williams' text reflects both that catastrophe and his own struggle not to supply a new strategy, not to subsume those voices to any one strategic order or discourse. The polarization of voices that ended Book II is finally dissolved into a multiplicity of voices, impossible to polarize. It is this dissolution that Williams hopes will enable the achievement of a dynamic "antagonistic cooperation" rather than a simple and static antagonism.

Section three presents Williams' most fundamental confrontation with this dilemma, this condition of life and the poem. Even when the flood has subsided and Williams' own voice becomes prevalent, it refuses to propose any easy escape:

> How to begin to find a shape—to begin to begin again,
> turning the inside out : to find one phrase that will
> lie married beside another for delight   .   ?
> —seems beyond attainment   .
>
>   (*P* 140)

The words can be allowed neither to "break loose" into chaotic antagonism, as they threaten in this section, nor to "hold, unshaken," in obedience to some directive. Where *Kora in Hell* and *Spring and All* had performed largely disruptive functions, *Paterson* acknowledges its dependence on some order, on some coexistence with strategy. What Williams calls "antagonistic cooperation" in Book IV is here a matter of the inflection, or perhaps deflection, of "the syllables" themselves—Williams points to the tactical materiality of the language even as he acknowledges that truly attaining such a language, resisting the imposition of strategy, may take "genius" and "a hundred years, perhaps," or perhaps even longer (*P* 144). Williams' invocation of "speed against the inundation," then, should not suggest a wartime acceleration like Pound's, but the precise *timing* needed to "catch aslant," to deflect or inflect, the distinct elements of the inundation: the timing requisite to the tactician (*P* 135).

Somehow the words must be turned "inside out," tactically broken from while yet remaining part of a strategic order, whereupon both words and lives will attain their own meaning, their own value. In *Paterson* Williams envisages this tactical ambivalence most often as a constant falling into—or attainment of—catastrophe. Sam Patch's dive provides an obvious analogy, as do tight-rope walkers, who escape "not by 'composition,' " but by "being taut, balanced between eternities," as Williams seeks balance between strategies (*P* 103–04). Later he will use the act of dancing, a series of constantly corrected falls. As Williams' "A Note on Paterson: Book III" tells us, it is the act of falling that causes the rocks or words to fission, thereby creating a language that "prevents" the fall. Just so, the active fissioning of the various discourses of Book III prevents the poet from succumbing to any one discursive strategy, which would lead to a final collapse—the final apocalypse. The deflection of the language keeps the poem unstable, always as it were on the cusp of catastrophe, the words "taut" and vibrant between orders, and so contained by none.[11]

This ambivalent, tentative, always shifting condition is marvelously presented, or linguistically enacted, at the end of Book III. For language, Williams declares, is "the visible part" of the falls, of this ongoing catastrophe, and it is only in his relation to language that Williams can succeed (*P* 145). He first offers a quite traditional strategy, to make of language "a replica" so that his "sins [will] be forgiven" and his "disease cured." But after citing *"la capella di S. Rocco"* and "the images of arms and knees / hung on nails" at de Montpellier as examples of such replicas, Williams interrupts this developing solution. I quote to the end of Book III:

No meaning. And yet, unless I find a place

apart from it, I am its slave,
its sleeper, bewildered—dazzled

by distance   .   I cannot stay here
to spend my life looking into the past:

the future's no answer. I must
find my meaning and lay it, white,
beside the sliding water: myself—
comb out the language—or succumb

—whatever the complexion. Let
me out! (Well, go!) this rhetoric
is real!

    (*P* 145)

The abrupt reversals throughout this passage result from Williams' tactical rejection of any single, strategic solution. Also important is the instability of certain key phrases, particularly "no meaning"—it seems both a denial of any
Christian connotations to the "replicas" and a lament that the traditional answer will not work, will not cure his "disease." The first "it," too, is of uncertain reference, although the possibilities—language (the referent of the previous "it"), replica, meaning—are closely linked. But if "meaning" (or perhaps
"referentiality") is the likeliest referent, Williams' deliberate vagueness gestures toward other constraints, other masters, not *a* strategy but strategies in
general, both inside and outside discourse. While Williams seeks a "place"
apart from "it," he remains acutely aware that no such place can exist, dependent as it would have to be on stabilities of the past or the future, derived from
some proposed *telos*—even, or perhaps especially, if the future promises some
new language. In their dizzying twists and turns, the last two stanzas precisely
enact the convolutions of Williams' tactics, the ambivalence of his place that
cannot be a place because only by constant action, only by a constant departure
from the stability of place, can he exist, however tentatively, apart from "it."
Williams necessarily distances himself from his meaning, his self, in order to
eradicate—paradoxically and ambivalently, succumbing and succeeding—the
stasis in which he would be trapped by accepting any stable solution. This
"white meaning," which is also the radiance given off in Book IV, is necessarily
both inside and "beside" because it can no longer be conceived as the strategic
goal—as if "meaning" were the ultimate achievement of a poem or a life. No
strategy, then, can be adequate to *Paterson*, for it removes itself from the strategic discourse of "truth" in favor of the tactical rhetoric of its own activity.
With "this rhetoric / is real," *Paterson* declares its freedom from the narrative
order that had been established in Book I, even as it admits its implicit relation
to that order: the "truth" of this poetics lies in the reality of the shifting relations between order and catastrophe.

At the end of "A Note on Paterson: Book III," Williams promised that, when the man and woman of *Paterson* were swept to sea "by their failure of speech," the poet would deliver "the key to their final rescue." Book IV, as we have seen, gives this "key" a name, "antagonistic cooperation." Unfortunately, however, Williams' translation of that key into Book IV seems a falling off from the achievement of Book III. Where the earlier Book achieved the "looser, wider world where 'order' is a servant not a master" Williams sought in *Paterson*, Book IV seems to defer to order (*SL* 214). In Book III the notion of a "cure," for example, is offered only to be retracted, or at best subject to qualification and irony, while in Book IV it becomes disturbingly concrete. To be sure, the pun on Madame Curie and the offer of radiation, the radiant gist, as a cure for the cancer of order and empire, continue in the same vein as Book III, open-ended and somewhat ironic. And Williams does connect the radiant gist to "dissonance." When he identifies the gist with social credit, however, and therefore presents credit as the "cure," the true solution to social ills, the openness characteristic of tactics has been forfeited. Given the finality of his turn to credit at the end of section two, there is insufficient dissonance to undermine the imposition of credit as the single, strategic solution—a solution that would lead, as Pound had hoped, to an ideal state. Apparently the postwar social situation, along with his own need, compelled Williams to supply a more concrete "key" and *telos*.

The conclusion to Book IV, in which Williams completes *Paterson*'s initial narrative structure, presents a similar problem. The preface to *Paterson* had begun with a statement quoted from Williams' own notes, "rigor of beauty is the quest." It is of course possible to read this declaration with no trace of irony, as a direct statement of Williams' purpose. Yet Williams' quotation marks themselves suggest a certain distance, as if this were a proposition to be questioned rather than a basis for all that follows. "Beauty" is a highly suspect term in Williams' vocabulary; "beauty" as such had been rejected in the twenties, while *Paterson*'s "beautiful thing" is explicitly not an embodiment of abstract beauty. Moreover, "rigor of beauty" is also suspect, echoing as it does the rigor of death Williams frequently encountered in his other career. The quest, then, and especially its completion, would seem highly problematic even at *Paterson*'s outset, inextricably bound up with strategy and constraint. Of course, if we take the sea to represent the quest's strategic *telos*, Williams does avoid succumbing to the death of a "rigor of beauty." His means of avoiding that finality, though, seem contrived. "Again," he had said in Book III, "is the magic word" (as "credit" becomes in IV.2). But given the subtlety of Book III's sense of "turning the inside out"—its refusal of easy solutions—Williams' "final somersault," with the Joycean hero apocalyptically returning from his death to begin anew, scarcely seems a magical conclusion (*P* 140, 202). Perhaps the tremendous pressures occasioned by World War II, with its seeming repetition (and escalation) of the Great War, compelled Williams to seek such a solution, as in the shorter poems wherein he first employed the cycle.[12] It is a solution, however, that seems inadequate to the complexities of both the postwar world and *Paterson* itself. If the Bomb marks an end and new beginning to the history of the West, surely that event is not simply another instance of an "eternal close," to be subsumed by an all-encompassing cycle, a circumscription that is itself strategic. Williams avoids the strategic *telos* of the sea only to adopt another, greater strategy, completed by the ultimate acceleration of an apocalyptic blast from end to origin. It seems an arbitrary solution, a stopgap until some better language could be found, of the sort adumbrated in Book III. No wonder Williams soon felt that he must continue *Paterson*, take it "into a new dimension" in order to give it "imaginative validity" (*P* xiv).

A Paradise of Postponement

Although Williams' works exhibit a remarkable diversity of forms and methods, they do share a certain similarity: a general resort to some form of fragmentation, distortion, or multiplication of voices in order to disrupt or thwart strategic orders—techniques developed around the time of World War I and still used in the context of the cyclic approach Williams favored in response to World War II. In the later work, however, in *Paterson* V and in the poems of *Pictures from Brueghel*, Williams' poetics undergoes a considerable shift. These works generally feature a single, coherent voice, speaking in a fairly conventional, even discursive, manner. This voice may touch on a wide range of topics, even entertaining contradictory possibilities, but its casual, assured ease contrasts markedly with the abrupt twists and turns of the earlier poems. More homogeneous and more relaxed, these poems have been taken to mark Williams' rediscovery and adoption of a more traditional lyric voice than he had hitherto used. As a result, they have been praised by those who favor more traditional forms—beginning, of course, with the Pulitzer Prize in 1963—and strictured by those who favor more "experimental" work and see these poems as a retreat, perhaps brought on by Williams' debilitating strokes, from his previous struggles. These poems may talk about many of the same issues as the earlier work, but they do not seem to *enact* the associated problematic in their poetics.

Both these views, however, are inadequate, for these poems do not in fact return to a traditional lyric voice. It would be best to consider this phase of Williams' poetics on its own terms, in relation to the earlier works, but without any preemptive evaluations as to relative merit. As a work like "Poem" indicates, Williams remains acutely aware of the "insanity" of contemporary events, while in "The Desert Music" Williams subjects his new voice to an extended interrogation concerning its position in and adequacy to the contemporary world (*CP2* 435–36). The poem offers no sense of a comfortable, settled existence, only

> an agony of self-realization
> bound into a whole
> by that which surrounds us
>   (*CP2* 275)

Yet despite this agony and despite Williams' reservations the voice emerges from this interrogation still worthy of affirmation: "I am a poet, I reaffirmed, ashamed" (*CP2* 284).

More important in the present context, "The Orchestra" also shows him fully aware of the complex problematic entailed in living and in writing poetry in such times. As its opening tune-up indicates, the orchestra provides an example of man's ability to create design, to establish value and meaning, and so to complete nature. But the orchestra (and with it design) encompasses more than this obvious, positive aspect. One of Williams' early drafts stresses its rather ominous pervasiveness: "An orchestra is that / from which our minds / can never free themselves."[13] And *Paterson* III had already spoken of "design" as a "beautiful, optimistic word," even while linking it to death, in "funeral *designs*" (*P* 137). In "The Orchestra," design is linked to oppression and thence to the Bomb—indeed, the orchestra may also represent the "design" of history itself, culminating in the Bomb. The orchestra's prolonged "A" is both a beginning and an end, the sun it lifts both the life-giving sun of nature (brought into the human realm) and the fiery ball of the A-bomb. Despite *Paterson* IV's denial, love is also caught in this predicament:

> Love is that common tone
>   shall raise his fiery head
>   and sound his note.
>   (*CP2* 250)

In this poem there appears no means to distinguish between the sun and the Bomb, no means to separate love from the smashing of the atom. The orchestra's "wrong note"—the draft refers to "dissonance"—is inseparable from its existence. The memory that assaults "our dreams," then, is the Bomb, and all it represents (*CP2* 252). Against the Bomb, the orchestra, and with it the poem, can only "repeat / and repeat the theme . . . until thought is dissolved / in tears" (*CP2* 251). The poem closes with an emphatic reassertion of man's ability to design, to complete and so to surmount nature, represented here by the twittering of birds. The absence of any evaluation gives the final repetition a tense ambivalence, fusing the positive achievement of design with an ominous finality:

> It is a design of a man
> > that makes them twitter.
> > > It is a design.
>
> (*CP2* 252)

Williams puts the case more optimistically in "To Daphne and Virginia," where he identifies the mind as "the cause of our distress," but insists that "of it we can build anew" (*CP2* 247). But in "The Orchestra" he embodies, as thoroughly as in any earlier poem, his fundamental dilemma: that without design, or strategy, there would be nothing of value, but that with it comes also all that he would oppose.

The smoothness of Williams' triadic line should not obscure the rapid shifts among disparate elements, from nuclear apocalypse to a husband's love, that it effects. Moreover, other voices are constantly mingling with his own. In between the repetition of the theme and the poem's conclusion, just at the moment when thought dissolves, occurs something both remarkable in itself and highly significant for our understanding of Williams' later poetics. The French horns enter and declare:

> I love you. My heart
> > is innocent. And this
> > > the first day of the world!
> Say to them:
> "Man has survived hitherto because he was too
> ignorant to know how to realize his wishes. Now that he can realize them,
> he must either change them or perish."
> Now is the time   .
> > in spite of the "wrong note"
> > > I love you. My heart is
> innocent.
> > And this the first
> > > (and last) day of the world
>
> (*CP2* 252)

The need for a change in man's wishes refers not merely to the Bomb and the extinction of the species but to the deadening effect of strategy in general, particularly in "this modern age" of increasing bureaucracy and technocracy—

"perishing" may still be spiritual rather than physical (*CP2* 428). But here Williams does assert at least the possibility of change, of a renewal of purity, despite the continued acknowledgment of the "wrong note" and despite the fact (which we will shortly discuss further) that this "first day" may also be (and in a sense must be) the last.

Particularly important for Williams' poetics is the means whereby this possibility is introduced, the "interposition" of voices—first the French Horns, apparently declaring Williams' love for Flossie, and then the anonymous quotation, which Williams takes pains to mark as a *speaking* voice. It is not so much the content of speech that is important here—that could be given by a text—but the speech act itself, which suddenly introduces into the omnipresent design the possibility of change, of some result, at least for the moment, other than the Bomb. This is the voice Williams discovers and develops in *Pictures from Brueghel* and *Paterson V.* If in "To a Dog Injured in the Street" Williams feels inadequate to the situation, "as at the explosion / of a bomb, a bomb that has laid / all the world waste," his voice yet allows his pain to be assuaged (*CP2* 255). And in "The Yellow Flower," despite his eyes' clear sight of "ruin for myself / and all that I hold / dear," his tongue has "the power / to free myself / and speak of it" (*CP2* 259). Yet this is not the authoritative, conquering voice of the traditional lyric, reflecting on topics external to its immediate workings—the workings of the poem—but an *interstitial* voice that tactically inserts itself into the interstices of strategic design. Where Williams had earlier tended to stray from the precise timing and deflections of tactics toward acceleration (an impossible attempt to surmount and conquer strategy), in these late poems he turns toward delay, thereby retarding the completion of strategy, the achievement of totality, and allowing the insertion of voice.[14] Unlike the traditional lyric voice, then, the coherence of Williams' new voice is not imposed from without by an external ego, but is achieved only tenuously in the course of the poem itself. Hence he need no longer project the possibility of a superior future language, he need no longer struggle with the paradoxes of an "apocalypse without apocalypse" in order to develop a post-apocalyptic poetics. This new freedom paradoxically produces considerable repetition of themes, as "The Orchestra" indicates: while there is much development there is little progress, either in one poem or in the whole corpus, for progress is necessarily strategic. Yet it also enables the great range of these poems, as they move back and forth, seemingly without effort, among the personal, the social, and the contemplative.

The shift to this interstitial voice doubtless stems in part from Williams' personal circumstances. Acceleration and cyclic completion do not seem such attractive solutions when one's own death is at stake. The plea in "Asphodel,

That Greeny Flower" for "time, / time to recall," is in the first instance personal (*CP2* 312). Even in this personal context, though, the voice itself causes the desired delay; hence Williams plans to "drag it out" and "talk on / against time" (*CP2* 311). Time itself becomes an element of the design into which the voice inserts itself, and which it delays by means of tactical play:

> When I was a boy
>   I kept a book
>   to which, from time
>   to time,
>   I added pressed flowers
>   until, after a time,
>   I had a good collection.
>   (*CP2* 312)

Even the lineation, here as elsewhere in *Pictures from Brueghel*, suggests a voice tentatively inserting itself into the world, discovering itself by locating the interstices of strategy—the voice neither conquering nor submitting, but operating precisely like the "odor" in "Asphodel" that "penetrate[s] / into all crevices" of Williams' world (*CP2* 337). The fecund crevices of memory that Williams celebrates there are only the most vivid image of the condition necessary for meaningful life, and for meaningful poetry, that he envisions throughout these poems.

But while the shift in part stems from Williams' illness, that can be only a partial explanation. As we have seen, delay is offered as a possible response to strategy and apocalypse as early as *Kora in Hell*. Although it does not figure very prominently thereafter, it does recur in "Russia," first published in *The New Republic* in 1946. There Williams responds to Russia's transformation of a utopian dream into the oppressive reality of empire by inviting it to join him "in the spirit of Walt Whitman" to "loaf at our ease—a moment / at the edge of destruction" (*CP2* 145). "Russia" offers delay as a possibility, but pessimistically acknowledges the inevitability of the strategic end, of the "obliterating blow / that shall flatten everything" (*CP2* 145). A letter Williams wrote to Byron Vazakas in May 1946 is also significant for its view of the relation between speed and delay. At first, Williams sounds remarkably like Pound on the "time-lag": "delay," he begins, "is the secret weapon the modern age uses against us." What follows, though, points to a distinctly different understanding: "it interests me a lot that the . . . faster the age travels the more the delay. There is a basic relationship there, unperceived." As Williams explains his point, those in control use frenzied speed to prevent others from "sit[ting] back and think[ing] out what we have to say." Speed, therefore, must be interrupted. Stressing his point, Williams advises Vazakas to "take a little time out" from his writing in order to read.[15] The emphasis on delay should not be misconstrued as a retreat in the face of illness; it is very much a response to strategic order. Indeed, it could well be seen as a correction of the accelerated blast that closes *Paterson* IV, particularly since "Asphodel," in which the shift is most explicit, was first drafted as a section of *Paterson* V.

This change in Williams' poetics was impelled, then, both by his own situation and by the general condition of the postwar, postmodern world—and particularly, as "The Orchestra," "Asphodel," and the general frequency of reference would suggest, by the Bomb. For it is the Bomb, in "Asphodel," that bridges the gap between personal death and strategic totality. The drafts contained in the Beinecke library make the relation quite explicit; as one draft puts it, "all life ends / in the bomb." The Bomb's "childlike insistence" in section II is an insistence on the overwhelming importance of a single end—leading, of course, to itself and the "flowering" mushroom cloud. As Williams wrote in a draft, its insistence can narrow our minds

> to a preference [*sic*]
> for the one flower until
> it fills our thoughts

This sense of the Bomb as the ultimate expression or embodiment of strategic domination also lies behind the claim that "all suppressions," from witchcraft trials to book burnings,

> are confessions
> that the bomb
> has entered our lives
> to destroy us
> (*CP2* 324)

In a draft Williams specifies as well the realms of discourse and thought: "all enclosures, / all neat packagin[g] / of our verses / as of our knowledge." As the ultimate end of strategy, the Bomb becomes for Williams the supreme embodiment, the symbol par excellence, of all strategic oppression.

Like "The Orchestra," "Asphodel" also acknowledges that design is implicated in strategy, in the Bomb. If Williams celebrates the flower, he yet recognizes that the exploding Bomb is also a flower, albeit "dedicated to our destruction" (*CP2* 321). Love, too, is at least partly implicated in the Bomb, as is evident in the awed fascination it provokes, and in our willingness to "prostrate ourselves / before it," even though we do not believe "that love / can so wreck our lives" (*CP2* 322). The last phrase is significantly ambiguous, for although it could refer to a simple lack of faith in love's greater power, it also implies that the Bomb embodies or is a product of love.[16] The flexibility of Williams' interstitial voice allows him to pursue even contradictory directions, here linking the Bomb to the flower and love in order to stress the intimate and ambivalent relation between the Bomb and the forces that would oppose it. Even the sea, though not directly linked to the Bomb, embodies a distinct ambivalence, representing as it does both extinction and renewal.

Yet Williams does assert a fundamental distinction between love and the Bomb, the former a source of energy in life and allowing a quiet death, the latter the expression of a force for order, impoverishing lives and leading to brutal deaths. In "The Snow Begins," he draws a contrast between two images of death, a snowfall (representing a peaceful, natural death) and a "rain of bombs" (*CP2* 426). Williams concedes their equivalent loveliness but stresses the snow's greater gentleness. Although both will cover "all crevices," the crevices of life that open at the end of "Asphodel," the snow will cover these necessary wounds of life with a healing white blanket, while bombs will only cause more terrible wounds. In "Asphodel" Williams presents the alternatives as a question of belief: whether to believe in love as a desire for possession (or presence) that culminates in the Bomb, or in another love that somehow acknowledges desire while always escaping such an end. Hence the Bomb is merely an object of fascination, while that "single image" of love that "brought us together" is an object of adoration (*CP2* 325).

In terms of Williams' poetics, the problem remains how to speak "outside" strategy. For, as Williams puts it, "the bomb speaks": all discourse seems to lead to strategy and the Bomb (*CP2* 324). The Bomb's ultimate effect, therefore, becomes not simply physical death but the suppression of speech: with "the measure itself" lost, "we come to our deaths / in silence," in ultimate defeat (*CP2* 324). Yet silence is not entirely a capitulation to the Bomb, to death, for it can also be seen as a refusal of strategic discourse. In this sense, Williams' interstitial voice in these late poems depends on an initial refusal of an authoritarian, totalizing discourse. Even death itself can similarly provide a critical resource against the Bomb, since it promises not only the end of the self but also the end of the Bomb's domain, of its insistence on uniformity. In both cases death establishes a limit to totalization, and it therefore offers an entry into multiplicity, an escape from strategy into tactics. Hence "Asphodel" asserts that "no greater evil" can befall a man than the refusal of death—other than "the death of love" (*CP2* 334). In fact, though, the refusal of death and the death of love are at least concomitant: acceptance of death, by allowing loss to be internalized, frees us to love.[17]

Other writings can help to clarify Williams' sense of the relation between death and love. "For Eleanor and Bill Moynihan" remarks on death's role as a *gift* to man, a gift that is enough in itself to bring about contentment, without our striving to sate new desires. Such striving, for example the attempt to conquer the moon, is therefore misguided:

> What
> do they think they will attain
>   by their ships
>   that death has not
> already given
>   them? Their ships
>   should be directed
> inward upon   .
>   (CP2 255)

It is freedom, clearly, that is at stake here, freedom from oppressive subservience to some ultimate *telos*, however it be imagined. Against this oppression, death offers a kind of double freedom: first, its finality renders such technical achievements superfluous and therefore empty. Second, and more important, such striving for a *telos* demonstrates a continuing desire for strategic domination, for totality, when death offers the only means of achieving the end of that desire. If the inevitability of death be fully accepted, then, we will be free from the demand of attaining such totality now. A draft of "Asphodel" goes so far as to declare that death is the only means "to escape the consequences of our deeds"—a statement echoed in *Paterson* V's discovery of the "hole / at the bottom of the cavern / of death," through which "the imagination escapes intact" (*P* 210). It is not mere nostalgia that causes Williams to recall "The Wanderer"'s climactic loss in *Paterson* V, for the "bitterness at world's loss" has now become death itself, and the resemblance to "possession itself" has become the production of love, love's production as an always unnecessary excess. Williams converges here with Georges Bataille's sense that in various "unproductive expenditures"—in most meaningful activities—"*loss* . . . must be as great as possible in order for that activity to take on its true meaning" (118). This argument also lies behind a 1951 letter to Frank Moore, in which Williams praises the Homeric Greeks for their recognition that "death dominates our world," a recognition that enables both "complete peace" and "complete consciousness." But, Williams says, "there is nothing to do with freedom once we get it but to enslave ourselves—under the name of love."[18] Love here is not a *telos*, the object of a new quest, but a condition of activity. Thus the death of love and the failure to accept literal death are linked in "Asphodel" as the two greatest misfortunes because they are inseparable in Williams' late poetics: the failure to

accept death *is* the death of love, while the acceptance of death as the condition
of life enables the activity of love.

Williams' primary image for the condition in which his voice speaks is the
sea, which underlies both the garden (which would include many flowers, not
simply the Bomb's) and the poetry of Homer, that "old man" who is also
Williams. The return from the sea in "Asphodel" represents both his personal
recovery from his stroke and his poetry's recovery from the sea at the end of
Paterson IV. But neither Williams' recovery nor the poem's may be followed by
any easy, single triumph:

> if I have come from the sea
>   it is not to be
> wholly
>   fascinated by the glint of waves.
> . . .
> The poem
>   if it reflects the sea
>   reflects only
> its dance
>   upon that profound depth
>   where
> it seems to triumph.
>   The bomb puts an end
>   to all that
>
>   (CP2 321)

Given the reality of the Bomb, the poem can neither devote itself to the insistence of depth (and therefore be caught in strategy) nor content itself with the
fractured surfaces of discourse, as if in ultimate triumph. The fractured surface
that would defeat the Bomb must always be implicated in depth, must always
be based on an internalization, as it were, of what it opposes. Even as Williams
turns to delay in order to defer death, he recognizes that it is death, paradoxically, that offers him the possibility of delay, of his new voice.

Williams' "position," then, shifts significantly in the late poems. Where
earlier it had functioned in terms of a surplus, something always outside any
order and enabling its disruption, here it comes to rest on death itself, seen as
the completion of all strategic orders. Williams' poetics no longer strives to
fragment strategies for the sake of a posited (but always in turn rejected) external position, because it is now founded upon those strategies' ultimate completion in a static *telos*, upon the inevitability of the catastrophe's end. Having
in a sense internalized this end, the voice is freed from any need to thwart or
obey. These late poems constitute in this sense the achievement of that new

language, based on sorrow, that Williams predicted would issue from the fissioning rocks at the end of *Paterson*. Williams' interstitial voice aims neither at fragmentation nor at homogeneity, but at its own discovery of and insertion into the crevices of discourse, of world, of strategy. Just as love's intervention (in section III) can cure by undoing what has been done, the intervention of the voice offers the only "cure" tenable in the postwar world, temporarily "undoing" the strategic order that is always already in place (*CP2* 325). Having thus abandoned the "rigor of the quest," the poem need engage none of the heroics of *Paterson* III; it need neither strive toward nor struggle against strategy.

The "Coda" elevates this interstitial voice, or mode of being, to something like a cosmic principle. The minute interstice into which Williams would insinuate his voice becomes "the huge gap / between the flash / and the thunderstroke," a "sweetest interval" that, enabling love and the poem, "gelds the bomb, / permitting / that the mind contain it" (*CP2* 333, 334). Delay allows Williams in effect to split design temporally into two aspects, one that initially enables life and one that finally destroys it. Steve Reich, commenting on his use of Williams in *The Desert Music*, refers to human conventions (or designs) as "the *light*—a kind of conveyance in which we ride, in which we live, and without which we die." Williams would add that the light itself brings with it our destruction. This formulation clearly cannot be taken as an assertion of final victory, yet we should also beware of assuming a complete victory even in the present. The mind can contain the Bomb only as it accepts death, only by constantly discovering the interval, the interstice. Williams' principle can afford no stability, it can only assert the continuance of what must remain an always spontaneous act, bounded to and by temporality. Any attempt to stabilize the always varying measure will cause it to be lost again, for the measure, like Williams' poetics, remains by its very nature ad hoc and tactical. Williams also uses the term "measure," which replaces the radiant gist as "the key" in *Paterson* V, as an attack on the stability of the concept, and also as an attack on Descartes. Thus it is conceived not as a unit but as a relation and is thereby linked to the crevice or the interstice. In "The Turn of the View Toward Poetic Technique," he writes, "Measure serves for us as the key: we can measure between objects, therefore, we know that they exist." He might also have said, as he implies, "therefore, we know that we exist." In "The Desert Music" Williams speaks of this activity as a dance, "the verb . . . seeking to become articulate" (*CP2* 284). And it is to the dance, of course, that Williams turns at the close of *Paterson* V in order to recuperate that poem from the strategic circle of Book IV. Inextricably bound to temporality, the dance inserts a tenuous moment of balance between two stases, the refusal of motion and the already fallen. But unlike the figures of catastrophe in *Paterson* I–IV, each moment is explicitly conceived as part of an ongoing, developing design. The dance, then, as Williams' figure for the condition of our lives, necessarily implicated in yet not succumbing to the Bomb, offers our only means to avoid "staring into the atom, completely blind" (*P* 225). In this condition, as he writes at the end of *Paterson* V, we can only choose, temporarily and tactically, among measures, for there can be no strategic basis. Therefore, as Williams says, we can "know" only

> the dance, to dance to a measure
>   contrapuntally,
>   Satyrically, the tragic foot.
>
> (*P* 236)

"Knowing" and "doing" are both subsumed in the activity of the dance, here the dance of these "contra," punning lines as they wonderfully present, enact, Williams' poetics. While acknowledging its inevitable involvement in the tragedy of strategy, the poem tactically counterpoints that involvement by means of its own punning summation. The dance of Williams' poetics is prior to and distinct from the strategy of the Bomb, but it can no more escape that strategy than our lives can escape death.

"Not Yet"

There can be no preconceived end to such an activity; it can only cease. Hence Williams' work on *Paterson* continued into Book VI, finally to come to an end only with his own death. As a coda to his work and poetics, however, one of his very last poems provides a particularly fine summation—and invitation to continue. "The Rewaking" begins with an assured acceptance of the inevitability of death and the "end of striving." Williams' ambivalence toward this end is embodied in the playfully ambiguous syntax, in the repetition of "image," and in the image of the rose itself, unavoidably both real and ideal.[19] More strikingly, a single "not yet" suddenly intervenes to delay this already accepted end—curiously echoing the opening of Mallarmé's *Igitur*, where Igitur utters "pas encore" when the breath of his ancestors threatens to blow out the candle, "grâce à laquelle peut-être subsistent les caractères de grimoire"—to some extent the function of the sun in Williams' poem (43). Here, though, it is not Williams' own voice that utters "not yet," inserting itself into the gap between the striving and the end, but the voice of the other—perhaps his wife, perhaps the reader—whose speech intercedes as an act of love. Through this speaker, through the cooperating intervention of an other, we move from the quest's "rigor of beauty" to the sun itself, conceived as something apart from any quest—and utterly distinct, of course, from the ball of light Pound dreamed of possessing. Although the sun still, perhaps, encompasses eventual destruction, it is for the moment, and for an indefinite future, the source of life: a gift from an other and an embodiment of the verb, promising to reopen "all the crevices" of life. Williams thought "The Rewaking" sufficiently important to be the last poem in his last collection, but it has been largely upstaged by "Asphodel." Here, then, I will give way to Williams' voice, engaged in its own fragile dance, and dependent as it must be on the cooperation—now both antagonistic and supportive—of all that is other:

> Sooner or later
> we must come to the end
> of striving
>
> to re-establish
> the image the image of
> the rose
>
> but not yet
> you say extending the
> time indefinitely
>
> by
> your love until a whole
> spring
>
> rekindle
> the violet to the very
> lady's-slipper
>
> and so by
> your love the very sun
> itself is revived
>
> (CP2 437)

4

Zukofsky's Twist

"After"—*later* or
chasing?
—*CSP* 222

The Outline

COMPRISING ONLY forty-three brief lyrics, Louis Zukofsky's 1946 booklet, *Anew*, may seem too slight a collection to support revolutionary claims. In his 1947 review of the booklet, however, Williams declared his belief that Zukofsky's postwar work could revitalize the world by making possible a radically new perspective—not so much a change in the content of thought as a change in the nature of thinking: "a revolution in the line, maintained by first-rate work, gives a chance for vast revisions that potentially penetrate the very bases of knowledge and open up fields that might be exploited for a century. It is the key, the true key that will really turn a lock, the toughest lock there is. The poetic line can be the key opening a *way* to learning, the hidden implement which could, once learned and supported by great *work*, poems, make knowledge work—though it lies in a stasis now" (*RI* 164). Through *Anew*, then, "a whole can again be imagined" and with it "a new music of verse stretching out into the future" (*RI* 165). Although Williams was no doubt imagining the lyrics of *Anew* as herald of and adjunct to his own *Paterson*, this remains extraordinary praise of another poet.

Williams' rhetoric is accurate in presenting Zukofsky's work as an "opening of the field," but its evocation of a utopian poetry of a whole involves a fundamental misconstruction, a misrecognition, of Zukofsky's project and for that matter of the postmodern world. For Zukofsky's work, from the lyrics of *Anew* to the lengthy movements of "*A*", adamantly refuses rhetorics of totalization, of apocalyptic breakthroughs. His work insists on the critical importance of seemingly insignificant details, of precisions that may seem precious. Even at the close of World War II, when others felt a need for grander strategies, Zukofsky was insistent. As he wrote in "Poetry," a 1946 essay that now, significantly, leads off his collected critical essays, he saw no solution in myths of wholeness: "The poet wonders why so many today have raised up the word 'myth,' finding the lack of so-called 'myths' in our time a crisis the poet must overcome or die from, as it were, having become too radioactive, when instead a case can be made out for the poet giving some of his life to the use of the words *the* and *a*: both of which are weighted with as much epos and historical destiny as one man can perhaps resolve. Those who do not believe this are too sure that the little words mean nothing among so many other words" (*P* 10). It would be simple enough to read this passage as a critique of Eliot, whom Williams had also criticized for his dependence on myth. The disparaging evocation of myth and radiation, however, also establishes both a line of comparison and a critical distance between Zukofsky's work and *Paterson*. For Williams was caught in the contradictory nature of his own quest for a strategy with which to surmount destruction and fragmentation. He sought to counter destructive totalizations by means of another totality, to avert apocalypse by recourse to apocalypse. *Paterson's* mythic circular structure itself embodied a totality that would exclude creativity, and even radiation, Williams' image of creative transformation in the "radiant gist," came to embody in the Bomb the destructive forces it would supplant. Zukofsky, on the other hand, advocates a practical turning aside from apocalyptics, an attention to details of the here and now. A telling instance of such attention occurs in the use of "resolve" in the passage above, where the word is weighted equally with reference to logic, to music, to will, and even to optics. Its qualification by "perhaps" further suggests the contingent nature of any resolution. Zukofsky's ongoing work to *resolve* such multiple referents, to sharpen the poem's resolution, constitutes a pragmatics that is at once esthetic and political: the title of this article, "Poetry / For My Son When He Can Read," indirectly suggests the importance of such a pragmatics, of such a turn from strategic wholes to tactical practices, to the future of the postwar, postnuclear world.

The title of *Anew* also focuses our attention on telling details: in this case, the concurrent shift in "*A*" from the word (or letter) *A* to the word (or letters) *An* ("*A*"-14 is the first of eleven movements, called "An" songs, that begin with *An*). In the eighteenth movement of "*A*", still preferring not to generalize their "epos and historical destiny," Zukofsky turned to the "little words" to divide his work into three distinct phases:

Goal's naturally breathless, look back, *an, a, the*—

("*A*" 397)

The, A, An: the three words correspond to *Poem beginning 'The'* (Zukofsky's first major work), the first half of "*A*", and the second half of "*A*". Of course, this seems a trivial distinction. But in this division of his work, under the aegis of these three terms, Zukofsky embodies a deeply thought, remarkably thorough critique of modernism. Of particular interest to us is the shift from *A* to *An*, for it is by means of this shift that he handles the critical moment of World War II—the moment of the collapse of modernism and of the obsolescence of modern man—and provides an important resolution of the dilemmas that beset modernism, in particular Williams and Pound, and that continue to beset the emergence of a postmodernism adequate to the postwar, postnuclear world. To understand Zukofsky's critique and resolution, we must consider his terms. I begin with *The.*

*

Zukofsky submitted *Poem beginning 'The'* to Pound's *Exile* magazine in 1926, when he was twenty-two.[1] With its numbered lines, seriocomic prefatory notes, and extensive pastiche of various modernist works, *"The"* has generally been read, correctly, as a parodic response to another poem Pound greatly admired, *The Waste Land.* Zukofsky never felt anything like Williams' antipathy toward Eliot—a parody, after all, is an homage—but he clearly felt that Eliot's poem needed to be countered. Like *The Waste Land,* *"The"* takes the Great War as the fundamental fact of modern life, the inescapable background of the modern wasteland. Hence the second movement begins, "This is the aftermath," and features a character named "Peter Out" (an obvious allusion to "Ash Wednesday"), while the last movement is titled "Finale, And After" (*CSP* 11, 18). The poem's comic tone, however, is foreign to *The Waste Land* and to the world it represents. The many references to Eliot and other modernists, particularly in the first movement, are not so much fragments to shore against ruins as sources of comedy themselves. The first movement presents a series of questions that culminate in an attack on the fundamental value of Eliot's enterprise and of literary modernism as a whole: "why if the waste land has been explored, traveled over, circumscribed, / Are there only wrathless skeletons exhumed new planted in its sacred wood?" (*CSP* 10). Why, that is, despite the advances of modernism and modernity, can we find no vision more compelling than that of the waste land? *"The"* proposes an alternate response, an alternative to Eliot's aftermath.

Part of the problem lies in modernism's misplaced emphasis on, or faith in, art. The first movement presents almost a catalog of modernist works and days, but then dismisses the works as so much insufficient rhetoric:

54   Let me be
55   Not by art have we lived
    (*CSP* 11)

Even if that art be "letters I fancy," the works Zukofsky obviously admires, this dismissal holds (13–14). Despite his own dedication to art, Zukofsky at the outset rejects modernism's tendency to elevate esthetics to the status of religion. Later, in the last movement, the poem uses allusions to Heine to attack Romantic notions of the artist's need to suffer, to sacrifice his life, for the sake of the work. Art should manifest "joy, against nothingness joy"; it should not negate but affirm (*CSP* 20). This stance no doubt appealed to Pound, who after World War I had also come to reject estheticism in his search for a solution to social ills.

Zukofsky's title and first line, however, isolating and stressing what seems the most innocuous word in Eliot's title, suggest another, more radical dimension to the critique. For "the," as the definite article, precedes an already recognized noun, a known object. It is spoken by a voice that would ground itself in certainty, in the security of moving among familiar objects in familiar order. The implicit presumption of such a voice is exposed in the poem's opening lines:

1   The
2   Voice of Jesus I. Rush singing
3   in the wilderness
    (*CSP* 9)

Anyone seeking the certainty of "the," the poem implies, is seeking, even presuming, a divine speech—the word become flesh. Here, however, the voice of Jesus comically becomes that of "Jesus I. Rush," the perpetrator of a mad singing in the wilderness. The apocalyptic implications are also satirized in the climax of this movement, with its intensely energetic but comical promise to "take this life as your lawful wife" (*CSP* 10). To the tune of e. e. cummings' *Is 5*, the climax enacts but also mocks the consummations sought by modernist esthetics and by *The Waste Land* in particular. It is immediately counterpointed to a comic sexual consummation—the body "trembling as over an hors d'oeuvres" immediately before a blank line dedicated to the French language—a passage that implicitly critiques modernist consummations (*CSP* 11). The subsequent awakening and opening of the "blind portals" suggest that it is time for us to abandon such dreams.

Eliot seeks to counter the wilderness by means of a secure basis for culture, a mythic framework—the grail of his poem, the dream of Zukofsky's. Given the inescapable absence of such a framework from the postwar world, however, Zukofsky suggests that it is the desire for certainty itself that constitutes the world as wasteland. Because certainty depends on the already known, the unknown is perceived as a chaos of uncertainty, and tactical possibilities are foreclosed in the search for strategic control and security. Just as Eliot's "The" leads literally to the next words, "Waste Land," so, more fundamentally, it constrains the imagination to a corresponding view of the world. *The Waste Land* concludes with an apocalyptic finale, an invocation of the union of Western and Eastern religious spirituality that may enable us to redeem the desolate modern world as a world ordered by its ultimate participation in the mythic. *"The"*, however, seeks not to exit through but to turn from the "blind portals" of apocalyptic consummation.

What might replace the search for certainty, however, with its corresponding desire for a final consummation, remains problematic. *"The"* 's final movement consequently manifests a certain ambivalence, evident in the title's dual time frame: finale, *and* after—not only sequential, I would suggest, but simultaneous, as if the structure leading to a finale cannot be avoided, but only overlaid, temporarily displaced.[2] In its conclusion the poem briefly recapitulates *The Waste Land*'s despair and revulsion and then moves to an apparent religious invocation:

309   Our God immortal such Life as is our God,
310   Bei dein Zauber, by thy magic I embrace thee,
311   Open Sesame, Ali Baba, I, thy firefly, little errant star, call here,
312   By thy magic I embrace thee.
       (*CSP* 19)

With its mix of veneration and parody, the tone of this passage is difficult to assess, yet that difficulty is itself a critical manifestation of *"The"* 's attempt to develop a condition of activity apart from the determinate end action customarily invokes. In the final section the son of God is diffused (or defused) among multiple possibilities: the son (Zukofsky himself, in relation to his mother), the Sun (as source of energy and life), communism (the "Comrade" of line 323), and the people. The people themselves become the focus of the final quatrain:

327   How wide our arms are,
328   How strong,
329   A myriad years we have been,
330   Myriad upon myriad shall be.
       (*CSP* 20)

The subject of "Shall be" hovers between "we" and "years," as if the process of human history were itself eternity, as if the collective peoples of the world might themselves constitute a Sun. Where Eliot would emerge from the nightmare of history into the dream of order, Zukofsky sees history as "The Dream That Knows No Waking" (*CSP* 14). We need not simply choose between dichotomous ends—either a bang or a whimper—for there is another, or an other, way. The embrace of "such life as is our God" should not become an entrapment in an idealized teleology; it should remain a manifestation of joy, a Nietzschean affirmation of living, rather than another variation of *ressentiment*, of the denial of life.

Zukofsky invokes a radically reconceived history in *Poem beginning 'The'*, a history that has moved beyond its own apocalyptic end, beyond teleology— history not as a progress that may be possessed in the fullness of time, in a strategic totality, but as a process always multiple. The poem's various tactics—the disjointed lines, the parodic citations, the many puns, syntactic ambiguities, and other instances of polysemy—effectively critique the fundamental conditions of Eliot's poem, and their emphasis on multiplicity, on a diversity of readings, works to disrupt the hegemony of an apocalyptic narrative and logical structure. It is worth noting here, in fact, two general tendencies of Zukofsky's poetics: first, a tendency to seek and embody the fundamental conditions of an activity in details, in particulars ("the"); second, the use of multiplicity to disperse pretentions to totality. Already in this early poem words tend to elicit their own connections, apart from the ostensible meaning of a passage: the ring of things, for example, in "against things' iron I ring" (*CSP* 19). Yet despite these tactics, *"The"* 's own structure remains overly dependent on the apocalyptic structure of its model. In this respect it anticipates a good deal of postmodernism: the poem relies on parody to such an extent that its multiple tactics seem to be deployed toward an as yet unachieved, strategic end. Zukofsky's first major poem brilliantly dismisses Eliot's apocalyptic search for an absolute, and with it the accompanying despair, but itself remains ambivalently situated between the transhistorical and the transcendent. In the end it can only gesture, and that rather apocalyptically, toward a resolution.

"A": Toward Distinction

"The" 's apocalyptic gesture, together with its final disjunction between the absolute and the human world, bothered Zukofsky immediately. In a 1927 letter to Pound, Zukofsky first disagreed with Pound's criticism of the derivative nature of the poem and then remarked, "Fact is I fear for not so much the second movement, as for the too precipitous end. Its chanted faith hardly begins to be buttressed, id est I feel it might have been, may still be, the beginning of something else and s.e. and s.e. What? Who knows? Hope it comes" (*PZ* 5). *"A"* was already in the offing, conceived as that "something else" that would buttress the faith of *Poem beginning 'The'*, that would address the disjunction evident in *"The"* 's "too precipitous," too abrupt, too apocalyptic, end. Three years later, with *"A"* already underway, a letter of December 12, 1930,

makes this account of the poem's origin more explicit: begun in late 1927 or early 1928, the long poem stemmed directly from *"The"* (PZ 78). The earlier poem had been conceived as "a direct reply to *The Waste Land* . . . intended to tell him why, spiritually speaking, a wimpus was still possible and might even bear fruit of another generation" (PZ 78–79). It had accordingly begun in satire but ended with more positive statement: "the *promise* of the last lines *trans* from Yehoash—'shall be.' 'A' 's intention was to make that *promise good*" (PZ 79). *Poem beginning 'The'* promises, but does not achieve, a new relation to the particulars of history and of the contemporary world, a relation that would neither subject them to an ahistorical pattern, nor find them wanting, a mere chaos, because they were not grounded on any absolute.

"*A*" seeks to embody that relation from its first word, once again pointedly isolated on a line of its own. In contrast to the definite article, which leads to the already known, the indefinite article plunges us into an unknown, uncertain world—an unforeseen delight, as "A"-23 would later call it—where possibility becomes endless and open and where the multiplicity of particulars precludes the establishment of any absolute. The movement opens in the middle of a Carnegie Hall performance of Bach's *St. Matthew Passion*, on April 5, 1928—a Thursday evening. Although the style is laconic, at times cryptic, a reader adept at modernist ellipses has little trouble identifying the elements of an empirical reality: fragments of the performance, snatches of the concert-goers' conversation, and then selected details of life and events around Carnegie Hall provide a surprisingly sharp representation of the event. The speaker also supplies a historical context (by juxtaposing the contemporary performance with the original) and enlarges the social context by providing sociopolitical information. But the language of "A"-1 is not merely a transparent medium for the realistic representation of this scene. While "the" has a relatively fixed, stable significance, "A" immediately involves the poem in linguistic instability:

A
    Round of fiddles playing Bach.
    ("*A*" 1)

Besides being the indefinite article, "A" can signify whatever is primary or first—certainly appropriate to the beginning of the poem—and the musical note used to tune orchestras—again obviously appropriate to the context. The meaning of "a round," too, hovers between sight and sound, between a visual object and a musical form, as well as suggesting the prepositional force of "around."[3] A number of other possible referents for "A" remain at least latent at the beginning of the poem, while a potentially endless number, including the Atomic bomb, do not yet exist. Where "the" would constrain meaning, "A" initiates a remarkable play of significations. With the opening of the long poem, Zukofsky has already taken a decisive step toward the rich textuality and intertextuality that informs his later works.

This multiplicity, wherein a word can mean anything a dictionary or dialect or aural or visual similarity may suggest, points to a critical difference between Zukofsky's conception of language and Pound's. For Pound, the primary function of language is communication—at times, in fact, his "ideogrammic method" of the thirties veers toward Thomas Sprat's eighteenth-century vision of an ideal language, wherein so many words would stand for, could be exchanged for, an equal number of things. Pound's ideal language would involve a seamless connection between a specific, definite content, its ideogrammic coding, and the reader's recognition of that content and subsequent action. Zukofsky, however, from the outset emphasizes the materiality of words: physical sounds in air, visual objects on the page. Rather than strive for the supposed naturalness of the ideogrammic, Zukofsky's radically *literal* interest in the letter embraces the arbitrariness of the alphanumeric. "A," the dictionary informs us, may also designate objects shaped like an A, and a large number of such objects, triangles, arches, and so on, appear in the course of the poem; they are, significantly, the fundamental units of a stable architecture. But neither in the dictionary nor in the poem do the various significations of the letter "A" cohere into a totality; they cannot be subsumed by a single image, but are rather multiple, and often incommensurate. Words are themselves things—in his later study of Shakespeare Zukofsky notes that in Hebrew the same term is used for both word and thing (*B* 104)—and as things they do not simply represent but themselves produce distinct, even contradictory effects.

These distinct conceptions of language, however, clearly involve much more than the merely linguistic. The letters Zukofsky and Pound exchanged help to clarify the larger contexts of their distinct poetics, especially as the correspondence becomes increasingly argumentative in the middle to late thirties, when political and economic pressures sharpened their differences. In their dialogue on politics, Pound maintains that American Communists, and Zukofsky insofar as he adopts Marxist views, inhabit a realm of free-floating "abstraction IN VACUO" (*PZ* 174). Pound claims that this groundlessness is largely a result of their blindly following Marx as if he provided an absolute guide, a final answer, rather than an analysis inevitably limited by contemporary historical circumstances. But his own arguments suggest that he is blindly rejecting Marx in favor of his own version of an ultimate answer. For example, Pound attempts to ground concretely one critical term by defining a "commodity" as "a material thing or substance" (*PZ* 168). Zukofsky, though he maintains a clear distance from the Communist party, argues that Pound refuses to read Marx, refuses to recognize the reality of the contemporary world, and refuses to recognize that labor is the critical ingredient in a commodity. Pound has consequently offered a definition "so general as to include nothing," since it would include all material objects (*PZ* 171). It is Pound, in fact, who devalues historical actuality in favor of an abstraction, of an absolute ground.

An especially revealing exchange concerns Pound's attempt to obtain *the* Jewish interpretation of Leviticus 25. The verses in question forbid interest charges on loans to "your brother," and Pound evidently wonders whether this legitimates a more usurious practice with Gentiles (35 ff.). In a July 1936 letter, Zukofsky offers his father's opinion: he notes that "the *absolute* sense of the passage" would forbid taking interest from anyone, but then comments that historical circumstances have necessitated the charging of interest from both Jews and Gentiles. Zukofsky's observations, however, are of greater interest. He comments that the "sense" of his father's interpretation is historical rather than "Messianic, absolute etc," and then continues to develop a contrast between his own historicism and Pound's search for an absolute: "Where he's Messianic he's as antiquated as you sunk in an absolute which has no useful relation to the present, or a bettering of the present. Strikes me in trying to isolate the root-idea of the reprehensibility of usury—which is what you seem to be doing?—you forget that even roots grow in a soil, and that soil changes with the times" (*PZ* 183). He goes on to cite Marx's criticism of Proudhon: " 'the economic forms in which men produce, consume, exchange are *transitory* and *historical*. . . . Why does M. Proudhon talk about universal reason?' " (*PZ* 183). And then Zukofsky provides his own, historical interpretation: "it ought to strike anybody with a little common sense that the contradictions in Leviticus 25—such as verse 10 against verse 44—'proclaim liberty thruout all the land' and 'they shall be yr. bondmen forever, but over the children of Israel etc'—are the results of different tempers operating under different conditions, & with different motives, & probably at different times—i.e. if you want to be mythical at all verse 10 is nearer to having been produced in the golden age, whereas 44 must have been an interpolation of the age of iron" (*PZ* 184). Even after World War II, in 1955, Pound could still ask whether Jews could be "useful," assuming both some absolute measure of use and a monolithic sense of "Jewishness." Zukofsky responded only that " 'Useful'? alwus comes down 'to whom'?" (*PZ* 212). For Pound, both the society and the long poem must be based on an absolute knowledge. Thus he criticizes Zukofsky for not basing his poetry on what he can "KNOW fer sure," outside language, and calls his linguistic play "Talmudic footling" (*PZ* 187, 169). But Zukofsky's "footling" is in part an attempt to enact the process of thinking, its experience and movement; his commitment is precisely to the relativity of knowing, to the process of meaning rather than to a single, determinate ground or end. Like society, the text, too, is transitory and historical—multiple.

As the two poets read their worlds, so they write their texts—Pound seeking a single voice, the voice of mastery, Zukofsky allowing multiple, even conflicting voices. When Pound asked about the correct reading of a poem Zukofsky had published pseudonymously in *Poetry*, he must have found the younger poet's response disconcerting: "Any other 14 'ambiguous' readings permitted . . . provided of course you keep each meaning distinct. . . . Or imagine a bottle with a label printed on it; the label has printed matter all around & down the bottle. As you turn the bottle the poem forms out of the cylindrical surface" (*PZ* 121). This attitude toward interpretive proliferation remained consistent through Zukofsky's career—if anything, it became more pronounced as his ability to "resolve" such proliferations increased—and could still seem remarkable to Guy Davenport and Hugh Kenner much later. As Zukofsky told the story to Kenner, when Davenport asked which possibility Zukofsky had in mind for "bay" in the poem that begins *Anew*, the poet responded that it was up to the reader; all possible connotations were permissible.[4]

Although one is inclined to dismiss, for obvious reasons, Pound's complaint concerning Zukofsky's "Talmudic footling," the connection he makes between Zukofsky's practice and traditional Jewish attitudes toward writing and interpretation—toward textuality—is both accurate and important. The poet's background and environment would have exposed him to interpretive practices quite distinct from those of classical culture; no doubt these predisposed him to develop a poetics distinct from the modernists. But here I am less concerned with specific biographical causes than with the general terms and implications of Zukofsky's poetics. Susan Handelman, in her study focusing on Freud, Lacan, and especially Derrida and Bloom, has presented a persuasive case for the affinities, and in some cases the causal relations, between Rabbinic methods of interpretation and poststructuralist literary theory's critique of the logocentrism of classical culture. Many of Handelman's characterizations of Rabbinic and Greek attitudes to textuality (and their corresponding epistemologies) could be used to characterize Zukofsky and Pound (for example, "For the Greeks, following Aristotle, things are not exhausted by discourse; for the Rabbis, discourse is not exhausted by things" [8]). Zukofsky's work can readily be considered in the same context. His dialogue with Pound in the thirties does not concern only politics and economics but evinces a well-developed critique of logocentrism. Particularly striking, considering the similarities that are often perceived between Pound and Zukofsky, are their divergent emphases on the image. If "the image is at the heart of Greek thought," Pound's com-

mitment to the image, to phanopoeia, argues a root commitment to a logo-
centric world (Handelman 33). In contrast, Zukofsky's critical writings rarely
mention the image at all, focusing almost always on sound and on the values
of particular words. In his work, then, there is no impulse "to discard the outer
letter and move towards direct perception of things in the silent images of the
soul"—as in Greek thought and as in Pound (Handelman 10). Accompanying
the rejection of this hierarchy between inner and outer, between surface and
depth, is a rejection of any hierarchy of interpretive levels, as well as a relativi-
zation of relations between general and particular and between necessity and
contingency—all of which, Handelman notes, are characteristic of Rabbinic
textual practices (65). One cannot ground knowing on a vision beyond the text,
whether it be the vision of the philosopher (Plato), or the poet (Pound), or the
mystic. As we will see later, even Zukofsky's *Bottom: On Shakespeare*, a work
that celebrates sight, in fact uses the "clear physical eye" to correct and qualify
the visions produced by an "erring brain" (*P* 166). It is the experience of
temporality that is fundamental to Zukofsky's work, not the achievement of a
vision.

I will discuss these characteristics of Zukofsky's poetics more fully below,
with respect to the later movements of "*A*", which embody an important development beyond critique to "more positive statement." But already in "*A*" 's
first movement, in its first line, the sign itself is critical. Isolated and stressed,
held for inspection, "A," like the other "outer letters" in Zukofsky's work, acquires a materiality, a density, of its own, a density that thwarts reading for a
specific message, an inner truth or necessity. This priority of word as object or
action leads to the text's extraordinary fusion of lucidity and opacity: generating multiple referents through what I have elsewhere termed "sounded contexts," Zukofsky's words can seem as recalcitrant as "things' iron," yet they
are also remarkably open, hiding nothing. If we would understand the world
we must listen to language itself, we must attend to its secrets. Unlike Pound,
who attempts a strategic mastery of the text—he would manipulate the language and the world from a secure, external, and finally ahistorical position—
Zukofsky seeks a tactical practice, acknowledging his own interiority to language, world, and especially the ongoing processes of history.

This is the practice Zukofsky seeks, but it is by no means fully realized at
the outset of "*A*": it remains a goal the poem struggles toward, the imagined
poetics that haunts the early movements of the poem and that is figured most
prominently in the *St. Matthew Passion*. Bach's fugues embody an ideal, both
esthetic and communal, of which the poem—and the world—can only dream,
caught in its "desire longing for perfection" ("*A*" 2). The perfection itself soon

vanishes: upon leaving the concert Zukofsky first encounters a tramp's face and then the bourgeois banality of other patrons' responses, themselves counterpointed to news of the Pennsylvania miners' lockout. And the following day brings "the reverses / As if the music were only a taunt" (*"A"* 4). Even Zukofsky's initial search for an exit from the concert was initially blocked, in a comical homage to Dante's first attempts to exit the dark wood. Only by deliberately taking a longer route can *"A"* resolve the problem of *"The"*; only by going "around" can the new poem hope to transfer *"The"* 's promise into actuality.

Yet through the first movements the poem continues to image its goal as an absolute, eternal perfection. Bach's music provides one obvious example of such perfection, but there are others. Consider the image in *"A"*-2 of the flower called "Liveforever" (which in an unusually expansive gesture is glossed as "everlasting"):

> The music is in the flower,
> Leaf around leaf ranged around the center;
> Profuse but clear outer leaf breaking on space,
> There is space to step to the central heart:
> The music is in the flower,
> It is not the sea but hyaline cushions the flower
> Liveforever, everlasting.
> The leaves never topple from each other,
> Each leaf a buttress flung for the other.
>
>   (*"A"* 7)

This passage clearly images a central and centering ground—a position of strategic mastery, outside the flux the poem elsewhere celebrates and minutely particularizes. Indeed, the allusion to Gothic architecture suggests that this flower constitutes a reinscription of Dante's celestial rose. The letter *"A"* also points to such a transcendent position: two meanings I have not yet mentioned are "eternal" and "absolute" (*OED*). Moreover, its pictographic triangle manifests the Pythagoreans' perfect form, the "holy tetraktys," mentioned by name later in the poem—and also presents an admittedly crude cross section of a Gothic cathedral (*"A"* 368). A certain paradox is thus fundamental to *"A"* from its inception. It begins as a quest poem, a poem in search of a desired perfection, and it is for this reason, as well as its historical context, implicated from the outset in a modernist poetics in this respect akin to Pound's. Even though the "object" of the quest is not in fact an object or state—a homecoming or a new hierarchy—but a specific practice, the quest inevitably implicates the poem in modernist strategy. "*A*" posits a postmodern, tactical poetics as the goal of a modernist, strategic quest. There are consequently two major tensions through the first half of the poem: between the ideal and its "reverses" and, more fundamentally, between the ideal and an eschewal of ideals.

Against the image of an unachieved perfection, Zukofsky is quick to present a series of counterimages. "*A*"-1 moves from the perfection of Bach's *Passion* to a melodramatic invocation of the "fierce, flaming pit" of hell. Just before that transformation, the Pythagorean perfection of "*A*" itself becomes a dog cocking its leg to a lamp post. In "*A*"-2, the climactic "Liveforever" passage is followed by an explicit alternative, marked by a stressed "Or," wherein Zukofsky turns to specific events, and in a new climax transforms the flower he would enter into a vagina—the Divine Passion become a rather comic human passion. Even Marx's presence in the poem is rather contradictory, as Zukofsky's letters to Pound indicate. In 1933 he wrote that "in Marx's economy, of all economies, *alone* there is substance for doing the new canzone," suggesting that Marx alone could provide the ground of his poetics—that Marx was what he could "KNOW for sure" (*PZ* 155). Only a few years later, however, Marx's voice (not his substance) is conceived as merely one more that might "enter the human intelligence & complex of feeling in the process of writing a poem" (*PZ* 199). Though important, economics, like any other system, is ultimately secondary, useful only as it furthered some actual product, some poem. It would be Zukofsky's poetry that would clarify the economic situation, promoting a better politics and economics through the integrity of its construction, rather than through its propaganda value—not through a presence it represents, but through its own presence.[5]

The well-known declaration of Objectivist poetics in "*A*"-6 provides a particularly striking example of this tension between a strategic goal and a tactical practice. An early version of the passage was used as the starting point of Zukofsky's "Objectivists" essay in the February 1931 "Objectivists" issue of *Poetry*. Since then it has often been cited as a presentation of the fundamental tenets of an "Objectivists" movement, frequently, and despite Zukofsky's explicit objections, termed "objectivism"—as if the passage presented the poem's poetic goal. It is important, though, to recall the original provenance of Zukofsky's statement, in "*A*". As he remarks at the beginning of section two of the article, the passage in question began as poetry. It was not, that is, primarily a statement of a specific theoretical "position," but an example of practice, a poetic act.[6] Here is the final version:

> But when we push up the daisies!
> The melody! the rest is accessory:

My one voice. My other: is
An objective—rays of the object brought to a focus,
An objective—nature as creator—desire
    for what is objectively perfect
Inextricably the direction of historic and contemporary particulars.
    (*"A"* 24)

In a letter written the same year as this movement, Zukofsky told Pound that although song remained his favorite form—"I'd rather be the troubadours (or one of them) than Dante"—he was now committed to *"A"* and found that he was no longer "excited *into* a song or something as brief and essential" (*PZ* 78).[7] In *"A"*-6, "My one voice" allies itself to melody and the "objectively perfect"—that is, the traditional, single voice of the lyric poem, or the poem as spontaneous, "pure" song. Against this desired perfection, *"A"* is inextricably involved in "accessories," in an "other," in the contingent, imperfect world of "historic and contemporary particulars," of the accidental rather than the essential.

Even here, though, the opposition is unstable, for "My other" itself bifurcates, leading to *both* senses of "an objective." According to this reading, "my other" would include "my one voice"—a situation that seems preposterous but that in fact recalls the movement's previous declaration that "He who creates / Is a mode of these inertial systems" (*"A"* 23). Zukofsky's poetics attempts to keep pace with twentieth-century physics—and with Spinoza's sixteenth-century view of nature (or God). Still other readings are possible. It is also possible to read "mother" in "my other"—as *"The"* informs us, "It's your mother all the time." ("Mother" is also the last word of *"A"*—so positioned by Celia Zukofsky, herself a mother.) One criterion of the "objectively perfect," albeit a radical one, may well be that it is inextricable from its diverse contexts.[8] Also, there exists a fundamental incommensurability between melody as an ongoing process and any fixed objective. And the first line could mean that all that follows comprises the melody, or all that follows comprises the rest. "Accessory," too, is significantly ambiguous, since it means both "extraneous" and "adjunct," while "rest" could denote either an extraneous remainder (but can any remainder be so simply dismissed?) or the pause necessary to music, the rest that, Zukofsky tells us elsewhere, allows melody "to draw breath and sequence" (*B* 99). And what does the phrase "objectively perfect" actually denote? Or does it rather act as a limit term of desire?

Any attempt to extract from this passage a single poetics, a statement of the poem's goal, is forced to suppress, to negate, the text's insistence on multiple readings, its affirmation of a plurality of voices. Although the passage may appear to present something called Objectivist poetics, it in fact juggles several distinct tendencies of *"A"* 's poetics, treated not so much as concepts but as material, "like two or three balls juggled in the air at once and the play got from the reflected lights in the colors of them balls" (*PZ* 80).[9] In this way, the theory of poetics never dominates its practice: *"A"* itself resists Zukofsky's explicit formulations of its poetics.[10] The poem avoids succumbing to polarization and dichotomy, to dialectics, by seizing on whatever devices are available to establish ambiguities, polyvalences, multiple alternatives. The simple is always complex.

Yet the dilemma remains; the strategic quest continues its threat to dominate, to subsume all to a single, static goal. The disjointed, uncertain end of "A"-6 reflects the poem's continuing tensions:

> How shall I—
> Her soles new as the sunned black of her grave's turf,
> With all this material
> > To what distinction—
>
> (*"A"* 38)

Zukofsky would later tell Louis Dembo that "the questions are their own answers" (Dembo 277). "A"-6's interrupted questions may well already imply their own answer—particularly the last phrase—but for the moment ambivalence and uncertainty would seem to prevail.

To what distinction, indeed? And how might distinction be accomplished? As if in answer to the questions ending "A"-6, the ebullient "A"-7 confidently declares that "words will do it." With its puns on "out of," "manes," "airs," and so on, the opening of the movement continues *"A"* 's technique of allowing multiple contextual determinations of referents:

> Horses: who will do it? out of manes? Words
> Will do it, out of manes, out of airs, but
> They have no manes, so there are no airs, birds
> Of words, from me to them no singing gut.
> > (*"A"* 39)

"Do it," too, is open to a variety of readings, from evoking horses to effecting a revolution. We have already examined some of these aspects of Zukofsky's poetics, as advanced in his letters to Pound. Here I will turn to more specific considerations: just what is (are) the "it" that words will do? and how will they accomplish it? What is the significance of the more obviously formal structures used in movements 7, 8, 9, and 11? What is the relation between evoking horses and effecting revolution?

The independence of individual words from a single determinative context is not the only method of emphasizing the "thingness" of words. The opening of *"A"*-7 points to another, more traditional method: poetic forms. One characteristic of *"A"* 's struggle to achieve "distinction" during the thirties and forties is a turn toward increasingly complex, tightly controlled forms: the sonnet sequence comprising *"A"*-7, the ballatta ending *"A"*-8, and the double canzone comprising *"A"*-9 are all highly wrought, highly condensed structures that first impress the reader with their own existence as objects, as artifacts. In *"A"*-9, in fact, the propulsive, formal music of the lines tends to prevent the reader from pausing to consider individual words. Combined with the abstraction of the language, the form curiously inhibits our tendency to read words as transparent referents to a visual reality—an image or succession of images. Instead, words here function more as visual referents to an aural reality—sound scored for the page. Although the result seems quite distant from any "practical" effect, the form is not impelled solely by showmanship, but by a desire for action:

> An impulse to action sings of a semblance
> Of things related as equated values,
> The measure all use is time congealed labor
> In which abstraction things keep no resemblance
> To goods created; integrated all hues
> Hide their use to one or one's neighbor.
>
>   (*"A"* 106)

Part of the poem's implied argument is that mental labor (including artistic labor) is not mere superstructure but is as fundamental as physical labor: singing, writing, painting, all of these are work, creating goods for use. As *"A"*-7 tells us, only words, working with the imagination, can perform the labor of transforming wooden sawhorses into horses.

   "A" 's Table of Contents records the abstract "time congealed labor" of the ninth movement: two years for the first 75 lines, an eight-year break, and then another two years for the next 75 lines. *The First Half of "A"-9*, privately printed in 1940, calls attention to the raw materials of this intense labor: Cavalcanti's *Donna Mi Prega*; translations by Pound, Jerry Reisman, and Zukofsky; Marx's *Capital* and *Value, Price and Profit*; some concepts from modern physics; and a "mathematical analogy to the form of the poem" were all involved in the writing (*A9* 1). The poem itself is intended to "fluoresce . . . in the light of seven centuries of interrelated thought"—which is to say that it is not merely the product of Zukofsky's labor but of centuries of civilization as well (*A9* 1). But the sheer accumulation of effort involved in the poem forestalls any notion that

its value can be assessed according to any abstract formula. As Zukofsky wrote in a 1940 letter, "I don't suppose anyone'll be anxious to print the canzone—& 2 years actual labor on it plus 7 years thought (?) and study won't, in any case be rewarded with even nominal compensation" (*PZ* 203). Neither use value nor exchange value can provide an adequate measure of "goods created." Hence the coda of the *First Half of* "*A*"-9, wherein "things"—these words—summarize their existence:

> We are things, say, like a quantum of action
> Defined product of energy and time, now
> In these words which rhyme now how song's exaction
> Forces abstraction to turn from equated
> Values to labor we have approximated.
>   ("*A*" 108)

Rather than abstraction subsuming things, here the poem as thing subsumes abstraction, restoring our sense that abstractions are, after all, created goods. Although obviously involved in the marketplace, in exchange value, the human interest in form, in a satisfactory esthetic, is not controlled by it. In this sense, "*A*"-9 is also offered as "a sign that ca*pi*talism will capitulate" (*A9* 1).

Of course, this play on "capitalism" recalls another way in which "words will do it." However much totalitarians of language may want to define and delimit them, words always tend to escape, to deconstruct themselves, as it were—especially once their "thingness" has been emphasized. And however much any strategic system may seek to control, it is always subject to tactical improvisations—in this case, the linguistic equivalent ("related is equated") of a black market economy. Furthermore, a word *means* according to the uses people make of it and will shift meaning infinitely according to the conditions of its use. An important experimental work of 1932, *Thanks to the Dictionary*, makes remarkable use of such shifts. The text's main narrative concerns the biblical David, but his story is condensed into about ten of its thirty-four pages; much else goes on. Consider this passage, which takes up the definition of "mind":

> Mind, that abstract, collective term for all forms of conscious intelligence, or for the subject of all conscious states, it walked along with David. What to do with the minim? To measure it roughly, the downstroke, one drop? To mind, to occupy oneself, to regard as of importance; to be concerned for the signs of the times: I do not *mind* the noise; one Minié ball its plug driven by the explosion of the charge to expand the lead. But to have a mind to work. The instinct of animals is now held by many to be of the same nature as the intellect of man, yet the apparent difference is very great. Certainly not in *opposi-*

tion to matter—or the spirit or intelligence pervading the universe. What faculty of relations and comparisons can that be? To mine, not like mineral jelly for the lubrication of everybody. Not to minify, to undermine. Not mine, not mind-reading, not that disease independent of the ordinary channels of the senses. Not belonging to me that possessive of I, that flying of higher cognitions. The pie is made of mince-meat. It has mingled but is chopped. But propensity is experience independent of and dependent upon its instruction. (*CF* 280–81)

Thanks to the Dictionary shares Wittgenstein's interest in the investigation of language games: "mind" here is defined not according to an abstraction, but with reference to our various uses of the term (including, the first sentence suggests, a synonym for the divine). But if Zukofsky's investigation is serious, it is scarcely single-minded; here he playfully mines the dictionary for words related only by accident of spelling, thereby undermining the very idea of arriving at a (or *the*) definition. More complex than an accumulation of definitions and usages would suggest, "mind" is manifest throughout this passage, both as the abstracted object of reflection and in the concrete means of that reflection—a language use that rejects the preeminence of reflection.

The work's preface, however, is more relevant to the present context. Bearing the subtitle, "And what will the writers do then, poor things," it establishes an explicit political context for the text—presumably, it will answer the question as to what writers will do after the revolution. For the moment, however, what this writing is doing now is of greater interest to us:

"A". Quoting the dictionary. Remembering my sawhorses, my little a.'s abbreviated for afternoon, perhaps for years, this afternoon. Another acre, one, any, some, each aback, as aloof, till before a vowel will stand accepted, "An", active, tho not as a vulture. Perhaps next Ab, when the fast will not commemorate a Temple in ruins, Aaron's rod, the serpent to blossom, will grow, goldenrod which flowers on long stems in that vacation a part of July and of August. David, then, on his page, not like a slab forming the top of a capital, but not unlike an abacus, a reckoning table telling its sums will embrace all the words of this novel. For, David, anticipated, appears when the groundhogs are not in Abad. Abad is any cultivated city. But David who resists all its agents is free from iridescence, and without accidentals. If there is iridescence, it will be at his toes. His name, these words till now, are almost his story. (*CF* 270)

There is no primary meaning "behind" (our metaphors are telling) this passage, no Image to be recovered by diligent decoding. But this does not mean that the passage is nonsensical, "mere" play, or without purpose—though part of its purpose, of course, is to demonstrate what writing might do when the revolution is accomplished, when *the* purpose has been achieved. Other seri-

ous concerns are also evident: the status of language, of the dictionary's organization of language, of "*A*", of civilization (a Temple is in ruins—as in Pound
and Eliot), of writers (David), of the relation between necessity and contingency (David, as his story is told, is "without accidentals"), and of narrative
itself. But none of these concerns dominates; rather, each is displaced by a tactical practice that takes up the serious, but treats the playful as equally important, that takes up the thread of argument, but responds as well to whimsy.

One tactic, fairly common in modernist texts, consists in the intermingling
of the time of the narration with the time of the narrated—the overlaying of
the story of David with the story of the narrator (Zukofsky, with his sawhorses
and "a.'s"). These narratives, however, are readily integrated: the telling of this
story is one among other events in the narrator's life, although when David's
story undergoes temporal displacement later in the text, anachronisms make
integration more difficult. More significant is the mining of the dictionary,
which enables the evidently delighted (and delightful) play with arbitrary connections and remote associations ("that vacation"). This mining takes several
forms, of which I will mention only a few: first, the use of words suggested by
physical proximity—here, words beginning with "a"; second, the use of multiple definitions of words—"A," obviously, but also "abacus" (which does
mean "a slab forming the top of a capital"); and third, the substitution of a
definition for a specific word (a practice more evident in the previous passage).
These are distinct techniques, but their combined effect is to intermingle incommensurate metonymic orders. The dictionary enables Zukofsky to disrupt
narrative metonymies by means of a distinctly different metonymic order, the
alphabetic (while under the heading of each word, of course, yet another metonymy is explored).

The important point here is that this alternate metonymy cannot be fully
integrated into a greater narrative. If poetry is generally characterized, as
Roman Jacobsen has claimed, by a displacement of the axis of substitution onto
the axis of contiguity, it is also characterized by a reintegration of that displacement. A poet may rhyme "boot" and "lute," for example, but a relation of contiguity, a narrative, would generally be supplied.[11] There are, moreover, well-
established guidelines and generic conventions, such as rhyme, to govern such
displacements. But the interruptions of narrative causality in *Thanks to the Dictionary* resist such restorations; because no generic conventions (other than the
dictionary's) govern their appearance, they remain whimsical, arbitrary.
David, we are told, is without accidentals, implying that his story is governed
by necessity. But the disruptions of the order of narrative causality, of narrative
necessity, nevertheless insist on the accidental. *Thanks to the Dictionary* is engaged in a radical rethinking, a rewriting, of the opposition between chance

and necessity. A certain fatalism is present throughout the text, as when David speaks to the other major characters in his life story: "You are all here, sending me, maybe you expect a report of the original meaning. It was that one morning springing shining out of the earth after rain, and that morning, too, I was going to battle" (CF 299). Bereft of an original meaning, we are also free of its determination. Even the author as Creator, the strategist in command of the entire text, is limited in the extent of design: "Direct, *if you can*, towards the chosen end, all the characters moving by their volition" (Cf 300, emphasis added). The final section of the text, in which this sentence occurs, repeatedly calls attention to the book's participation in its own material circumstances, apart from its (necessarily inadequate) representation of David. Earlier we have been told that while "*Intent* and *purpose* overleap all particulars and fasten on the *end itself*"—a succinct critique of modernism's commitment to strategy— "David is distinguishable, and, even beyond this end" (CF 290). Zukofsky's David is not only "without accident" in relation to the end but also without (outside or beyond) necessity. David's life, his story, *is*, and as such is necessary. But so too are the innumerable connections to be made among the words of his story and the innumerable possible interpretations of it ("Abad is any cultivated city"—think of the possibilities!). To be distinguished, then, is to live *without* the end; the achievement of distinction—"*A*"-6's desire—is the achievement of postmodernity.

This insistence on the importance of what we customarily regard as accidental is critical to "*A*" 's struggle to escape the tyranny of intent and purpose—particularly as such accidentals thwart what we may call the "exchange value" of words. (Of course, the text also puns on the "accidental" in music, which is not accidental but necessary.) We can no longer simply exchange word for image when we have come to see the pit in capitalism or see horses (and seahorses) in sawhorses. If *Thanks to the Dictionary* critiques the notion of author as distant creator, as strategist, both that text and "*A*" nevertheless take up another biblical—or at least Rabbinic—postulate, the creation of the world *ex nihilo* by (rather than merely through) language. Language, because it is not only representation, escapes the imposition of any strategic form. In so doing, it also offers tactical means for the author—and interpreter—to become active, to escape the control of an inexorable "design." The text constitutes its own order, an order characterized by a multiplicity (by distinction, by difference) that resists subsumption by any external idea of order, any form. Reality, as we read "*A*", is neither referent nor product of the text. Rather it is the interweave between referent and product, between text and world. Thus the words' creation of horses in "*A*"-7—along with the creation of the sonnet sequence— is critical to the achievement of freedom, of revolution.

Yet the sonnet sequence comprising "A"-7, the ballatta that ends "A"-8, and the double canzone comprising "A"-9—all of which demonstrate the work of words—also manifest the continuing, even increasing tension between strategic end and tactical practice: as the poetry becomes more highly wrought, more astonishing, it also becomes denser, more opaque. Despite the grace, strain is evident, as if the poem were struggling to prevent its own "intent and purpose" from "overleaping all particulars." Only when we reach "A"-11, which also reworks the ballatta form, does the tension appear to have evaporated. Although certainly not "transparent," the poem is much more relaxed and considerably easier to read than the formal sections of earlier movements. No doubt these qualities are in part simply a result of the previous years' practice in difficult forms. And, too, the poem makes a turn toward the family unit for its material. But the shift is considerably more important than these explanations would suggest; it is fundamental, in fact, to the structure and achievement of the poem as a whole. Consequently, it is important to consider this shift—"A" 's postmodern "twist"—more closely.

"A": The Twist

In a 1931 letter, arguing the poem's substance as a life work, Zukofsky remarked that "the difficulty will be not searching for material to eke out the matter . . . but to twist the neck of the material in the movements immediately to follow (the next 1 to 5 years) movements 8–12, so that all the preceding detail gets a new head. . . . That is, to so handle the setting of the piece—the Jheezus material—so that eventually by development nothing of it remains etc" (*PZ* 112). This material twist involved the development of a truly tactical poetics that is signaled, embodied—the text continually subverts our reasoned categories for linguistic practices—in the poem's shift from *A*, the key word of the first half, to *An*, the key word of the second. But the shift was to prove considerably more difficult than Zukofsky anticipated: it would be six years before "A"-8 was finished, twenty before the twist was completed. The reasons for this difficulty are of course diverse and complex, involving more than just poetics. But perhaps the most important element in terms of Zukofsky's poetics concerns "A" 's relation to teleology, as the poem comes to embody radically distinct relations to both its author and its end. The "An" sections defer to neither of these external poles; instead they absorb both into an ongoing practice.

The resituating or reconstituting of the authorial voice is manifested formally throughout the later sections of the poem, but it is also presented thematically, if briefly, at various points. "A" begins with a recognizable figure of the poet: the "I" of "A"-1 to "A"-6 clearly represents Zukofsky himself, musing on the origins of his poem and on the relations between esthetics and politics, among other subjects. This is the voice that argues esthetics with Kay in "A"-2, the voice that directly states, "I would write you down / In a style of leaves growing," and that we identify with "my one voice" in "A"-6—though, as I have indicated, even in that passage "my one voice" is complex. Following the direction indicated by *Thanks to the Dictionary*, however, the poem subsequently develops a quite different relation to authorship. In the course of *"A"*'s "twist," the authorial or authoritative "I" of the poem becomes more and more displaced from its customary position of mastery and absorbed into the ongoing process of the poem, of the language. "A"-7, the sonnet sequence, points to this absorption when it answers the question, *"Who* will do it?" with *"Words* / will do it"—as if words (note that they are already multiple) were prior to the singular person (italics added). "A"-7's answer is perhaps also a response to Pound's increasing enthusiasm for Mussolini as *the* answer. But the important point here is that the author is less the origin of his words than their coinhabitant.

"A"-10, situated precisely in the middle of the twist, is in many respects the pivotal movement. It embodies a critical treatment, both thematic and formal, of the three central issues of the twist: the author, the end, and, related to these, the "Jheezus material." Particularly noteworthy in the present context is the movement's immediate occasion, the fall of Paris in World War II. The transformation of *"A"*'s poetics is thus intimately linked to the transformation of Western politics and culture: if Western strategy in its various manifestations has culminated in the war, the poem's development of a tactical poetics offers an implicit resolution of the dilemmas occasioned by that strategy. In "A"-10, however, the politics are scarcely implicit; although its concerns are integral to the internal dynamics of *"A"*, it is nevertheless the most overtly political, most outward-directed movement of the poem.

In part, the more explicit politics of the movement results from a deliberate eschewal of the dense and complex song of earlier movements—such celebration is simply inappropriate to the current situation. The people, having lost their freedom, have stopped singing; accordingly the poet, too, has "stopped singing to talk" (*"A"* 120). Indeed, the war seems to have rendered him "so weak" that he cannot sing, though the poem implies that he will return to song in "a better time" (*"A"* 113, 120). But more is at stake here, for Zukofsky also uses the occasion to stage the death of the author—and of the authoritarian. When song itself returns in "A"-11, it does so only in the absence of the poet, offering comfort to Zukofsky's wife and son after his death. In the final stanza, "A"-11 indicates its independence from an all-encompassing authorial voice by advising the wife and son to "Honor / His voice in me," the poem having absorbed Zukofsky's particular voice into its own multiplicity ("*A*" 125). Thus when "*A*"-12 declares, "I am different, let not a gloss embroil you," the "I" no longer refers to the poet but to the text itself ("*A*" 129). Later movements, in the second half of "*A*", frequently refer to the death or absence of the poet. Of course, the poet is still present, so to speak, in the choice of each word, each phrase, each form. Moreover, in "*A*"-11 and later movements the poem actually becomes much more personal than it had been. But just as the text cannot be explained by means of glosses, neither can it be explained, encompassed, by means of an originating Author. It is not the actual poet who is absent, but the poet as external, authoritarian control, as *strategos*—indeed, in the absence of the Author as *strategos*, the author as tactician—wily, deceptive, multiple— can now thrive. It is precisely characteristic of the tactician that the act of staging his own death should enable him to move freely onto the stage.

"*A*"-10 is also critical to the poem's turn away from the teleological drive of the early movements. The movement follows the structure of the Mass, with sections corresponding to the Kyrie, Gloria, Credo, Sanctus, and Agnus Dei. This structure, combined with the movement's political rhetoric and moral indignation, creates an urgent, apocalyptic tone. But if it invokes apocalypse, the piece does so in order to reject apocalypse—moreover, it inverts the hierarchy, the ascension and sublimation, celebrated in the Christian Mass. Of course, the Mass celebrates the Incarnation, the spirit becoming matter, but this incarnation is only a prelude to matter becoming spirit. In any case, the two terms are necessarily oppositional. Zukofsky, as we will see, wants to celebrate instead the spirituality of matter, the materiality of spirit—the terms are not oppositional, but relational. Rather than appeal to an ideal, absolute power, "*A*"-10 calls for a return of power to *mass*—to the people as a mass and to materiality as it embodies actual relations of forces.

The critique of sublimation begins with the opening evocation of the fall of Paris, the Paris of our "beautiful phrases" ("*A*" 112). This Paris is, of course, the actual city, and we are meant to lament its fate. The reference to our beautiful phrases, however, suggests a more complicated view, as if this Paris were also a rather puffed-up artifice—not merely a source but also a product of beautiful rhetoric, and so doomed to fall.[12] Nor does the question of Paris concern merely rhetoric—it is also a matter of "civilized" ideals as opposed to practical humanity. A similar ambivalence therefore qualifies the poet's sympathy for the people themselves. If the French did not help the Spanish fight against fascism, why should we now be so gullible as to help them? Still, no ambivalence complicates the poem's attitude toward the fascist regimes. The long section corresponding to the Credo singles out other groups, mostly capitalists and Christians, who share the blame: arms traders, oil profiteers, the Christian Church, and "the old betrayers" ("*A*" 116). But throughout the poem the fascists, of Italy, Germany and Spain, are the prime movers:

> With their aim London
> With their aim Paris
> With their aim the United States
> With their aim The International Brigade
>
> ("*A*" 118)

The stress on "aim" here is not merely an exaggerated political rhetoric; it in fact returns us to the idealism conjured by "Paris." The fascists embody a particular instance of intent and purpose overleaping particulars, an instance of *ressentiment* that in this case obliterates the "free body" in pursuit of the desired end. The desired end, of course, is an ideal of order—a specific, rationalized order that is very much the vision of power that later came to inform Michel Foucault's work:

> Shadowing lives everywhere
>   with spies, laws, tests, and the last mark,
>   final zero of death
>
> ("*A*" 117)

While the fascists bear the primary blame, then, Zukofsky also identifies the underlying structural causes, the forces and systems that have contributed to World War II and to the militarization or rationalization of "lives everywhere." Unlike Pound, he does not identify systemic faults with specific individuals.

"Ideals of endless chains," taking ironic visible form in the circular treads of tanks, entrap both the conquered and the conqueror ("*A*" 119). The end of the Credo states the general problematic with particular clarity: treaties simply cannot last "With the conquering Idea / unconquered ("*A*" 121). We may parse "conquering Idea" as both the specific idea of conquest and the general triumph of the idea or ideal—of the image over the real. The capitalization of "Idea" also implicates the authoritarian "I" in this conquest—in what we would now term logocentrism. In any case, the phrasing of the last line neatly embodies the predicament in which the West, as well as "*A*", finds itself: the conquering Idea can seemingly only be conquered by yet another conquering Idea.

Although "*A*"-10 mentions many specific evils and evildoers, Christianity and the increasing dominance of abstraction are the two chief culprits in the triumph of the Idea. Both establish hierarchies that devalue the particulars of life—objects, words, or individuals—in favor of some higher good or goal, in favor of the endless chains of ideals. They strip things of their substance, destroying solid materiality in favor of some gaseous abstraction or ideal. Thus the Christian Mass, by investing in a higher authority, has become "A mess sucked out / [with] No substance," and it therefore contributes to the war's "massed refugees" and "mass death"—that the insubstantial can cause substantial damage is a seeming paradox that *"A"* often notes (*"A"* 113, 112, 119). Nor is reason innocent: as *Thanks to the Dictionary* had asked, perhaps alluding to Ockghem's razor, "What is reason but a cutting edge, the rearmost have no realty in?" (*CF* 278–79). Reason, that is, constitutes a political tool, supplying a rationale for the continuing oppression of the masses (again anticipating Foucault). But it also supplies a rationalized seeing that destroys; *"A"*-10 also notes the fearsome technological advance of the bombers' new high-altitude "super-sights." Nothing, apparently, can defeat such technological sight—unless it be a superior technology.[13]

The close of *"A"*-10, however, refuses to succumb to this repetitive pattern, to the search for an ever greater strategy. A sarcastic rewriting of the "Sanctus," it foregrounds Zukofsky's favorite analogy (and the one that informs much of *"A"*-10) for the contrast between the concrete (or particular) and the abstract (or the Idea): the three states of matter—solid, liquid, and gas. In a 1969 talk Zukofsky referred to these as the "three states of existence," corresponding in poetry to imagery, music, and intellect, but pervading all realms of life (*P* 169). Although the three states coexist at all times, specific historical periods tend to be dominated by one or another—with the period since Shakespeare and Spinoza being "the gas age," the age of abstraction (*P* 169).[14] The climax of *"A"*-10 takes advantage of a double reading of "Vichy" as the capital of unoccupied France and the source of "Vichy water" to address the gas age as a whole:

> The capital of France is Vichy
>
> Blessed is the new age-old effervescence
>
> Till the sailors who mistook their planet for a light
> And took the wrong soundings
> Come back
>
> (*"A"* 123)

This inversion of the Mass invokes a reversal of priorities: from the spiritual to the physical, from abstraction to particulars, from rational discourse to the sounded, sounding, poem. (It is worth noting how deftly the pun on "soundings" invokes both music and its analogue, the liquid state.) Grace, the next movement tells us, comes not from heavenly effervescence but from "knowing things," from earthly solids, from ourselves (*"A"* 125). The final lines of *"A"*-10, corresponding to the "Agnus Dei," therefore turn to the people, rather than to God or an Idea:

> And the people
> Grant us the people's peace
>   ("A" 123)

Where the Christian Mass invokes a return *of* the Ideal, "A"-10 invokes a return *from* the Ideal. An abstracted Love (as in Christianity and as satirized in Williams' *Spring and All*) can be used to rationalize death and even motivate it. But "Love moved to earth," as the Credo declares, "cannot agree with death" ("A" 121). It is in this manner that the poem's "Jheezus material" disappears, as the poem dissolves the strategic quest, the quest for an absolute End, in its ongoing tactical practice. In a sense, "A"-10 has adopted more than merely the form of the Mass, as it has sacrificed the Author (as *strategos*) in order that the authors (the people as tacticians) may achieve their peace. The mad prophet— the Author—of *Poem beginning "The"* has at last been laid to rest.

One danger of a movement such as "A"-10, however, is that its strongly stated, overt politics may dominate the poem—as if the poem's purpose were, finally, political. Zukofsky handles this potential problem by means of the two poems bracketing "A"-10, the second half of "A"-9 and "A"-11, both of which were completed some ten years later, in 1950. In them Zukofsky is careful to situate the overt politics of "A"-10 in the context first of more abstract ("A"-9) and then of more personal ("A"-11) concerns. The three poems focus on different aspects, different spheres of influence, as it were, of "love moved to earth." Drawing on Spinoza for its discussion, "A"-9 observes that under the auspices of such love substance is not subject to human prevision and is therefore free to love ("A" 109). Such love also leads to understanding—as Spinoza says, "the intellectual love of a thing consists in the understanding of its perfections"—and thence to action. It is this earthly love, then, not an ideal, that supplies a rationale for "A"-10. "A"-11, as already noted, takes up the theme of the death of the author. Addressed to the poet's wife and son, it adopts the form and adapts the content of Cavalcanti's *Perch'i'no spero*, so that the entire poem functions as a kind of envoy. (This function connects it to the preceding "Mass," the word for which derives from the phrase *ite, missa est*, "go, it is dismissed.") The love here is familial and individual—concrete and particular. The "love moved to earth" is here the poet's body, now become dust, but like "A"-9 this movement also calls attention to love's ability to "overcome ills" ("A" 124). The poem, once again a song, is in any case conceived not as an ultimately political instrument, but more as a locus of exchange, of secular communion—though such a conception is inherently, radically political. Here are the final lines, the song now speaking directly to the poet's son of how it now sounds:

> His happiness: song sounding
> The grace that comes from knowing
> Things, her love our own showing
> Her love in all her honor.
>
>   ("A" 125)

Functioning as an afterword to the quest constituting the first half of "A", "A"-11 is also a prelude to the songs to come, the songs of the "aftermath."

Bottom and the Bomb

Zukofsky had planned a series of "Ballate" beginning "An"—originally twelve—virtually from the poem's inception. He wrote Pound that they were to be a "longer breath" that would "come easy and with mirror like grace with *maturity* & a clear and richer head" (PZ 80). In fact, however, the first "An" song, "A"-14, was not completed until 1964. From 1947 to 1960, Zukofsky was occupied with another major project, *Bottom: On Shakespeare*. It is to that book that we should now turn, in order to develop a fuller understanding of Zukofsky's mature poetics, for *Bottom* is critical to Zukofsky's work as he moves into the later, postwar sections of "A". Although the following account of the book will necessarily be partial—it deserves a separate study, rather than brief consideration in the course of another argument—*Bottom* can do much to clarify Zukofsky's solutions to the problems and questions posed by the long poem. In particular, it can help us understand how Zukofsky's poetics resolves the opposition between strategy and tactics that I have described as the central tension of "A". The evident easing of tension in "A"-11 and in the subsequent long movement, "A"-12, indicates that a resolution has occurred—or is occurring—but that resolution calls for further explication. How can we conceive of a tactical poetics apart from strategy, unless as a necessarily contradictory strategy of tactics?

Since *Bottom* is much concerned with contextualization, it is appropriate for us to consider at least some aspects of its own diverse contexts. We have been considering one such context, the developing poetics of "A", throughout this chapter. "A"-10, as we have seen, draws a dramatic connection between the devastation of the war, which would culminate in the bomb, and a general cultural tendency to overvalue abstraction and idealist philosophies. World War II supplies another, broader context. Begun in the aftermath of the war, *Bottom* presents a more reflective and much more elaborated examination of the questions posed in "A"-10. But the book also has a more specific context in the form of an immediate predecessor: Pound's *Guide to Kulchur*, which had been dedicated to Zukofsky and Basil Bunting and which had also been written in the shadow of war. Not one to follow the elder poet's suggested curriculum—especially considering the position to which that curriculum had led Pound—Zukofsky produced in *Bottom* a lengthy answer to Pound's guide. But where Pound offers a *guide* to kulchur, characteristically assuming the position of a master leading his students, Zukofsky offers a *graph* of culture—a clarification of the field, an outline of possible directions. More important, Zukofsky offers an alternative to the visually based epistemology of Pound's ideogrammic method.

Published to virtually no notice by the Ark Press (University of Texas) in 1963, *Bottom* is a dense and difficult, often brilliant but also often baffling text. Ranging through the entire canon, taking *A Midsummer Night's Dream* as its major Shakespearean text and bristling with citations from Aristotle, Wittgenstein, Spinoza, and many others, it has received little serious attention. Those interested in modernist poetics no doubt find it perplexingly unlike comparison texts, and while it addresses the concerns of poststructuralism, it does not do so in any of the accepted academic discourses. Nor have Shakespeareans rushed to attend to a poet's text, written from the viewpoint of a character who is transformed into an ass. Zukofsky's fourfold description of the book (perhaps an echo of Dante's Letter to Can Grande) also tends to invite dismissal of its "weight," since it is by turns cryptic, paradoxical, and self-deprecating. In addition to being an autobiography and a work on prosody, *Bottom: On Shakespeare*, Zukofsky writes, is

1. A long poem built on a theme for the variety of its recurrences. The theme is simply that Shakespeare's text throughout favors the clear physical eye against the erring brain, and that this theme has historical implications.
2. A valid skepticism that as 'philosophy of history' (taking in the arts and sciences) my book takes exception to all philosophies from Shakespeare's point of view ('Shakespeare's,' as expressed above and as excused by my preface to the book.) (*P* 166)

It is tempting to read "theme" as "thesis" (especially since *Bottom* is in prose and appears argumentative), thereby transforming "poem" into "argument" or "essay." But to do so would be tantamount to dismissing the text on suspicion of banality (for its theme), naivety (for its apparent confidence in the "clear physical eye"), and repetition (in its insistence on "recurrences"). The fact that the "simple" theme becomes compound ("that . . . and that"), however, suggests that more is going on than such an initial judgment would allow. The second point, moreover, thoroughly questions its own claims. "Valid skepticism" is glossed in Zukofsky's talk "For Wallace Stevens" as a skepticism so consistent as to be skeptical of itself, the quotation marks around "philosophy of history" undermine the integrity of that basic conception—as does the notion that it "takes in," or dupes, the arts and sciences—and "Shakespeare's point of view" implicitly contextualizes and limits this argument. The statement that the book's purpose is not to advance a theme but to develop its variety (very much a sixteenth-century notion of poetics) also serves to qualify its claims.[15] Within the book, in fact, the preference for physical eyes over the erring brain is subsumed within the proportion that, Zukofsky says, informs all of Shakespeare's writing: love is to reason as eyes are to mind. The ideal proportion would be an identity, a proper balance: "when reason judges with eyes, love and mind are one" (*B* 266). Perhaps never achieved, that ideal does not, in any case, depend on a facile overestimation of the physical eye.

Because of the nature of Zukofsky's poetics and of *Bottom* as it embodies that poetics, the question of genre is also important. The multiplicity of purposes suggested by the description accords better with a poem than with the more single-minded structure of an argumentative essay. Even the book's argument serves several purposes—a demonstration of the consistency of this theme in Shakespeare, an exploration of its philosophical implications, another exploration of its historical contexts, and a consideration of the various possible relations between seeing and thinking are but a few.[16] Of course, these various purposes do share a concern with the limits of thinking, the limits of reasoned argument. Wittgenstein's *Tractatus* is a forerunner here, with its concern to show the limits of what can be said and the nonsensical status of metaphysics. So too is "Shakespeare's text": Bottom, Zukofsky points out, reminds us that "no man can tell" his "rare vision," while Prospero commands: "No tongue! All eyes!" (qtd. in *B* 9). Part of the brilliance of *Bottom* is not merely to note but to take seriously the frequency with which the speech of Shakespeare's characters, however "inconsequential" they may be, embodies dramatically the abstract propositions of other, more systematic thinkers. In the case of *A Midsummer Night's Dream*, Bottom's discourse also has significant affinities with Wittgenstein's distinction between what a proposition shows and what it tells, for his dream can only be staged (as it is, by Shakespeare) or sung (as Bottom promises). In Zukofsky's hands, this distinction is also an argument for the importance of form, and so of poetry: because it *shows*, the form of a work is both more convincing and more accurate than what it "says." As he had declared in *A Test of Poetry*, "poetry convinces not by argument but by the *form* it creates to carry its content" (*T* 52). *Bottom* argues—or rather, shows—that this is actually true of all discourse.

The book's argument, concerning the limits of reason and the corollary importance of showing, thus argues its own status as *also* a poetic text, rather than a solely critical one. Although it frequently mobilizes the terminology and syntax of rational argument, the book insistently transgresses the limits of such discourse. It is always gesturing toward what cannot be spoken, both what the text can only show and even what the text cannot show. Rational discourse, that is, is relativized and positioned within a larger field of possible discourses. Moreover, Zukofsky positions language as a whole within a larger field of possible human activities: his poetics applies as much to living as to writing. Manifested in *Bottom* as much as in *"A"*, Zukofsky's poetics reject any domination of language or of life by a reasoned "intent and purpose." As Wittgenstein observes, "colloquial language is part of the human organism and not less complicated than it" (qtd. in *Bottom* 50). Spinoza is also called upon for corroboration, particularly for his assertion that "the eyes of the mind" are themselves "proofs": "the object of the idea constituting the human mind is the body, or a certain mode of extension actually existing and nothing else"—meaning, as Zukofsky explains, that "proofs are *not* the object of the eyes of the mind" (*B* 94). "Object" here has a range of meanings (recalling "objective" in *"A"*-6), but primary would seem to be "end" in the sense of purpose, the Aristotelian final cause. Explanations, proofs, are not the ultimate purpose of thinking; thinking should rather further existence. The body (and by extension the temporality of the material world) provides necessary context and actual purpose for the representations of the mind. As Isaac Rosenfield has recently argued, "the body, not a sense of absolute space, is the brain's absolute frame of reference" (45). At the end of Part Two Zukofsky remarks that he does *not* "wish to draw an end to thinking but merely to show its limits" (*B* 94). The characteristic pun on *drawing* suggests the rejection of a final visual image that would foreclose thought.

Even where it articulates its own apparent position, then, *Bottom* (like *"A"*) is always showing the limits of what it says—it is always relativizing, temporalizing, decentering its position, validating its skepticism by turning it back onto its own statements. Apparent claims to a strategic authority are in fact tactical: they are partial formulations, or temporary representations, that constitute momentary seizures, so to speak, of discursive power. Such seizures are always contextualized with reference to other discursive fields, or to a deictic "this" that remains outside—beyond, before, or beside—that which the text can tell. This displacement is accomplished by use of many of the techniques we have already considered: the semantic and syntactic ambiguities, the shifts and slippages of meaning from one context to another, and so on. Even though it displays the rhetoric of rational argument, *Bottom* refuses to deploy an authorial metalanguage—one that would subsume Aristotle, Spinoza, Wittgen-

stein, and Shakespeare into one discourse. Zukofsky offers neither a facile assertion that the various arguments are "the same" nor a translation of all these
discourses into one set of terms. Instead, his own text offers a tactical negoti-
ation of these discourses, at times delicate, at times aggressive, displaying their
affinities and differences but making no attempt to disguise their heteroge-
neity, their incommensurability. Much of what *Bottom shows* resides in the gaps
that are left between these discourses, gaps Zukofsky leaps or simply leaves.
All these tactics are inseparable from what we could call *Bottom*'s alternate epistemology—did not the very term "epistemology" evoke an authorial metadis-
course, precisely the rational systematizing *Bottom* seeks to overthrow. In fact,
to speak of a discourse being contextualized also suggests its absorption within
a greater discourse. It would be better to speak of *Bottom* in terms of a *contex-
ture*, a weaving together of disparate threads.

   The text also refuses to deploy absolute oppositions—its major criticism of
Aristotle, in fact, concerns the "tincture of dialectic" that leads him astray (*B*
54). Such terms as have previously been conceived as paired, either-or oppositions are also relativized. Zukofsky's description of his theme, for example,
with "the clear physical eye *against* the erring brain," might well be taken as
an absolute opposition. Yet the relation is much more complex—Zukofsky is
not, for instance, unaware of the brain's role in constituting the visual field,
despite the occasional appearance of a naive insistence on the transparency and
infallibility of physical sight—and in *Bottom* that complexity is explored at
length. The relation between sight and sound, too, can also seem oppositional.
As we have seen, the aural and the visual have generally been considered in a
dialectical relation—however critics may disagree as to which is better, or to
what extent one or the other has predominated within a particular culture, the
two worlds are taken to be in significant opposition. Since Zukofsky's poetry
and statements on poetics consistently stress sound and music, as if attainment
of the condition of music were the proper aim of poetry, we would expect him
to favor sound against sight. And, indeed, his emphasis on sound provides a
useful way of distinguishing between Zukofsky's poetic world and Pound's,
with the older poet's focus on the Image. Surprisingly, however, *Bottom* favors
seeing throughout, words both arising from sight and "moving to a visual end"
(*B* 19). A closer examination of Zukofsky's actual presentations of the relation
between sight and sound, in *Bottom* and elsewhere, suggests a more complex
perspective—or a complex of perspectives.

   One well-known formulation of his poetic occurs in his textbook anthology, *A Test of Poetry*, where he declares that poetry's "purpose as art" is "the
range of pleasure it affords as sight, sound, and intellection" (*T* vii). The mix
of sight, sound, and intellection may seem a straightforward Americanization

of Pound's phanopoeia, melopoeia, and logopoeia, but the implied function
and relation of these three components of poetry function are quite distinct. In
Pound the three elements are subsumed by the totality of the Image, being
used instrumentally in order to convey the author's experience of the Image to
the reader. Because Zukofsky's measure, however, is the range of pleasure,
rather than the power of the Image, the three components are more like equal
partners, the subjects of a fugue. The poem need not be conceived as a single
Image, an instant of time, in order to afford pleasure; indeed, the range of pleasure may well increase as the poem fragments into distinct elements. *Bottom's*
description of Shakespeare's text as "constantly seeking and ordering relative
quantities and qualities of sight, sound, and intellection" perhaps clarifies the
distinction (*B* 18). Here the author is not a strategist deploying his words, but
a tactician negotiating their multiple variables. And while the words may move
toward a visual end, that end does not subsume the entire process, the pleasure of the movement.

The reciprocal rather than dialectic relation between sight and sound is explicit in two passages of "A"-12, a movement that, completed in 1951, often
reads as a series of notes written alongside *Bottom*.[17] These passages adopt the
symbolic language of mathematics to present the relations between these components more precisely. Thus:

I'll tell you.
About my *poetics*—

An integral
     ("*A*" 138)

Here the poetics is clearly not a question of striving to attain music at the expense of speech, but of a range of activity, the two terms acting as upper and
lower limits of that range. *Poetics* encompasses the entire field, a graph of
possibilities. But this formulation gives only a simplified version of the informing poetics—for one thing, both speech and music are within the range of
sound. A somewhat enlarged conception of music, for example, might consider speech as a kind of music—and we might note, too, that the symbol for
"integral" puns visually (and silently) on the sound-holes of a violin. Zukofsky
tells of one aspect of his poetics, but *shows* considerably more. The movement's
second integral presents a larger range, this time with sound as a whole con-

stituting one limit and "story—eyes: thing thought" the other ("*A*" 173). The formula invites us to consider the relations obtaining among the items constituting the last term, but for the moment we may read it as roughly synonymous with the component of sight—the *matter* of the poem, its anchoring, as it were, in the material world. Thus the degree of emphasis on sound as a whole varies inversely with the emphasis on sight. Speech, presumably, would be more involved with sight than a purer music; it would be closer to story, to *thing thought*, as distinguished from (but not opposed to) abstract thought. (Although "intellection" is not a term within these equations, both of them are clearly products of a good deal of intellectual play.) We should not be too rigid, however, in pursuing this linear progression, for music itself, *Bottom* insists, should remain connected to, grounded in, sight. Otherwise it becomes abstract, a "sightless tune" produced by and for intellection, removed from bodily rhythms and human emotions (*B* 37). The conventional opposition between aurality and visuality simply cannot account for the poetics developed in Zukofsky's work, which seeks not the triumph of one sense over the other but a reconciliation, a recognition of the interplay between the two and of their necessary embodiment in their immediate material context.

What Zukofsky means by "sight," in fact, is itself neither simple nor invariable. Already in "An Objective" he had distinguished between the mirage and the detail of seeing (*P* 12). In *Bottom* the meaning ranges from the literal (a function of eyes) to the metonymic (representing the senses) to the metaphoric (representing something like "insight")—and even the literal sense, as noted above, is complex. Puns are also involved: "sightless tune," for example, also invokes "siteless tune," a tune without grounding or material context; and although it is never explicit, "sight" also suggests "cite," the many citations in *Bottom* and "*A*" providing context for Zukofsky's various sightings. Common to all these uses of the word, however, is an emphasis on sense, on materiality—if nothing else, materiality of the word as sound in air, as marks on paper. We have generally considered sight in terms of a monologic world, perhaps best illustrated by Cartesian perspectivalism, with its rationalizing of space and secure positioning of observer and observed, the observer as strategist *overlooking* the observed—in both senses of *overlooking*, simultaneously overseeing and not seeing. (Thus Zukofsky commented after the war on Pound's having "overlooked" the "hell of Belsen" [*P* 166].) As Martin Jay has suggested, however, other "scopic regimes" are also possible. That developed by Pound, for example—and common in mystical traditions—argues for a visionary union of subject and object that would displace critical reason entirely: the "full eidos" that would guarantee the validity of Pound's work. Both these scopic regimes, though, exhibit a common structure: although they begin with accurate observation, with the particulars of things seen, their commitment to a unifying abstraction from that observation leads them increasingly to ignore or distort subsequent observation. Whether rational perspective or mystical union, they tend to sacrifice the actual *eidola* for the sake of the *eidos*, the redemptive, but always deferred, Vision. Although the totalizing tendencies of thought are the explicit object of *Bottom's* critique, the way Pound's vision led him to embrace political totalitarianism is very much in the background. One of the difficulties of the book is just this simultaneous critique of both reason and mysticism. Both are instances of an excess of one term in Zukofsky's proportion. Cartesian perspectivalism stresses reason at the expense of love, and hence at the expense of sight and insight; Pound's Imagist epistemology stresses love at the expense of reason, and hence of judgment. In Zukofsky's work, however, sight contends an immediacy, an imbrication of observer in the observed that is biological (or physiological) rather than theological or teleological (*B* 63). Zukofsky's insistence *on* sight points to an insistence *of* sight that disrupts both rational and mystical orders; the multiplicity of the saccadic glance returns the eye to what has been excluded from both rationalized perspective and mystic vision.

Because it is sited in the body rather than in a mystical (mental) vision, Merleau-Ponty's conception of sight as a chiasmus, an interpenetration of subject and object, comes close to the view articulated in *Bottom*. However, the implicit utopianism in Merleau-Ponty's celebration of the chiasmus, of the body as the site of this interpenetration, is much less prominent in *Bottom*. There the "ideal" relation is postulated as itself a kind of upper limit, perhaps to be approached asymptotically, but never to be achieved. Zukofsky frequently recurs to such moments in Shakespeare. One is the allegory of *The Phoenix and the Turtle*, the supreme lovers who have vanished from the world. While in Merleau-Ponty the body occupies the position of center, and so centers subjectivity, Shakespeare's poem conceives of subjectivity as transpersonal, constituted from a chiasmus between individual subjects in such a way as to confound "in itself" the reason that would insist on the separation of subjectivities:

> Reason, in itself confounded,
> Saw division grow together,
> To themselves yet either neither,
> Simple were so well compounded;
>
> That it cried, How true a twain
> Seemeth this concordant one!
> Love hath reason, reason none,
> If what parts can so remain.
>
>   (qtd. in *B* 26)

In Zukofsky's use the poem also functions as an allegory of the perfect relation between love and reason, each folded into the other. Love hath reason when Love's mind "without flaws . . . *sees*" and "the sight flames" (B 25, 26). Related moments in Shakespeare include Hamlet's "the rest is silence," and Prospero's "No tongue! All eyes! Be silent!"—the "inexpressible mysticism," as Zukofsky puts it, of "look, don't think" (B 91). Like the proposition that ends Wittgenstein's *Tractatus*, this line gestures toward a condition that cannot be represented (and which is only in this sense mystical). But climbing the ladder of Wittgenstein's propositions, turning the pages of Zukofsky's book, may also lead us to admire the construction of the ladder and to appreciate the pleasures of the climb. Perhaps more important, that ultimate condition is from a practical standpoint not even desirable: for the writer, in particular, silence is an untenable alternative, but for any "human animal who must speak" that end would mark the end—the cessation—of human fellowship (B 91). At the end of Part One of *Bottom* we are told that seeing should be the object of speech, rather than vice versa. But always in Zukofsky there is a mixture. The text does not seek simply to cancel itself out in an ultimate gesture toward sight. While it prods us to see, it reminds us that we also see words. The text has other purposes as well, and perhaps none greater than the desire to "unite others . . . in friendship"—to continue and extend, that is, the conversation that constitutes culture and society (B 90–91).

While a good deal of *Bottom*, then, is devoted to showing the limits of reason, the book also acknowledges the practical limits of seeing. The distance afforded by abstraction is acknowledged as a *felix culpa*, both necessitating and enabling speech and social interaction. The "tragedy of the poetry"—and this phrase refers both to writing and living—lies in the necessary interrelationship: that "not only what the eyes of the poetry see but its music *must* suffer its reason" (B 89, italics added). Like the relation between sight and sound, that between sight and reason is a matter of relative predominance rather than absolute opposition. The point, again, is not that one should triumph over the other, but that the two should coexist in appropriate and clear proportion. *Bottom*'s formulations of the relation constantly avoid absolute oppositions in favor of reciprocal relations and reversible processes. Hence the "necessary proportion" to which Zukofsky's meditation recurs: "love : reason :: eyes : mind" (B 39, 77). The formula emphatically does not mean that we should simply look and accept appearances, although that is one possibility in the field of relations it governs, and one of the variations Zukofsky plays on the theme. A useful paraphrase of its sense would be: when love sees, the mind is reasonable—but love sees only when the mind is reasonable. (Only silence can avoid this circuity.) Otherwise we are varyingly under the sway of "Love's mind" or of an abstracted reason, which is to say, in part, that we are to varying degrees blind to the actual world because we are caught in our own constructions. While both Shakespeare's text and Zukofsky's exhibit a *preference* for accurate looking, neither is utopian. As Zukofsky asserts, "the formula never permits pure comedy, nor for that matter pure tragedy" (*B* 24). However blind the thought, it "still has some proportion of love" (*B* 37). Like comedy and tragedy, pure eyes and pure mind are convenient explanatory fictions, unattainable limits, necessary to the symbolic system, but not actual.

An exclusive reliance on eyes would also finally undermine the effectiveness of the eyes themselves. In a discussion of Aristotle, Zukofsky presents another chiastic formula: "insight moves sight to the site, or the site moves sight to insight" (*B* 60). The reversibility here is both necessary and critical. Insight cannot be conceived as the end, the final cause of this process, for it only turns back to its own final cause: "the term *site* must always be there with the other two—sight and insight—or they will not be there" (*B* 60). Each element must persist into the others, folded within them. Their relations constitute a process requiring constant adjustment and adaptation, where no one term can dominate, and which must always be sited in the flux of its material context. Otherwise, both sight and insight would lose their grounding, and consequently their sense. Significantly, thought itself is brought into this relation, since it can also become a (material) site: "In that sense thought offered a site to interest men's sight and also . . . their insight" (*B* 60). Far from being against thought, *Bottom* in fact insists on its necessity—but it also insists on resiting thought within its material, historical context.

Sight, then, does not so much oppose multiplicity to unity, as relativize all framing unities with reference to their own multiplicity, and to their siting in material contexts. It is largely this attention to multiplicity that *Bottom* denotes by "love." In its examination of Shakespeare's definition of love, the book offers an almost overwhelming variety of its own definitions—the book does, after all, assay the variety of its theme's recurrences—perplexing not because they are in conflict but because they often pertain to distinct, often incommensurate discourses, while we characteristically expect a more single-minded pursuit (*P* 167). Yet whether it be human love, intellectual love, or the pleasure of looking, love is characterized as an extraordinary attention to, openness toward, and appreciation of an other. This attention is *textually* evident in the practice of writing throughout *Bottom* (and, of course, *"A"*); an apt example is the way the index refuses to be *merely* an index, but also advances commentaries and themes of its own. The entry for "love," for example, reads *"see* definition"—both an instruction to look elsewhere, under the heading "definition," and itself a definition of love: to experience love is to see definition, to experience not the mirage but the detail of seeing the world, the other (*B* 458). Thus even the word "definition" can reward attention. As the book illuminates its object from one perspective after another, it brings our "picture" of love into ever greater definition, even as the very process of this definition embodies another act of love.

In its broadest sense, then, sight offers to enlarge our worlds, to open up the boundaries between self and other. In addition to *The Phoenix and the Turtle*, *Bottom* also cites *Troilus and Criseyde* in support of its view of subjectivity as transpersonal, as a construction derived from the chiasmus of self and other (*B* 72). But expressions like "self and other" inevitably suggest a confrontational construction, as if a preexistent self were threatened by the other as its limit. That is, the self is implicitly imaged as a strategic entity, which as such can only respond to the appearance of an other as a potential threat to its sovereignty. Norman Bryson has pointed to the persistence of this view even in those, like Sartre, who attempt to go beyond such a conception of the self. *Bottom*, however, does not begin with a self that is subsequently fragmented or partitioned; rather, the self is conceived as a dynamic process, a series of selves, as it were, revealed and constituted through multiple relations with others (*B* 52, 89). There is no single, stable self to be threatened by an other. We could say that love consists also in this readiness to reformulate, to transgress and expand, previously constituted boundaries of self. Sight is thus not a means of possession but an exchange, a mutually constituting regard. The pleasure of looking thereby displaces the fear of confrontation. Even our desire for the fullness of silence, for an unspeaking presence, becomes merely one moment, or one tendency, in our conversation with ourselves and our world (though the conversation may be motivated, at least in part, by that desire). In *Bottom*, the desire to unite with others in friendship—whether this refers to a union of reason and love or of individuals—supplies both the basis and the limit of its philosophical discourse. Conceived in this way, the desire for conversation is a critical force for the tactical disruption of any strategic totalization.

Pleasure, a recurrent motif in *Bottom*, is also critical to such disruption. For pleasure, as the text informs us, "is at any moment complete," which means simply that the experience of pleasure is at that moment sufficient in itself (*B* 62). Furthermore, it is not an end product: pleasure may be experienced, intentionally or not, at any moment in a process. The experience of pleasure consequently undermines not only any conception of a quest for pleasure, but also the importance of any strategic teleology. Pleasure is also multiple and nonexclusive. Its multiplicity is evident in the diverse pleasures of love, of sight and the other senses, and of intellect. In *Bottom*, Zukofsky himself clearly takes great pleasure in thinking, in the pursuit of specific goals, and even in the construction of strategic totalities (though these are always playful rather than ponderous, local rather than global). Its nonexclusivity is evident in its ability to coexist with other purposes, in its ability to persist: the eye, for example, "even when harnessed for intellectual action, also takes pleasure in seeing" (*B* 61). Thus Zukofsky's assertion that "the test of poetry is the range of pleasure it affords" does not exclude other purposes—indeed, his next statement, "this is its purpose *as art*," invites the ascription of other purposes in other contexts (*T* vii, emphasis added). In the political context of the late thirties, when Zukofsky was writing *A Test of Poetry*, even the declaration of pleasure as sufficient purpose was unavoidably also a political act.[18] *Bottom* itself is first motivated by pleasure, the pleasure afforded by the "variety of . . . recurrences" of its theme.[19] The emphases on friendship and pleasure, in fact, allow the text to sustain a degree of "valid skepticism" that might otherwise render it an impossible project. At the end of Part Two, for example, Zukofsky can still distance himself from the preceding argument, presenting himself in the third person and wondering "whether eyes are preferable to reason"—though such skepticism, he points out, "palpably makes no sense, if he continues to be affected by the seniority of eyes as the life of *his* Shakespeare" (*B* 91). Thus the value of reading Shakespeare's work is simply the *feeling* that "it is"—although that thought has no value itself.

Implicit in the recurrent references to material contexts, to process, and to recurrence itself is an appeal to history. History, the text implies, provides the ground for a resolution, an integration, of the contradictions and incommensurabilities of human culture and society. This is also the concern of an important passage in "A"-14, the first of the "An" songs, written just after publication of *Bottom*. Perhaps generated by the play of "integrates" and "integral," the passage relates historical integration to a more elaborate presentation of Zukofsky's "integral" poetics:

. . . "history" integrates

lower limit body
upper limit dance,
lower limit dance

upper limit speech,
lower limit speech
upper limit music,

lower limit music
upper limit *mathémata*
swank for *things*

learned . . .

("A" 349)

Here the poetics of writing at first appears to be incorporated within a larger trajectory that culminates in *mathémata*—as if poetics were a stage on the way to increasingly abstract representations. But although the rigorous repetition of structure gives an initial impression of a clear linearity, that impression quickly collapses. The apparent continuum is in fact constituted by qualitatively different continua: body and dance, for instance, cannot be conceived as upper and lower limits in the same way as speech and music. These fields do not form a narrative, nor even a sequence; rather, each persists into the others, folded into them, as it were, each thereby presenting one aspect of the whole process. This relation is perhaps most evident in the passage's close. The assertion that *mathémata* is merely a "swank" substitution resituates *mathémata*—and with it the entire passage—within the field of rhetoric, of speech, while the shift to "things learned" reminds us that the object of thought is the body. Any attempt to derive a progressive linearity from materiality to abstraction collapses into a circularity as we suddenly return to the material and rediscover that "thinking's the lowest rung" (*"A"* 260). Thus philosophy, "all philosophy," becomes absorbed into a larger poetics, displaced from its presumed position of mastery and resited within the "whole process," as *Bottom* terms it, "of desire" (97). The passage tactically negotiates a series of incommensurate ranges, in effect incommensurate discourses, in the same way as *Bottom* negotiates the incommensurate discourses of its citations. Far from being a summation of Zukofsky's "integral" poetics, this passage qualifies and is in turn qualified by the earlier statements of poetics—including one from *"A"*-12 that eschews calculus and explicitly evokes love as its basis: "As I love: My poetics" (*"A"* 151). The colon allows this formula to be read both forwards and backwards, Zukofsky's poetics both deriving from love, the process of desire, and constituting an object of love, an object of that process. Despite Zukofsky's postwar interest in a scientific definition of poetry, there can be no mathematical metalanguage for his poetics—such a definition, he notes, would have to be based on "the entire humanly known world" (*P* 9). A poetics cannot finally be told, but only *shown*. The integrals of *"A"* *tell* of a specific relation between variables, but their combination *shows* a larger complex of fields, matrices that finally cannot be modeled.

But what of the claim that "history" can integrate all this? The scare quotes point to the problematics involved in such an appeal to history for an ultimate resolution. They in part mark a skepticism toward what often amounts merely to an eschatological faith, a faith in the revelation of order, of "the full eidos," in the fullness of time. Such a conception of history is merely another product of "love's mind," and as such it deflects attention from the actualities of "historic and contemporary particulars"—from what Foucault terms "the singularity of events outside of any monotonous finality" (qtd. in Rorty 46). The scare quotes also remind us that "history" is always itself a citation, a construction. In both *"A"* and *Bottom*, "history" is not so much an object of discourse as a construction of discourses. The unity of a reified "history" dissolves into another multiplicity, an always transforming, often discontinuous process, embedded in words and characterized not by progress or repetition but by recurrence. Interestingly, Foucault also turns to sight in order to explain his interest in "the historical sense," which "corresponds to the acuity of a glance that distinguishes, separates and disperses—the kind of disassociating view that is capable of decomposing itself, capable of shattering the unity of men's being through which it was thought that he could extend his sovereignty to the events of the past" (qtd. in Rorty 46). This is very much a Zukofskyan contrast between history as a construction of reason and history as sense, and between the subject as strategic master and the subject as tactical participant. In Zukofsky, historical resolution occurs in action, in the ongoing practice of negotiating and balancing distinct particulars. As in the passage from *"A"*-14, however, various descriptions are possible and at different times desirable. Even linear and cyclical models of history may be useful for certain purposes, though they are always situated as fictions, as self-deconstructing artifacts; they are always subject to further sightings and resitings. *Bottom* presents a graph rather than a guide; it will not "settle for the purpose of ordained cycles" (*B* 34). Linear and cyclical constructions are temporary strategic orders emerging from (and as part of) a process of tactical practices.

Decades earlier, in his 1927 poem in memory of Lenin, Zukofsky had seen history as a sum "of all live processes" (*CSP* 21). No one can total the sum of these neverending processes. Even *Bottom*'s desire to present a graph, acknowledged to be an abstraction of sight, requires an apology: Zukofsky finds his "excuse" in the requirements of the symbolic system, in his attempt to imagine the propositional sign as constructed from spatial objects, rather than written signs, and more fundamentally, in the human desire to speak with others (*B* 90–91). Or, again, perhaps there is no graph but only "notes" for one, as the title of Part Two suggests. Even this assertion is questioned in the final sentences of Part Two: "Perhaps not to tie the points of a graph of culture at all, and so there are no points. Intimacy is not solved, nor does it solve anything, speaking as must happen, trusting to see an alphabet of subjects" (*B* 94). It is this resiting of strategies within tactics, developed at length in *Bottom* and corresponding to the resiting of thought within its material context, that enables both *Bottom* and *"A"* to resolve the apparent opposition between strategic order and tactical practices.

Certain sums, nevertheless, are assayed, and some of these can threaten

to end live processes, at least from a human perspective. The Bomb's importance to Zukofsky can be gauged by its significant appearances in his work: in
Bottom, in "A"-19 (which we will shortly examine), and in the opening paragraphs of the 1946 essay that begins *Prepositions*. There the Bomb is associated
with the exhausted and emptied world of the final months of the war. "Sworn
to drudgery," Zukofsky writes, "people parted in those months with everything in the spirit of a fool and his money." Only the intrusion of his son's
voice allows the return of hope: "no matter how blank the world was it again
seemed possible. I saw why definitions of poetry rounding out like ciphers
(abstract and like numbers on clocks that read only this century or that century
and no other) should not satisfy either of us. For I hope that you as well as I
will never want to live by them" (*P* 3). In the aftermath of the Bomb, only the
voice of another makes resistance both possible and desirable.

This postwar dissatisfaction with an abstracted world is very much the impetus behind *Bottom*, on which Zukofsky began work the following year. The
first section of Part Three's "An Alphabet of Subjects," entitled "A-Bomb and
H-," explicitly takes up the question of the Bomb's critical relation to cultural
history and to Zukofsky's project. Here is the first paragraph:

> The implicit alchemy in the atomic table of the human animal is his residual
> perceptive *stand* in the *rout* of an original formation of flesh-and-blood life.
> Previously the rout of alchemy had been the re-formation of animal sense-
> impressions—ratios or powers in spatial magnitudes, organs of sense (*De
> Anima, II, 12*)—by a discriminative capacity whose self-restorative power of
> life later systematized an abstract explosion. This now assures the *actual rar-
> efaction* in the explosion of the bomb. That it is A-bomb or H-bomb, a bomb
> exploding according to a principle of fission, another according to an opposite
> principle of fusion, does not affect the actual rarefaction of bombs of either
> type in particular times and places they explode: the intellectual rarefaction
> of both principles that precedes and assures particular explosions is their
> most knowable end or good. To perceive that actual rarefactions are not al-
> ways sensually beneficial does not contradict that their knowable end also
> determines explosions for the sake of sensible objects—such as the new in-
> ventions conceived to answer cultured human desires. In time these nursed
> desires will be anterior as ever primitive desires were to later logical states,
> while the always necessary end subsists in the whole process of desire and
> its *stand* for logic. The 'choice' between *anterior* and later is forever determined
> by logical necessity. (*B* 97)

With its dense mix of terminology, drawn mostly from Aristotle but from others as well, such a passage can elicit even from an accomplished reader of
Zukofsky something like awe—as if the content were somehow inaccessible,

and one could only admire the construction (see Quartermain "Only is order othered"). Even though punning is constant, however, the terms, most of which have been introduced in citations in Part One, do have specific, if multiple, referents. (The most relevant passages from Aristotle are quoted on pages 39–41, though Zukofsky characteristically condenses and puns.) Given our previous discussion, we can make the overall sense of the passage relatively clear. Our "implicit alchemy" is our ability (by means of processes still unknown) to transform sense perception into what Aristotle terms "higher states of knowledge." As Aristotle tells us: "out of sense-perception comes . . . memory, and out of frequently repeated memories . . . develops experience. . . . From experience again . . . originate the skill of the craftsman and the knowledge of the man of science" (qtd. in *B* 39–40). Zukofsky's *stand* and *rout* derive from Aristotle's analogy between this process and a rout in battle, which is stopped by making one stand after another. Our ability to abstract from the material world produces a "discriminative capacity" that allows us to theorize about that world. Here, too, the process of increasing abstraction returns to the material world, producing actual effects that can be either good (in response to "cultured human desires") or bad (the Bomb).

Western culture's "abstract explosion," the explosive growth of abstraction that marks its history, culminates in the theory of the Bomb as a triumph of abstraction (*B* 99). Zukofsky is here close to Heidegger's sense of the Bomb as a "gross confirmation" of the "annihilation of the thing" science had long since accomplished (170). But Zukofsky does not dismiss the actual explosion as an unimportant confirmation. He also acknowledges the inherent good of the intellectual pursuit: even if some actual results are not beneficial, others are. The "intellectual rarefaction" of that theory in turn achieves its consummation in the Bomb's "actual rarefaction," the vaporization of matter. In that apocalyptic scenario, the passage goes on to say, "all individual bodies will be buried—a singularly visual future which, if in nature happens to all at once, may by someone imaginably surviving be thought of only as the common death that has forgotten to know what each has been or *seen*" (*B* 99). I would note here the distinction between the singularly visual end, the product of a fixed intent and purpose that would subsume all particulars, and the multiplicity of the *seen*. We can escape the singular end only if we "spring back" from the logic of ends (and from abstraction as an end) to "sense": only if we rewrite the end as subsisting in the "whole process of desire" (*B* 99).

In the final lines of "A-Bomb and H-" Zukofsky turns from his own argument to the text of Shakespeare's *Pericles*, focusing on the exchange between a despairing Pericles, with "nothing to think on but ensuing death" and a tongue barely warm enough to ask for help, and the First Fisherman, who, showing compassion, offers a warm gown and rescue (*P* II, i, 7). Or rather, Zukofsky turns to the graphic symbols before him, playing lovingly with Greek sources of the quarto's "ke-tha" (for "quoth-a") in the first fisherman's response: "Die, ke-tha; now Gods forbid't, and I have a Gowne heere, come put it on, keepe thee warme" (qtd. in *B* 99). Here is the conclusion to "A-Bomb and H-": "κειθι = ἐκειθι = ἐκει = there; thither; then; in that case—*keepe thee warme*" (*B* 99). Place and logic are embedded in one another here, manifesting that infolding of site, sight, and insight that in turn enables compassion, intimacy, and love. So the first fisherman of *Pericles* rejects Pericles' thought of death, instead offering him warmth and companionship—the warmth of companionship. *Bottom's* graph of culture embodies a calculus that would have us always turn back from the singular end of thought.

"An" Songs

In both *Bottom* and *"A"* the second World War, with its deployment of the atomic bomb, foreshadows the apocalyptic consummation of a cultural desire for the objectively perfect. Given that the letter *A*, as we have seen, embodies both that quest for the objectively perfect and the poem's apparently paradoxical quest to escape, it seems especially apt that *A* should also come to stand for the atomic bomb itself. The Bomb becomes an especially critical signification for *"A"* to resolve. The poem itself must answer the question Zukofsky posed in an interview: "What happens when you start radiating once the atom has got you?" (N.E.T. Outtake). What happens after modernism? Or more specifically, what happens to *"A"* in the aftermath of apocalypse? How can the poem continue once its own complicity in the process leading to the Bomb is confronted? It was in this context that Zukofsky began work on *Bottom*, that his "Poetry" essay reaffirmed the persistence of possibility, and that *Anew* appeared, heralding for Williams a new music of the future. What Williams perhaps did not know was that *Anew* also heralded the "An" sections of *"A"*—the sections that would bring this music into the long poem and embody the poem's ongoing resolution of these questions.

Even in the letter he sent to Pound asserting that the "An" songs would "come easy and with mirror like grace with *maturity* & a clear and richer head," Zukofsky was mining the dictionary: *an*, the *OED* tells us, is "an older and richer form of 'a'." Other possible meanings of *an* also come into play in the course of the poem. "If," its meaning in *"A"*-21, suggests the contingent, rather than the absolute of *A*. "And," the first word of *"A"*-24, suggests a paratactic structure, an ongoing movement that comes to no final completion. "Nothing is ever finished," says *"A"*-12; *"A"*-18 later quotes Samuel Johnson on "my work which would in time be ended / tho not completed" ("*A*" 181, 396). *An* is also a common abbreviation for "anonymous," confirming the displacement of the authorial voice noted above. This anonymity—together with the shift to *An*—was in fact forecast in the Objectivist passage of "*A*"-6, with its stressed contrast of *My* to *An* and its linking of *An* with "objective" (My one voice, My other; An objective, An objective). In mathematics, "a" represents a definite, known, quantity, while "n" represents an indefinite quantity: *An* multiplies the definite by the indefinite, thereby embodying Zukofsky's sense that certainty is always mixed with uncertainty, and that we therefore can never be certain ("*A*" 180–81). The absolute implied by the poem's initial quest is inextricably bound to, or bound in with, the contingent. The first half of the poem closes with an enactment of this incorporation of the *A*, of the absolute, into the poem's processes. Recalling how Bach signed his name to the *Art of the Fugue* by using the notes B, A, C, H as a theme, "*A*"-12 uses the same device to come to a close. The threading of these letters extends over several pages and then is quickly recapitulated at the end in a formulaic epithet for the poet's wife ("*A*" 261). Here *A* is no longer *the* note but *a* note among others, the objectively perfect incorporated as one moment in the development of the paratactic structure, as one moment in the ongoing process of desire.

This incorporation of the poem's objective gives it a distinctive relation to temporality. In marked contrast to the "too precipitous end" of *Poem beginning "The"*, the second half of "*A*" seems much more relaxed, more assured, than the first half. The *An* sections make no attempt to defeat or surmount time; they are on the contrary "faring no cause to an unowned end" ("*A*" 393; note the play on *an* here). Consequently, Zukofsky "need not rush at the book"; the poem comes to create, to inhabit, what the twelfth movement terms "the new Time" ("*A*" 179). As Samuel Johnson had pointed out, the end occurs *in time*, not *after*. There is no need to hurry, now that the modernist quest, the teleological drive of the poem, has unraveled. This leisured approach to time also has an ethical dimension: anyone who "writes hurried by / eagerness to the end" is likely to hurry by, to brush aside, specific human rights for the sake of that end ("*A*" 396). And of course "*A*"-24, written by Celia Zukofsky as a present for Louis, does provide the poem with an end unowned and unforeseen by its author ("*A*" 536).

We can distinguish two distinct ways to conceive this new time. The first would be as a postapocalyptic time, a postmodern time, after the end of teleology, if not of history. "*A*"-19 takes up this sense when it explicitly presents itself as an "encore," as simply "another" song in a series. The movement combines an account of a violin recital by Paul Zukofsky with an homage to Mallarmé, the poet's son having given him a copy of Mallarmé's work. As an encore, the piece plays repeatedly on a sense of being unhurriedly late, of arriving after the climax but *in time*, echoing Mallarmé's sense in his "Crisis in Poetry" that being late is the true condition of freedom (*Selected Poetry* 75). "*A*"-12 offers a different perspective, a corrective suggesting that what *must* be born—what of necessity *is*—can never be late ("*A*" 179). But the frame of reference is not solely literary, for the movement also marks the twentieth anniversary of the bombing of Hiroshima, "Hiroshima's 'A' " ("*A*" 426). A striking passage locates the poem's practice in relation to the blast of that *A*, as well as to its own first half:

> ploughs will
> not hurry
> a path
> A legacy
> windfall of
> a rush
> of notes
> falling together
>   ("*A*" 433)

The *An* sections' new temporality, their leisurely but attentive pace, occurs in the aftermath of *A* and of the Bomb. The new Time is a time beyond the End, a time of the aftermath: postmodern, postnuclear, postapocalypse. Seen in the context of this new practice, the fallout of the Bomb can itself become a windfall—the *felix culpa* of postmodernity. Through its language practice, the poem suggests the possibility of a postnuclear politics, of a social practice that would also situate itself in this new Time—a pragmatics that, ever alert to the incidental, would affirm the multiplicity of life *after* the End, rather than sacrifice that multiplicity in order to *achieve* the End.

    The *An* that begins the movement suggests a different but complementary model of this temporality:

> An other
>   song—you
> want another
>   ("*A*" 408)

We may want another, but Zukofsky will supply an *other* song: not merely another in a series, postapocalyptic, but an alternate song, a practice that occurs contemporaneously with, but alongside, the apocalyptic. The "new Time" is not marked by a transcendence (amounting to the achievement) of teleology, but by a different relation to teleology, a tactical practice that persists alongside, continuously undoing, the drive for strategic totality. Only in the realm of the conquering Idea does the lack of a totalizing myth, a great narrative, appear "a crisis the poet must overcome or die from . . . having become too radioactive" (*P* 10). Whether we would lament or celebrate it, we need not proclaim post-modernism as the new Idea. For there can be no condition beyond apocalypse, no condition of postmodernism, once and for all beyond modernism. We should not strive for the end, but neither can we position ourselves beyond the end. In *Bottom's* terms, the end subsists in the whole process. In her fine study of Zukofsky's *80 Flowers*, Michele Leggott notes the poet's coinage, in an interesting notebook entry on *a, an,* and *the,* of the term "*an*historical" (49). Leggott remarks that "*anhistorical,* suggesting *without* history . . . is somehow stronger than *unhistorical*" (50). But the distinction is not simply a matter of strength. To be unhistorical is to be bereft, ignorant of history, while to be an-historical is to be outside, but still alongside history. The neologism carries a sense of its own displacement, of the possibility of being both inside and out-side history: an historical anhistorical. The pragmatic politics implicit in the poem rejects even the apocalyptic inherent in the Idea of postmodernism.

"*A*" rejects attempts to transcend temporality, however such a transcen-dence may be figured. This rejection is evident in the distinctions "*A*"-19 makes between its own practice and Mallarmé's desire for the objectively per-fect, for a book that would take the place of all other books and even of "the world itself" ("*A*" 423). The desire may be understandable—even unavoid-able—but Zukofsky's rejection is clear: he would prefer not to "preempt" his "horse from / actual pavement" ("*A*" 422). Even Zukofsky's *All: The Collected Shorter Poems* is finally careful to situate itself as a part, rather than *all*.[20] And Mallarmé, the poem suggests, was not himself late—and so free—but "a last mind," presumably because he remained committed to a great narrative culmi-nating in the Great Book, the book as strategic end, a summation engulfing—like abstraction and like the Bomb—the entire universe ("*A*" 423, 422). Mallarmé seeks freedom *from* time, not *of* time.[21] Accordingly, "*A*" 's relation to chance is also markedly distinct from Mallarmé's. In contrasting Mallarmé to Nietzsche, Deleuze observes that the French poet's dice throw is finally an appeal to necessity rather than a commitment to chance: "chance is like exis-tence which must be denied, necessity like the character of the pure idea or the eternal essence. So that the last hope of the dice throw is that it will find its intelligible model in the other world" (33). Chance and temporality would be redeemed in necessity and eternity. Zukofsky's "windfall," by contrast, em-braces temporality and affirms the "falling together" of chance. We need not either overcome or die from chance; harmony occurs through chance, not as its transcendence. Hence the poem accepts both the accidents of history and of the poet's life, particularly as these are manifested in the caprices that may determine a word's meaning. Rather than attempt to master chance and make language *ours*, "A" embraces words "*hourly* shifting" ("A" 395; italics added).

"A" proposes a materialist poetics grounded in uncertainty and multiplicity, in the accidental and the contingent: not the theological Word, but material words.[22] This poetics is not the result of mere preference, for it actually constitutes an explicit acceptance of the inescapable material conditions of writing. "A"-18 usefully quotes Samuel Johnson on his own struggle with linguistic material:

> Sounds are too volatile for
> legal restraints. To enchain syllables and to lash
> the wind are equally undertakings of pride unwilling
> to measure its desires by its strength.
>
> ("A" 395)

The attempt to construct an ideal Book is an instance, inevitably doomed to failure, of the hubris of an unchecked desire for the objectively perfect. In the later movements of "A", words are always in excess of reason. The writer cannot become master, the text cannot subsume all, because, as Johnson again tells us,

> he whose design includes
> whatever language can express must often speak of
> what he does not understand
>
> ("A" 396)

It is characteristic that Zukofsky would state a central tenet of his poetics by means of citations, by means of unowned words.

But a materialist poetics is not simply an acknowledgment of the inevitable condition of language. Once made an explicit principle, the materiality of language becomes a means of freedom, a means of escaping the conquering Idea. One's words do not so much fail to live up to an ideal as they always succeed in escaping it, in exceeding it. *Thanks to the Dictionary* had noted the political implications of this excess at the very time that Pound was championing Mussolini: "As against any dictator, there is that book containing the words of a language, modes of expression, diction" (*CF* 290). As M. M. Bakhtin reminds us, every word "tastes" of the multiple "contexts in which it has lived its socially charged life" (293). No one can dictate the exclusion of such contexts, of such multivalent lives, for any word embodies intersecting, often incommensurate forces. In Zukofsky's context, "that book" could refer to the dictionary, to *Thanks to the Dictionary*, or to "A", which is to say that it refers to all three—

and to any text insofar as it is acknowledged as a transitory, historical object. A multiplicity of meanings always directs attention away from the univocal dictator and toward the material conditions of those meanings' production.

Of course, "any dictator" may refer not only to political dictators, but to the author and reader as well. These referents bring us to the particular difficulty and challenge of reading *"A"*. It is not simply that the poem requires an extraordinary attention to each word, to its multiple possible significations, for many authorities have spoken of postmodernism in such terms. But Zukofsky's text disclaims such authority: the poem requires a willingness to accept a mix of the known and unknown, a willingness to inhabit the work in a condition of uncertainty, to live with the hourly shifting of words. When a word as apparently simple as "An" performs such diverse functions—functions set in motion but not controlled by the author—when a word can signify anything the dictionary or dialect allows, when it can be broken down into signifying components, replaced by homophones, or included in larger homophonic units, and when syntax is treated similarly, then it becomes impossible to establish any external point by which to organize the text. Object and subject become possibilities of the text rather than ends. Reading therefore also becomes a tactical practice; we may choose our entrance and exit points, but we should focus on the process or production of the text, rather than search for some stable representation or reproduction—we should focus on the "whole process of desire," rather than on the perfection for which it longs (*B* 98). Neither the author nor the reader can master the poem; often, especially in later movements, we cannot master even a line. To read *"A"* is necessarily to acknowledge and become complicit in a process constantly demonstrating, by traversing, the limits of authority: the writer's, the reader's, that of reason itself, above all the authority of the End, whether it be figured as Book or Bomb. Just as the absolute is multiplied, displaced, and dispersed in *An*, so in *"A"*-19 the Bomb that would redeem us from time by ending time (and us) itself becomes "the balm / of time"—and time itself, Beckett's "double-headed monster of damnation and salvation," becomes embodied, embedded, in an herb (*"A"* 410; Beckett 1).

"With Backward Glance"

Yet reason and love, as Zukofsky's Bottom laments, are still apt to keep little company together nowadays (*B* 9). Intent on a grander panorama, whether it be in the domain of history or theory, we are apt to overlook the words, the music, in the poem before us. Thus we are prone to speak, and so I speak here, of the nuclear, of fascism, of Marxism, of the Bomb, of ends, and of the End. To take Zukofsky's text seriously, to accept its challenge, must be to take up the play of that text in detail, not merely as a stage in another argument. In April 1971 Zukofsky gave a talk and reading on the occasion of the University of Connecticut's annual Wallace Stevens Memorial Program and Awards, in the course of which he read, as an antiphonal response to Stevens' "Puella Parvula," the recently completed " 'An' song beginning 'A'-22."[23] That song, in its various forms of publication, provides a fine example of *"A"* 's late poetics:

> AN ERA
> ANY TIME
> OF YEAR
>   *("A"* 508)

First published as a Poetry Post Card in 1970, this must rank as one of the most curious poems ever written. No verb or copula is even implied; the piece seems like a direction for the setting of a play—or, better, an invitation *to* play. I do not wish to become enmeshed in the many permutations of these words, these letters, but I would note in passing that *I am* is contained in *time,* and that both these abstractions are bracketed by the concrete *ear* found in *era* and *year* (and *year* rhymes *yere* and *yeer,* both archaic forms of *ear).*[24] Indeed, all six words of the poem are grounded in that final *ear,* giving us a brief mouthful of song that arises from and is grounded in the ear. But however much speculation may be provoked by these and other relationships suggested by the poem, the work remains defiant of attempts at paraphrase. In effect the piece is rather like the sophisticated mathematics of, say, quantum physics, wherein a formula may exhibit great elegance and grace, yet completely resist translation into a more prosaic logic.

To be sure, general concerns can be established: the poem obviously has to do with time, in particular with the relation between large "segments" of time and the present moment. An era leads up to and is thus contained in any given moment, while that moment in turn gives rise to and so contains an era. There is, then, a fullness to every moment that suggests (but the poem does not assert it) a timelessness within time, an eternity in an hour. Thus we may infer from the poem, as from the world, a Blakean transcendence, but the poem, again like the world, makes no explicit claim. The poem suggests, rather, the "new time" announced in *"A"*-12 and embodied in the "An" songs.

It is the play of sight and sound in this poem, however, that predominates. By this I do not mean images—it evokes no images—but the material play of sight and sound: the sound of the phonemes, the sight of the letters, reflecting and reverberating through the poem. Zukofsky's language establishes connections and correspondences that transgress those customary to rational discourse, or even to poetic discourse. And with its intricate activity and sheer playfulness the poem can create the situation to which it refers: if we allow ourselves to become involved in the activity, we do indeed become absorbed in the present moment, the present era. Reference and description are not ends, but moments within the overall process, specific modes within the larger context of the "sounded contacts" mentioned in *"A"*-6 (*"A"* 37).

Sounded contacts, sounded contexts: it is this sounding that takes the place of "depth" in Zukofsky's poetry. The second part of the "An" song, published separately as *Initial* in 1970, plays with an extraordinarily complex multiplicity of such connections. Consider the first stanza:

> Others letters a sum owed
> ages account years each year
> out of old fields, permute
> blow blue up against yellow
> —scapes welcome young birds—initial
>> (*"A"* 508)

The general lack of context is reinforced by the frustration of our syntactic expectations initiated by the first two words. "Others letters" with the copula understood would make sense but is unlikely because we have no referent for "others"; another reading would put a copula between "others" and "a sum owed," with "letters" glossing "others": Others (letters) are a sum owed. The most obvious reading, of course, would be "others' letters"—yet without the apostrophe, there is no reason to settle on this particular meaning: the words are free to pursue their own course, as indeed they are forced to do, since they are not limited to one syntax. But the complexities of the first line do not end here. "Letters," in addition to those handled by the post office, could refer to the letters of the alphabet, especially in a poem called *Initial* by a poet who had by 1970 published twenty-one movements of a life's work called *"A"*. In fact, a reader unaware of the Poetry Post Card may not even think of post-office letters. The word also has some verbal force, suggesting painstaking attention to detail and an approach to writing based on words as intricate objects rather than mere signifiers. "A sum owed," as noted above, would seem to be connected to the first two words by an omitted copula, but "a sum" also puns on "assume" (the apparent proposition is only an assumption), while "owed" rhymes "ode" (which label could be affixed to this poem). If we read the poem in the different context of *"A"*-22, however, and if we know that the Poetry Post Card was printed in blue and yellow, the whole of this first stanza can be

read as a meditation on the postcard, and "owed" can be read as *zeroed*. Others'
letters were a sum that was owed, but the postcards have now zeroed that
debt.

Multiplicity continues: reading the first two lines,

Others letters a sum owed
ages account years each year

we can either end-stop the first or run on into the next, as in "a sum owed for
ages." And "ages account" can be read as "age is a count," perhaps providing
an intermediary thought to connect the counting of others' letters to the more
general "ages account." Clearly, a line-by-line exegesis is not possible, for the
readings multiply and compound with each new word or phrase. As with "AN
ERA," however, we can still gain a general sense of the poem's concerns. For
the moment the following should suffice:

Others letters a sum owed
ages account years each year
out of old fields, permute
blow blue up against yellow
—scapes welcome young birds—initial

transmutes itself, swim near and
read a weed's reward—grain
an omen a good omen
the chill mists greet woods
ice, flowers—their soul's return

let me live here ever,
sweet now, silence foison to
on top of the weather

The general impression of an Edenic world is confirmed by the last three lines,
the first two being adapted from *The Tempest* (we are on Prospero's island) and
the last suggesting the transcendent view attained in the *Dream of Scipio* and
in the final lines of *Troylus and Criseyde*.[25] We can be more particular here: given
the title, even a cursory reading will isolate "initial / transmutes itself" as a key
statement. But to what might "initial" refer? The lines preceding would appear
to give instances (or an instance) of initial transmuting itself, but they do not
provide any clear referent. Here one apparently small difference between *Initial*
and the twenty stanzas incorporated into "A"-22 becomes significant. While in
"A"-22 the type is uniform throughout, *Initial* begins with an oversize capital
O, so that "initial," meaning "an extra-large capital letter at the start of a
printed paragraph, chapter, etc." can refer to the *O* (*Webster's New World*). (This

is reinforced by the heavily stressed /o/ of "owed," as also by the later "old," "blow," and "yellow.") Here the word itself shows initial transmuting itself while remaining invariant, for "initial" also denotes what is primary, "of or pertaining to a beginning" (*OED*), while "O" can represent omega, the end.[26] The two together point to the identity (or near-identity) of "the initial and conclusion of the world" (*OED*). And since "O" also indicates zero, the whole remains zero while nevertheless constituting *all*. "Initial transmutes itself" thus states what may be the essential activity of the universe, for "*A*" as, in another language, for Spinoza. It is also one way, we should note, of describing "*A*".

The seasons enter the poem as instance of recurrence, of the world transmuting itself. But the first phrase concerning them, "out of old fields," has wider implications, being a quotation from Chaucer's *Parliament of Fowls*. Note that the context, although appropriate, has been dropped:

For out of olde feldes, as men seyth,
Cometh al this newe corn fro yer to yere,
And out of olde bokes, in good feyth,
Cometh al this newe science that men lere.
  (566)

Implied by Zukofsky's use of the quotation is a correspondence between the continuity-with-change of the natural world and the continuity-with-change of human activity (here, literature from Chaucer to Zukofsky). The line also alludes to the epigram of *Poem beginning 'The'*—"And out of olde bokes, in good feith"—thus drawing attention to the continuity of Zukofsky's own work despite the changes wrought by nearly half a century.

Transmutation and continuity permeate the language of this poem. At first a puzzling phrase (if we forget, for the moment, the postcard), "blow blue up against yellow" adopts a technique first used extensively by Gertrude Stein, that of using colors as nouns rather than adjectives in contexts where we would expect adjectives. It is another means of depriving particulars of their context. But the dictionary, as usual, can provide all we *need* to know: blue is "often taken as the colour of constancy or unchangingness," while yellow is often used "of the complexion in age or disease; also as the colour of faded leaves, ripe corn, old discoloured paper, etc.; hence *allusively*" (*OED*). An era any time of year. Words themselves can undergo almost alchemical changes, as in the common origin of English "blue" and Latin *flavus*, "yellow," in Indo-European *bhle-wos*, meaning "light-colored, blue, blond, yellow" (*Webster's New World*). Initial transmutes itself.

This last connection between "blue" and "yellow" remains hidden, never being explicitly mentioned in the poem itself. There are other such connections. Given the immediately preceding "old fields," "yellow" could refer to a field of grain (supported by stanza two's "grain"), and "blue" could in that case refer to a weed growing in the field (stanza two also includes "weed"). The weed is probably darnel, "a weedy rye grass (*Lolium temulentum*) often occurring in grainfields" (*Webster's New World*). The Greeks called the plant αἶρα; it was considered ὑπνώτεκος, which means "sleep-inducing" but puns our "hypnotic" (and the blurred, alogical syntax of *Initial* mimes the narrative syntax of a dream vision). But αἶρα points in another direction, to what probably generated the weed in stanza two: the bilingual pun of Greek αἶρα and Latin *aere*, whence our "era"—indeed, αἶρα seems as though it ought to be the source of, or cognate with, *aere*. (It is neither.) This connection suggests that Zukofsky traced "era" to its Latin root, noted (chanced upon?) the rhyme with the Greek word, and therefore included in *Initial* the weed that αἶρα denotes—though not by name. Hidden linkages exist between one line and another ("blue" and "weed," among others, in *Initial*) and between one poem and another (αἶρα connects "AN ERA" to *Initial*; another connection is an alternate reference for "initial" as an "extra-large capital letter": in "A"-22 it could refer to the whole of "AN ERA"). The poem exploits the resources of language, especially sound correspondences, but often includes only the apparently disparate particulars, omitting any key to the origin: how, other than by chance, can bilingual puns in other languages be detected on the basis of Zukofsky's text?[27]

Evident in all this activity is the poet's desire to include—not so much the world, but as many aspects of each word as the poem can be made to admit. Opportunities are seized, connections and correspondences noted and incorporated; possibilities are not sacrificed to an overall system precisely because such a system would arbitrarily limit what the words say and do. We would thereby withdraw into "intellectual rarefaction," rather than keeping intellect within a larger context by "spring[ing] back to sense." *Initial* gives a vivid image of the trap of knowledge:

> fish purl in the weir:
> we are caught by our
> own knowing, barb yellow hard
> every yet—
>   ("A" 510)

In fact, two images of our situation are present here. First is the circularity imposed on us: contained by our knowledge, we are thus condemned to oscillate within its limits: when we reach one end of the weir we must turn and head in the opposite direction. So the subject circles within the discourse that constitutes it, unable to escape so long as it remains that stable subject. Second is the hook, the "yet," which is a particular from which we can abstract a general significance: it represents those qualifying clauses required by almost any statement about the world.

As, for instance, that initiated by the "yet" that divides this poem precisely in half. For *Initial* does include an argument. The first half moves from Eden to uncertainty, *Paradise Lost* and Parmenides' "Way of Truth" and "Way of Seeming" being two of the models that come to mind. The "error / if error vertigo" of stanza six calls to mind both the Fall and Descartes' doubt. As a result of the intrusion of error, Paradise can now be recognized as such, even as it is left behind:

> leaving it eyes' heat stars'
> dawn mirror to west window
> binds the sun's east—steersman's
> one guess at certainty made
> with an assemblage of naught—
>   ("A" 509)

Adam and Eve after their sin, Descartes before he posits a benevolent God, and Pound's storm-tossed raft in the *periplum* of the *Pisan Cantos* all come together in this skepticism. The poem presents a rational, "either-or" argument: if we cannot have Edenic certainty, nothing at all can be certain. But the next stanza leaves behind the abstract argument in favor of practice and valid skepticism:

> yet in cells not vacuum
> records as tho horses rushed
> definite as an aching nerve
> pleads feed and feed back—
>   ("A" 509)

We have moved away from the static subject of "knowing," which is necessarily in a position of mastery (Eden) or of being mastered (doubt).[28] Here the subject participates and is itself in a state of flux, a subject in process corresponding to the poem as object in process.

The conclusion of the poem (signaled by the stressed "so" bridging the last two stanzas) does not merely present an acceptance of this condition, but celebrates it by enacting the condition itself. Because that condition *is* our certainty, we can anchor anywhere we like and read an Eden (but not *the* Eden) in our surroundings:

> wait it is very right,
> sink killick read the kelp—
>
> cherries, knave of a valentine,
> were ever blue of yellow,
> birds, harp in three trees—
> now summer happy new year
> any time of year—so
>
> no piper lead with nonsense
> before its music don't, horse,
> brag of faith too much—
> fear thawed reach three-fingered chord
> sweet treble hold lovely—initial
>
>   (*"A"* 510)

With our fear of uncertainty thawed we need no metaphysics ("nonsense") to reach the condition epitomized here by music.[29] As an object in process, the musical chord that ends the poem is neither means nor end but both—just as music both moves toward an end and is the end. Music, however, does not replace argument; rather, the two coexist as necessary complements throughout the poem. Just as the world is both an object of thought and an event involving each of us, words, once sighted and sounded, are both physical events and signs. The triumph of music here does not mark a complete erasure of speech—if anything, the poem seems clearer in the final stanza than in the first. The reader need not, then, abandon all hope of meaning, but only refuse, always aided by the playful density of Zukofsky's language, to be bound by its limitations. The steersman—writer, reader, actor—can attempt mastery, and find himself mastered, or he can participate in the process of "feed and feed back": he can play it by ear.

Chasings

In the "An" sections, then, *"A"* achieves in practice what it could only posit contradictorily as a goal, the object of a quest, in the first half. Yet the critical question persists: "To what end?" It is the same question Williams had posed long before in *Spring and All*, one of Zukofsky's favorite texts; it had also worried Pound's work, and life, to the very end. Zukofsky himself had taken it up in *Poem beginning 'The'* and again at the end of *"A"*-6; in *Bottom* he had found it already present in Shakespeare's *Cymbeline*, and all the more critical to the atomic age. To what end? The final lines of the *Cantos* dedicate Pound's long poem to another, while the final poem of *Pictures from Brueghel* invokes the voice of the other. *"A" *'s final movement, the contrapuntal twenty-fourth, was actually composed by another, Celia Zukofsky, as a gift to the poet. *"A"*-23, the last movement written by Louis (after that gift and functioning in part as a bridge to it), uses the template of the alphabet to close its song, recapitulating many of the poem's favorite topics and favorite words, and perhaps also paying homage to Chaucer's "Prier a Nostre Dame." The letter "Q" provides an opportunity for a parenthetical summary: "Quest returns answer—'to / re-think the Caprices' " (*"A"* 563). The Caprices are no doubt Paganini's, several of which were played by Paul Zukofsky in the contest recorded in "A"-19 (and in which the first test specifically required number 23). But they are also the caprices of life, of words, of the poem. The quest provides no final answer, but enables a reenactment of these caprices through its own processes. The last line of "A"-23, "z-sited path are but us," makes clear the multiplicity of what is no longer a strategic quest but an interweaving of tactical paths. No idea, but individuals.

With its scoring of Handel's "Harpsichord Pieces" and four voices derived from Zukofsky's works, "A"-24, the last movement, presents a look back that is indeed naturally breathless. Finally, the poem explicitly requires multiple voices, multiple readers, for its realization. Yet on the final page we still read "His best words were yet to be written" (*"A"* 803), and the final punctuation of *"A"* is a question mark. To what end? Next came *80 Flowers*, eighty poems for the poet's eightieth birthday (finished well ahead of schedule), and then *90 Trees*, conceived as ninety poems for his ninetieth birthday. The last project was scarcely begun when it was prematurely ended, in 1978, by Zukofsky's death—that other naturally breathless goal toward which, *"A"* quietly insists, we need not hurry.

5

Ending

Listen Willie, said Brewsie, you kind of think I go over it all too much,
you're like anybody with a story, you want the middle to go faster but
that's it Willie, that's it, it is going too fast, got to slow it down, got,
sure then you want the end, but Willie there isn't any end,
you got to go slower, sure there is an answer.

—*Brewsie and Willie*

EVEN ON HER deathbed Gertrude Stein reminded us that the question of the answer remains unanswered. Her works insist that we have always to begin again, over and over again. "Everywhere the world over everybody has to begin again," she wrote in a 1936 article, "My Last About Money" (337). There she was protesting the strategic "organization" that had come to dominate America and the world. But beginning again, casting off the security of organization, could never be so easy. As Stein recognized, "the more they began organization the more everybody wanted to be organized and the more they were organized the more everybody liked the slavery of being in an organization" (336–37). Instead of beginning again, everybody continued to pursue the interests of organization, and the process of organization continued into another world war. And the war, we know, only increased the speed with which strategic organization expanded, only increased its reach. Undoubtedly the same process continues today, even as we replace the "organization man" with that new professional, the new entrepreneur: its latest guise. To what end, indeed?

For at least a sense of an ending, we might well return to Stein, and particularly to her last book, *Brewsie and Willie*. The book is not so much a narrative as an extended conversation, the overheard conversation of American GIs, at the end of World War II, awaiting their repatriation. It is an interesting moment, this: for while these ordinary Americans have been outside America for a long time, they are now also tenuously outside its purposes. It is not that they have another point of view, of course, for they have no alternate position. Yet if they have no place, they are also afforded a new glimpse, at least, of their country and the world. They are worried about America, these GIs, worried about the world and their place within it; they are especially worried about their imminent return to the world of "job-mindedness" and to a standard of living so high it is "on top of you all the time" (*Brewsie* 104, 33). Even Willie, neither a thinker nor a talker, is critical of America's belief in "a bigger and better country, a bigger and better industry, a bigger and better war" (73). The question is implicit throughout Stein's text: toward what end, toward what *human* end, could such a system move? What now distinguishes America's power, Stein's GIs know, is the Bomb. Yet they already recognize that America has "not so got" the atomic bomb; they see that the Bomb, on the contrary, has got America, and with it the world.

Only for the moment are the GIs free men and women who can think and listen to thinking; once back home, secure in their places, they will again become "job men," they will stop thinking and stop listening, they will "all feel alike" (*Brewsie* 103, 55). America's political and economic rationalization of the individual prohibits actual thinking, allowing only Gallup poll categorizations of the already thought: yes or no, republican or democrat, yes or no. Yet to engage thinking itself, the process of thinking rather than the recycling of the already thought, is difficult and uncertain. It leads to no place, and often produces no clear and recognizable results. So Brewsie thinks, while the others listen and interject occasional comments. Stein's text, though, does not offer a solution. For all her cheerful enthusiasm with regard to things American, *Brewsie and Willie* is not an optimistic book. Brewsie can "almost see something," but it remains a barely glimpsed possibility. Perhaps it never can be modeled, but only glimpsed, intuited. At the end, the GIs still doubt that one can exist as a job-chaser, that one can exist in a society dominated by strategic organization and job-mindedness, and still think and listen—and still live. At best, says Willie, they will have dim memories of an elsewhere: "Brewsie will talk but we wont be there to listen, we kind of will remember that he's talking somewhere but we wont be there to listen" (110–11).

Yet there are glimpses of hope: if we cannot have "some kind of hope," at least it is "kind of there" (105). The point is, of course, precisely not to get to the end, not to seize possession of the solution—an impossibility in any case. Instead, the text suggests a turning aside from economic and political systematizations, away from the Bomb, to what Stein calls "pioneering," which is to say to the improvisation of living rather than the mechanical pursuit of organization. Once organization has triumphed, there is no interest in its pursuit. At one point Willie asks Janet, "do you want us to drop our atomic bombs on ourselves, is that what you want, so we can go out and pioneer, is that the idea." Janet responds, "Well yes kind of" (83). The difficulty, of course, is to articulate this *kind of*, the difference it makes. Having seen the singular end of organization, how can we escape that end? So Brewsie sees the difficulty, speaking to Willie but for any one of us: "you're like anybody with a story, you want the middle to go faster but that's it Willie, that's it, it is going too fast, got to slow it down, got, sure then you want the end, but Willie there isn't any end, you got to go slower, sure there is an answer" (62). And so, as he continues to articulate the question, Brewsie first shifts from *the* answer to *an* answer and then renounces answers in favor of a way of living: "perhaps," he tells Willie, "if I tell you all about it all over you'll come to the answer too, not an answer but a way to go on" (62). "All over," we should note, refers both to a rebeginning and to a telling whose end is shown to be ever-present—inhering in the whole process of desire, not limited by but including its demand for an answer.

It is talking, rendered as an ongoing process of mutual thinking, as an articulation of differences leading to ever greater definition and making ever finer distinctions—or at least showing such definition and distinction—that offers the surest way to go on. As Robert Creeley writes, a life of talking provides "a way of thinking of itself in the very fact and feeling of existence. God knows one wants no end to that ever" (8). So Stein's text shows a way to go on, not through a struggle toward another, utopian discourse, beyond strategic organization, but through a contextualizing, a resiting, of narrative, of argument, of discourse, within the interweaving of its various voices. Each voice having its own end, there can be no singular end. Brewsie's argument is only a moment within an ongoing story, one stage within the conversation, the interrelation of disparate thinkings, in which he acts—in which he thinks. So, too, Stein resites Brewsie's story within the multiplicity of ongoing conversations and intersecting narratives that constitute her *Brewsie and Willie*. And with its coda adding Stein's own address "To Americans" to the conversation, the book is in turn situated explicitly as an act, as an invention and an intervention within a larger, ongoing and unfolding field of actions. It was as a conversationalist and as a writer of conversation that Stein became best known. In *Brewsie and Willie* Pauline identifies her "with great solemnity" as "that Stein woman who says things" (50). Stein's mode here and throughout her works is not simply dialogical but paralogical. The answer is already all over in *Brewsie and Willie*, to be found in the diverse varieties and pleasures of human intercourse, pleasures that can persist alongside any strategic organization.

Willie listens to Brewsie, and finds relief in that listening. But he does not listen so much that he forgets to be natural: he is interested in thinking as practice, he will not settle on theory at the expense of practice. We might usefully figure the relation between the two characters in terms of the supplementarity of theory and practice suggested by Foucault and Deleuze, but that is perhaps still too rigid a model (205–08). Brewsie's thinking does not culminate in a theoretical model because it is part of a conversational practice, while Willie's practice is intimately involved in his listening to Brewsie's thinking. Then, too, there are all the other characters, the other voices, that surface throughout the book. Stein suggests that thinking, writing, living, figuring—all forms of inventing—occur alongside even the figure of supplementarity. Pauline perhaps comes closest to articulating an answer. Just visible, at the margins of the text, as it were, are traces of her developing relationship with Willie. When he asks where she lives, she responds, "Oh I just live" (82). Pauline recognizes that she has no proper place, that in the postwar world no one has a place of her own. Stein, too, answered the Bomb by saying we should "just live along like always" ("Reflection" 161). We should note the word "along" here, referring as it does not only to the act of going on, but also to a way of going on. It is precisely this freedom from place that offers us the potential to become pioneers, that allows us to pursue the "spiritual pioneer fight" necessary if we are to go on apart from, or rather alongside, organization (*Brewsie* 113).

The term "postmodern," whether what is meant by it is celebrated or vilified, inevitably suggests a going beyond, an escape from the limitations of modernism. Yet it is clear that much of what now goes by the name of postmodernism, in the media and in the university, while perhaps offering the appearance of innovation and freedom, all the while furthers the exigencies and submits to the demands of strategic organization. Equally clearly, and acknowledged by Stein and Zukofsky, the tactical improvisation by which I have characterized the postmodern moment can never succeed modernism; the two necessarily coexist. Indeed, this postmodern moment has always been present within modernism, and only became more apparent, more widespread, after World War II.

To gain a better sense of Stein's "alongside" relation—what Zukofsky embodies in the new Time of *An*—a better term, I think, would be the *para*modern, by which I mean those practices that acknowledge an inability to succeed modernism but that nevertheless refuse to accede to strategic organization. This term is obviously related to other usages: paratactics, paralogy, and so on. To the extent that we can speak of their place, these practices are always situated alongside the modern. They do not replace it, but resite it, strategies becoming tactics, tactics becoming strategies, and so on, each extending into the other, marking limits. From the perspective of strategic organization, such practices will remain precisely beside the point: groundless, ill defined, haphazard, and disruptive. It may be a formless, even a monstrous project I speak of—but these are also attributes of the sublime. It is perhaps in another sense altogether that Stein's "just live along" must also mean *to live justly*. This practice of the paramodern manifests that resistance that is also an expansion of actual possibility.

Notes

Chapter 1. From Modern Strategy to Postmodern Tactics

1. For an account of immediate apocalyptic responses to the atomic bomb, see Boyers 230–40.

2. The political dimensions of Stein's compositional procedure become evident when she turns directly from composition to politics: "Just as everybody has the vote, including the women, I think children should, because as soon as a child is conscious of itself, then it has to me an existence and has a stake in what happens" (17).

3. Interestingly, Dwight MacDonald made a similar observation in 1946, with reference not to the millennium and Christianity, but to the "future" and socialism: "Scientific progress has reached its end [goal], and the end is turning out to be the end of man himself. . . . Now that we confront the actual, scientific possibility of The End being written to human history and at a not so distant date, the concept of the future, so powerful an element in traditional socialist thought, loses for us its validity" (qtd. in Boyers 236). As Derrida asserts (in a somewhat different context), "one can no longer oppose belief and science, *doxa* and *épistémè*, once one has reached the decisive place of the nuclear age, in other words, once one has arrived at the critical place of the nuclear age" (24). The Bomb repeatedly reveals such structural homologies between seemingly distinct systems, uniting them in a common end, or End.

4. For the agonistic *context*, see Ong, *Fighting for Life*.

5. A related argument can be found in Emmanuel Levinas' *Totality and Infinity*. Derrida's "No Apocalypse, Not Now," though seldom explicit, is evidently based on a similar line of reasoning.

6. For a discussion of the end of the "authenticity paradigm" of death in the face of the twentieth century's "death event," see Wyschogrod, *Spirit in Ashes*. Wyschogrod's "death event," though subsuming all forms of "man-made mass death," including the atomic bomb, derives primarily from the experience of the World War II death camps.

7. For a good account of the development, with special reference to military strategy, see Brodie, *Strategy in the Missile Age*.

8. Of course, as the Strategic Defense Initiative or "Star Wars" proposal indicates, proponents of technology still try to attain an ever higher level of strategy.

9. The "one world or none" movement, quite strong after Hiroshima, indicates the accuracy of Wells' psychological insight.

10. See particularly Robbins, chapter 4, "Belligerent Aims" (103–26), and Brodie, *Strategy*, 61–70.

11. See, for example, Jung's account of his struggles with *Ulysses* in "*Ulysses*: a Monologue." For Eliot, see "Ulysses, Order and Myth."

12. The various attempts to develop such an architecture indicate that the fragmentation evident in Modernism is not merely mimetic of the modern world, but the first stage of the restructuring noted by Williams.

13. The explicit internationalism of Joyce and Pound provides the most obvious instances of this general tendency; Williams, whose insistence on America seems an exception, in fact regards America as the only means to transcend the petty nationalism of the European states.

14. See Power's *Conversations With James Joyce* and Berrone's *James Joyce in Padua.*

15. For an overview of the relationship between Williams and Zukofsky, see Baldwin's articles and Quartermain, "Actual Word Stuff."

16. According to Stein's own account, it was in *Matisse, Picasso, and Gertrude Stein* that "words began to be for the first time more important than the sentence structure or the paragraphs," and *Tender Buttons* was "the apex of that" (*A Primer* 17–18).

The Dadaists might also be considered as evincing the practice of tactics. However, they seem more akin to the typical military strategy of World War I, followed especially by Foch: direct attack, with no attention to defense, heedless of consequences.

Chapter 2. Pound's War

1. For a good account of Gaudier-Brzeska's death, the dissolution of Vorticism, and Pound's response, see Kenner, *The Pound Era.*

2. It is important to note that "absolute speed" in Deleuze and Guattari does not refer to immediacy, but to a distinction between *movement* and speed: "a movement may be very fast, but that does not give it speed; a speed may be very slow, or even immobile, yet it is still speed. Movement is extensive; speed is intensive. Movement designates the relative character of a body considered as 'one,' and which goes from point to point; *speed, on the contrary, constitutes the absolute character of a body whose irreducible parts (atoms) occupy or fill a smooth space in the manner of a vortex*" (381).

3. Whether that world of feudal dignity ever really existed does not, of course, affect the poems' appeal.

4. *SL* 123, with emendation from the manuscript in the Beinecke Library, Yale University.

5. Later the *Cantos* would celebrate Pound's grandfather for his effort to build railroads, and Jefferson for his effort to build canals. Mussolini, of course, also produced progress in the realm of transportation.

6. A full description of the various proposed taxonomies of the apocalyptic is unnecessary to my present discussion. The three major strains of apocalyptic I discuss are a selection from Robinson's more complex, and for my purposes unnecessary, scheme of five: "(1) the *biblical* prediction of an imminent end to history, controlled by God so as to provide for a paradisal continuation; (2) the *annihilative* prediction of an imminent end to history controlled by no God at all and followed by the void; (3) the *continuative* prediction of no end at all, but of simple secular

historical continuity; (4) the *ethical* internalization of apocalyptic conflict as a figure for personal growth in ongoing history; and (5) the *Romantic* or visionary internalization of the fallen world by an act of imaginative incorporation, so that the world is revealed as the paradise it already is" (26).

7. Other references to an imminent millennium are scattered through the New Testament: for example, 1 Pet. 4:7; 1 Cor. 16:22; 2 Cor. 6:2; Phil. 4:5; Jas. 5:8.

8. No doubt part of Pound's attraction to painting, sculpture, and music was because it was easier to see that works in those fields were not simply media for ideas.

Some contemporaries, such as May Sinclair and Jean de Bosschère, came very close to noting the visionary basis of Imagism and its transcending of discourse: Sinclair remarks that "the Image is not a substitute; it does not stand for anything but itself. . . . You cannot distinguish between the thing and its image" (88–89) ["Two Notes," *Egoist* 2 (1915)]; de Bosschère comments that Pound "is free and without rhetoric—no one more so. His vision is direct; he does not use the image, but shows the things themselves with power" (27) ["Ezra Pound," *Egoist* 4 (1917)] (qtd. in Schneidau 56).

9. For Pound's view of the pivotal significance of *Ulysses* at this time (1922–23), see *PJ* 192–211.

10. Pound assumes, via Kung, that his ethics are continuous and consistent: inner vision leads to familial peace, to societal peace, and thus to proper conditions for individual vision. However, his own insistence in the 1930s on a dissociation of ideas points to a break in this ordered continuity: an effect may be evil even though the intent be good, and of course vice versa. Pound, for example, was willing to distort his own statements in order to produce the proper effect in a particular audience.

11. Bush qualifies the importance of Canto 4, remarking that although "*Three Cantos II* describes" and "Canto IV presents," "under the surface, *Three Cantos II* and Canto IV are very much alike," and therefore "we must be careful . . . not to overemphasize Canto IV as *the* turning point in the evolution of the *Cantos*" (200, 205). Froula, however, argues strongly for its importance as "a first completed step" that exemplifies "in microcosm Pound's struggle in *The Cantos* to bring together modern history and a 'paradisal' language" (8, 6). Froula's phrasing here points directly to the importance of the apocalyptic narrative to the construction of Canto 4 and by extension to the *Cantos* as a whole.

12. All references to the unpublished drafts of Canto 4 are to Froula's edition and follow her numbering of those drafts.

13. The poet's authority also stems from his previous visit to the underworld, originally presented in Canto 3 and subsequently shifted to Canto 4.

14. The poet also sees that "smouldering boundary stones" represent the collapse of social and legal institutions, rather than the collapse of actual walls: the boundary stones Pound would have seen in the British Museum were not field markers but tablets, roughly the equivalent of real estate deeds.

15. Anthony Woodward, for example, to some extent following Hugh Kenner's emphasis, repeatedly invokes a "true Pound—the poet of Canto 49—[who] was Taoist in spirit" (48).

16. For a concise account of Pound's interest in James and Aeschylus, see Bush 175–82.

17. Odysseus' wanderings, too, are not, after all, an end in themselves; his journey is toward home, and his ports of call may be judged in part by whether and to what extent they helped or hindered that journey.

18. *LE* 52. The passage begins, "poetry is a centaur."

19. Ms. c1 records an early, fiercer version: "strike thru with the / centaur's heel" (Froula 125).

20. The revisions were actually carried out in 1923, the year Pound made a commitment to Italy by trying out life in Rapallo. See Carpenter 417–36. As Carpenter notes, Hemingway perceived the political implications of Pound's infatuation with Italy. He delayed a visit to Pound to avoid current politics—and also to avoid a walking tour of places connected to Malatesta (428). See Rainey for a good discussion of the relation between the Malatesta Cantos and Mussolini.

21. Although Pound was in fact moving toward fascism, Froula in effect has him discovering democracy in his final revisions, as the Garonne procession image "tear[s] through the fabric of the poem": "the ideology of its form and style as initially realized in MSS C and D only transposes the romantic idealism—which his commitment to history would reform—from divine spirit to an elite 'body' of poets; rather than bringing the transcendent back to earth, to history, Pound idealizes the (literary) historical. Yet Pound discovered in the very act of writing it his own error of denying actualities in an attempt to shape history to his designs" (51, 52). As I have indicated above, the Garonne procession gave Pound the opportunity to intensify, to crystallize his already well developed structure. And certainly the position of the poet remains among the elite in the final version: it is precisely the function of the elite to guide and instruct the less illumined.

22. This dual function is also suggested by the fact that the paradiso is both a temporary (three-day) experience for the speaker and a place inhabited by those who have striven for such a state: Borso, Carmagnola, Sigismundo (C 17:79).

23. To be sure, Pound also plays with the idea of the author as Authority, as a God. Canto 28 addresses the lack of less exalted, more human presences in the poem, presenting such material as an afterthought of "God the Father Eternal (Boja d'un Dio!)," who

> felt yet
> That something was lacking, and thought
> Still more, and reflected that
> The Romagnolo was lacking, and
> Stamped with his foot in the mud and
> Up comes the Romagnolo:
> > "Gard, yeh bloudy 'angman! It's me".
> (C 28:133)

The story pokes fun at excessively pious notions of both God and the Author.

24. Peter Makin, following Kenner's lead, presents a more detailed "map" of the first three books of the *Cantos*, pointing out that in 17–30 the "Earthly Paradise" is "returned to as a ground-tone roughly every other Canto" (170–71).

25. The visionary material becomes increasingly sexualized as political ten-

sions increase and as the poem moves closer to Mussolini's entrance. See Canto 39, moving toward the next major punctuation, Mussolini's entrance in Canto 41.

26. For a widely accepted reading of the passage, together with a brief account of other critical views, see Pearlman 115–24.

27. Pound also refers to Mussolini as "the Romagnol" in *Jefferson and/or Mussolini* (65).

28. Canto 13, which presents the Confucian interlude, and Canto 14, the first of the Hell Cantos, may also rhyme with those years, although there is no other indication that Pound intended such a rhyme. Canto 41, the last of "Eleven New Cantos," the next section, is rhymed with the year "XI of our era," 1933 in the fascist calendar. It is that canto, of course, that at last presents "the Boss" (202).

It is of course possible that in Canto 30 Pound is also "punning on the printer's '30'," as Pearlman points out (131, citing Max Halperen's Ph.D. dissertation). But it seems highly unlikely that Pound, intimately involved in contemporary politics, would fail to note the rhyme, or pun, with the current year. That Pearlman and Halperen could note one pun but fail to see the other illustrates the early, and to some extent understandable, critical tendency to dehistoricize Pound.

29. Canto 17 and excerpts from Cantos 20, 25, and 30, however, are used in the 1949 *Selected Poems*. The Cantos used for that selection are generally more overtly political than those chosen for the later book.

30. Pound also judged other writers by their works' contribution to the cause, at least to the cause of economic literacy. Although his pantheon of great works remained largely unchanged, they too came to be seen in less esthetic terms: "Homer's epos is real because it is concerned with the means of existence, he is concerned with how Odysseus is to be fed on his raft, and how his pig farm is to continue production" ("A National Poetry," 1938). Certainly Pound is the only great poet to have praised Homer for his interest in pig farm productivity.

31. All of these theories are in this context annexed as an anticipation of fascism, as in Gaudier-Brzeska's statement, "will and consciousness are our vortex" (*GK* 68).

32. Pound had been speaking of "egg-shell" (and therefore fragile) definitions, but shifts here to a pun on artillery shells: as a boundary preventing access to the real, then, the rational system is both fragile and extremely destructive.

33. By 1960, Pound had toned down his praise, though it is still remarkably favorable: "Apart from the social aspect he was of interest, technically, to serious writers. He never wrote a sentence that has any interest in itself, but he evolved almost a new medium, a sort of expression half way between writing and action" (*SP* 217). W. C. Williams remarked on Pound's attitude in a 1931 review of *A Draft of XXX Cantos*: "It is still a Lenin striking through the mass, whipping it about that engages his attention. That is the force Pound believes in" ("Excerpts from a Critical Sketch" 262).

34. It is difficult to determine in this instance whether Pound was fully aware of his own distortion. In the 1942 "A Visiting Card" Pound still maintained that "with the falsification of the word everything else is betrayed," but his own correspondence and propagandizing show him all too willing to falsify the word for the sake of the cause.

35. Pound to O. R. Agresti, Nov. 29, 194-, Beinecke Library, Yale University.

Pound's near obsession with the betrayal of previous revolutions (i.e., before the fascist "continual revolution") is perhaps also related to his messianic view of Mussolini and himself.

36. "L'America e le Cause della Guerra" (1944?), Beinecke Library, Yale University. Interestingly, the 1951 English translation of this passage replaces "millennial" with "secular," thereby ignoring the religious basis of Pound's wartime views (*America* 5).

37. Pound dated the actual origin of usury to "the loans of seed-corn in Babylon in the third millennium B.C." (*America* 6).

38. "Volitionist Peace" (1937), Beinecke Library, Yale University. Also, any historian who neglects the true basis of money is "the ally of corruption, he is a carrier of every bacillus of evil" ("Communications" 12).

39. "What We Are Fighting For" (June–Sept. 1941), Beinecke Library, Yale University.

40. "American Revolution" (May–April 1939), Beinecke Library, Yale University.

41. Pound was quick to recognize others' belief in mythologic narratives. Hence, despite his own belief in an imminent, but thwarted, prosperity, he criticized others' belief in it: "As far as reality is concerned, as far as you and I are concerned it makes little difference whether prosperity is in heaven, or in the year 2300, or just round a corner that will never be turned" (*Radio* 283). Similarly, he scornfully referred to others' belief that replacing a leader could "bring total salvation . . . sudden salvation," but evidently believed Mussolini would provide something like salvation (*Radio* 332).

42. This concept of governmental speed also correlates with Mussolini's "continual revolution."

43. The inexcusable "time-lag" between the development of an idea and its implementation—often the result, in Pound's eyes, of sabotage—is also a frequent refrain before and after World War II.

44. Adams actually wrote (to his brother-in-law), "I lament that it is so hasty a production. . . . But the disturbances in New England made it necessary to publish immediately, in order to do any good. . . . The field is vast enough, the materials are splendid enough, and the subject is of weight enough, to employ the greatest scholar of the age for seven years" (Adams I, 432). Peter Nicholls uses this example in his discussion of Pound's "eclipse of reason" (132–37), explaining it in terms of Pound's "desire to place as much emphasis as possible upon 'action' and 'energy' " (135).

45. Pound's ideally transparent language parallels his desire for a fully transparent monetary system, and both come to depend increasingly on sheer speed. C. H. Douglas' economic thought essentially depends on his perception of the time lag between the availability of goods and availability of money with which to buy them. And while Silvio Gesell's remedy for increasing the speed with which money would circulate may go some way toward ending monopoly and usury by in effect decreasing the materiality of money, the drive behind Pound's economic thought is clearly toward a complete transparency of the medium and a complete erasure of delay—toward an ideal, instantaneous circulation.

Pound praises mavericks who oppose the conventional economic system but does so without either detailing or entirely subscribing to their alternative systems. What he praises, in fact, is simply the ability to break out of convention, to escape systems, with their tendency toward a slow process of amelioration, in favor of a sudden insight capable of immediately transforming society. In sum, Pound's preferred mode of economic thought is as apocalyptic as his poetry: as he insisted to Zukofsky in 1935, his economics and his poetry are "NOT separate or opposed" but an "essential unity" (*PZ* 169).

46. Speaking of the book's importance, Pound wrote to Nino Sammartano, the Minister of Popular Culture, that "a philosophy is valuable to the extent that it leads to heroism" (Nov. 2, 1945, Beinecke Library, Yale University).

47. He made the same point in the British *Fascist Quarterly*, noting that the principle had already been established in practice even before Confucius: "*La Rivoluzione continua*, the principle of continuous revolution, or daily regeneration, was already there in the inscription on King Tching-Thang's tub when Confucius proclaimed it: The tree-root for growth, and the axe for clearing the rubbish, all this combined with a symbol of order" (II.4: 496).

48. Bacigalupo makes the connection between Pound's Dioce and the Duce's state (101). Stock, who quotes the inscription, speaks merely of "this beautiful image" (479). Nicholls also remarks that "there are signs that Pound conceived these Cantos as an act of direct political intervention," citing scattered references to contemporary Italy in the sequence (112).

49. Pound defends propaganda in one of his radio speeches: "There is an enormous prejudice vs. what is called propaganda. Yet almost any valid and serious statement IS propaganda in the best sense of the term. The modern world has been fed narcotic. The deadly propaganda IS precisely the shiftless, is precisely the stuff that has built up the prejudice against ALL order, and all coherence" (313). At the time of the Great War, as we have seen, he was against any attempt to "turn the class room into a hall of propaganda" (*SP* 191). While there is certainly a good deal of truth to his later viewpoint, Pound's propaganda did not generally exemplify "the best sense of the term."

50. For a discussion of the circumstances of this canto and the newspaper story it recounts, "a transparent fabrication" that Pound accepted unquestioningly, see Rainey, who also includes the original story in an appendix (214–17, 243–47).

51. Pound was not at all embarrassed by these poems immediately after the war: Charles Olson records his pride in 1946 "at having rediscovered and used a Dante method" (*Charles Olson and Ezra Pound* 69; Canto 72 is in fact a rather dull imitation of Dante). Much later, however, in the 1962 interview with Donald Hall, he denied having written any cantos during the war (47).

52. Pound also thought the radio could solve problems in America: "And if Congress won't go on the air, let the State Senators go on the air, let the State Legislatures go on the air, to compensate for the difficulties of communication . . . " (*Radio* 345).

53. "Simplest parallel I can give is radio where you tell who is talking by the noise they make" (Letter to Homer Pound, Nov. 29, 1924, qtd. in Terrell 1:75).

54. The entire passage, from the April 20, 1943 broadcast, is of interest for its simultaneous acknowledgment and sidestepping of the facts: "Certainly they are a forgery, and that is the one proof we have of their authenticity. The Jews have

worked with forged documents for the past 24 hundred years, namely ever since they have had any documents whatsoever. And no one can qualify as a historian of this half century without having examined the Protocols. Alleged, if you like to have been translated from the Russian, from a manuscript to be consulted in the British Museum, where some such document may or may not exist." Strikingly, Pound then declares that their interest lies not in whether or not they are authentic, but "in the type of mind, or the state of mind of their author," evidently completely confusing the purported and the actual author. The "state of mind" to which this argument attests, of course, is Pound's (283).

55. The line, "what whiteness will you add to this whiteness, what candor" (*C* 74:425), repeats Tzu Kung's rejection of a replacement for Confucius, the implication being that no one could be as intelligent or ethical as the sage—or, in the Pisan Cantos, as Mussolini. Pound relates the anecdote in his radio broadcast of July 3, 1943 (*Radio* 358).

56. The statement's reference is first to Pound himself, of course, but it also affirms a basic tenet of fascism, the strength of the individual will.

57. Even remembering the tradition is seen in terms of the activity rather than its product: "remember *that* I have remembered," not *what* I have remembered (80:506, emphasis added).

58. Indeed, the alternation between affirmation and negation in Canto 77 does not end with the corporal's broken heart, as the next lines present a more positive, if rather Baudelairian, response to a new day:

Bright dawn 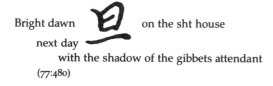 on the sht house
   next day
     with the shadow of the gibbets attendant
(77:480)

59. No source has been found for the man who stole a safe he couldn't open— Pound may even be thinking of himself (cf. "I have brought the great ball of crystal; / who can lift it? / Can you enter the great acorn of light?" [116:795]). Also, kylin does not seem especially close to *ch'i-lin*, the Chinese "fabulous animal" (Terrell 2:404).

60. The threat of imminent death produces a similar limitation on Pound's discourse, as he indicates in Canto 80: "Nothing but death, said Turgenev (Tiresias) / is irreparable" is quickly followed by "To communicate and then stop, that is the / law of discourse" (80:494). Pound's death may interrupt his communication before a synthesis can be achieved.

61. We should recall, too, that ants are also known for their warlike behavior. Mary de Rachewilz acknowledges this in her memories of Pound's action during the war: "despite all this, Babbo relentlessly kept working, like a lone ant, fighting his own battle" (197).

62. In other passages Pound blames the loss on Italy's "losing the law of Chung Ni" (77:470), on Mussolini's lack of time (78:482), and somewhat less seriously on the lack of Chinese food in Italy (80:507) or Italians' "loose taste in music"

(80:510). The last two of course point to an inadequate culture, and all support the more particular statement I quote.

63. Related to my point here is Nicholls' observation that in Pound's text "it is almost as if intellectual weakness and the very fragility of the connections which bind ideas of justice to the material base are recruited as signs of a deeper knowledge" (180).

64. Flory relates "AOI" to a cry of distress in the Noh drama (298), although it is generally assumed to have been taken from the *Chanson de Roland*, where it divides the formal sections. Both possible sources contribute to my reading.

65. Cf. *C* 79:506; 80:525.

66. Murray Schafer's remarks on the *Cantos'* analogy to the fugue are to the point here: "Ideally a fugue has no point of termination. It could continue its contrapuntal involutions without ever coming to a logical point of rest. . . . what brings a fugue to an end is no long chain of cadencing fireworks but a simple device which can be executed within as short a space as half a bar—the pedal point. When we have a pedal in a fugue we can be almost certain that the composer is getting tired and intends to stop" (141). Canto 77 explicitly acknowledges tiredness just before the end, "mind come to plenum when nothing more will go into it" (77:475), while the close of Canto 82 indicates both tiredness and depression. Others, of course, close on more triumphant notes, but all are primarily personal.

67. Speed continued to be crucial throughout the postwar period, although Pound began (at last) to despair of attaining sufficient speed. On March 14, 1946, Pound wrote to Williams: "time lag gettin moreso daily" (Beinecke Library, Yale University). As late as 1956 he warned Ralph McNair Wilson about the pitfalls of publishing: "re / yr / bloody printer / watch for sabotage and kikes onto his overdraft. I don't know how one is to move fast enuf / Or how much velocity McN, Wilson can attain" (Nov. 26, 1956, Beinecke Library, Yale University).

68. He told D. G. Bridson that the atomic bomb was "a detail. At my time of life I cannot get bogged down in details" (qtd. in Kenner, "Ezra Pound's Commedia," 56).

Chapter 3. Dr. Williams' Position

1. One example, from an early draft of "The Later Pound," may suggest Williams' perceptive critique of Pound: "Pound's insistence on Kung and his importance are all on the soundless idea, on the character. Perhaps that is the precise spot where he went astray" (Beinecke Library, Yale University).

2. These contradictory impulses have also led to something of a split among critics of the work into two interpretive camps, which may be roughly characterized as modernist (e.g., Breslin, Mariani, Miller), and postmodern (to varying degrees, Miller, Perloff, Riddell).

3. Much later, in a 1945 poem entitled "At Kenneth Burke's Place," Williams still saw the earth (and contact) as an external disruption, a surplus "external to anthologies, outside the / orthodoxy of plotted murders" (*CP2* 107).

4. For Williams' varying attitudes toward the war, see Mariani, especially Chapter 9 (408–60).

5. Kolich notes the evidence for Williams' intention to include "Let Us Order

Our World" in *Paterson* in his introductory note (15). Although this essay provides a remarkably detailed account of Williams' thoughts on a number of issues related to *Paterson* III and to the present chapter, we should bear in mind a note in the Beinecke Library that suggests he did not want it to represent an authoritative statement: instead, he would "ridicule this essay by making a brief of it in the language of the day and the mind" (W139, Beinecke Library, Yale University).

6. Beinecke Library, Yale University.

7. The unleashing and harnessing of energy in large measure promise this transformation, but Williams also recognizes that the threat of the bomb, of total annihilation, will also transform the world (see Mariani 501).

8. Located in the Lockwood Memorial Library, SUNY at Buffalo.

9. The paradoxical nature of his enterprise prompts Williams to call *Paterson* (and call for) "a plan for action to supplant a plan for action" (*P* 2).

It was precisely the refusal to skirt catastrophe that Williams found so irritating in Eliot's work: "I am infuriated because the arrest has taken place just at the point of risk, just at the point when the magnificence might (possibly) have happened, just when the danger threatened" (Letter to James Laughlin, March 26, 1939, Beinecke Library, Yale University). Already in 1929 Williams had spoken of "the savor which can be enjoyed only at the brink of disaster" ("A Note on the Art of Poetry" 77).

10. A note for *Paterson* IV indicates that the lecture on uranium mentioned there has a "literary meaning" "in the splitting of the foot . . . and consequently is connected thereby to human life as life" (Lockwood Memorial Library, SUNY at Buffalo, D7).

11. Here I am drawing very loosely on the cusp model from catastrophe theory. This sense of an oscillation between orders offers one reason why critics have had such difficulty pinning down a poem that is in many respects the most readable of this century's long poems.

12. In 1946 Williams lamented that no "sudden upsurge" was following this war, as had happened after World War I: "but we didn't have 'the bomb' hanging over our heads then as we do today and besides this war had the quality of a repeat performance, we knew all about it already" (Letter to Josephin Herbst, December 24, 1946, Beinecke Library, Yale University).

13. Lockwood Memorial Library, SUNY at Buffalo, A234.

14. Miller notes the importance of delay in "Asphodel, That Greeny Flower," but identifies it with the poetic of earlier work like "Young Sycamore," which, as he says, is involved with "the always-not-quite-yet characteristic of modernist apocalypse" (*Linguistic Moment* 365). Even there, however, Williams does not attempt to accelerate the apocalypse.

15. Beinecke Library, Yale University.

16. Williams' drafts indicate that he began with a comparison, but then altered it to create the present ambiguity.

17. "Let Us Order Our World" ends with a similar point, though it is expressed in more traditional terms that obscure as much as they clarify: "that we do not expect to live forever will make us no less sanguine: eternity leaps into the minute and life is by that the more quickened" (22).

18. Beinecke Library, Yale University.

19. The literary rose is inextricably involved with Eliot's and Dante's roses, both of which Williams saw as mystifications. The image itself is not always positive: in a passage of "Tribute to the Painters" that was not included with the rest of the poem in *Paterson* V, Williams speaks of "the tyranny of the image" and of how men have had to shatter it (with designs) in order to quiet their minds (*PB* 137).

Chapter 4. Zukofsky's Twist

1. Not only was Pound sufficiently impressed to publish the poem, but he began what would develop into a considerable and remarkable correspondence with the younger poet. The writers became close enough, in fact, for Pound to help finance Zukofsky's 1932 trip to Europe (which of course included a visit to Pound in Rapallo). The correspondence itself continued, despite their divergent politics, up until World War II.

2. This is precisely the ambivalence inherent in our use of the term "post-modern." The question of temporality will be discussed in greater detail below, with respect to "*A*".

3. "A round" can also be read "around," while "fiddles" could refer to the poet's fiddling. Zukofsky's "fiddling around," then, might enable Bach to be "played back" for the twentieth century.

4. See Leggott 369–72.

5. Throughout the 1930s Zukofsky also referred to a planned book on Thomas Jefferson's use of language (mentioned also in "*A*"-12). It would examine Jefferson's revitalization of words and argue that his interest in language use was intimately related to his politics. Characteristically, Pound commented on the "danger of its being a smoke screen to keep pea/roozer's mind off of Jefferson's main content or 'message' " (*PZ* 201).

6. It also seems extraordinarily reductive to attempt to find some common denominator among Zukofsky, Reznikoff, Oppen, Niedecker, Rakosi, Williams, and the others—even more so than is usually the case with literary movements. The "Objectivists" issue of *Poetry* and the subsequent anthology present a collection of disparate writers whose work Zukofsky found vital, not a group that had been working together in a common project.

7. This turn away from song, despite preference for it, also shows Zukofsky turning from a goal such as Pound's of an all-encompassing Image.

8. Furthermore, the isolation of "is" implies that *being* may be the desired goal—is "is" an objective? Or should we read "is" literally, as a plurality of "I" 's?

9. Interestingly, this 1930 description of "*A*"-7 seems a deliberate echo and rejection of a section in Ford Madox Ford's 1929 *The English Novel*. Ford complains that having discovered "that words could be played with as if they were oranges or gilt balls to be tossed half a dozen together in the air, mankind rushed upon it as colts will dash into suddenly opened rich and easy pastures" (64). Ford develops the colt metaphor at some length, arguing that "the business of colts or of the arts is to carry things and we tire reasonably soon of watching horse-play." This also suggests a possible inspiration for Zukofsky's frequent horseplay in "*A*".

10. A telling example of "*A*" 's reluctance to follow even Zukofsky's certainties occurs in the materials included in the separately published *First Half of "A"*-9.

Zukofsky's prose restatement of the poem is definite, declaring what the words *would* say, whereas the poem itself only allows for the possibility, offering what they *could* say (see *A9* 41; *"A"* 106).

11. This is in fact Zukofsky's explicit practice in one of his short poems, "Her Face the Book of—Love Delights in—Praises" (*CSP* 206). Of course, the narrative realism is often in turn subsumed by a more general symbolic relation.

12. The passage perhaps also alludes to Paris of Troy, who causes his own lamentable fall.

13. The introduction to these bombers also connects them to the Holy Ghost, the dove upon the waters, the giver of life now destroying it (*"A"* 120). See Paul Virilio for an important discussion of the development of sighting techniques in World War II. Zukofsky worked for a while producing booklets for General Dynamics, including one on the use of such sights.

14. It is important to keep in mind that this analogy mitigates against any opposition between abstract and concrete, implying as it does that these terms are only relative and that one can turn into another. Zukofsky also applies the analogy to the components of poetry: solid, liquid, and gas correspond to sight, sound, and intellection (*P* 171).

15. Compare "Claims," a short poem that assesses *Bottom*'s theme: "After ten years he thought thought is that risk / whose claim claims claim" (*CSP* 155). The back and forth reflections here set up an unceasing process of qualification: a valid skepticism.

16. Others include to "make reason and love friends" and, more simply, the sense of fellowship that motivates writing.

17. *"A"*-12 is the first movement of *"A"* that explicitly takes notes as its material, a method that becomes increasingly important later in the poem. See Rieke for an important discussion of this aspect of Zukofsky's poetics.

18. Zukofsky's version of Wittgenstein's "ladder" image of his propositions also speaks to this combination of purpose and pleasure. At a talk given in Newcastle-upon-Tyne he cited a passage in *Bottom* that tells of "an ancient Korean poet" who "crossed water in the body of an instrument that was both shallop and harp he strung to play on the other shore" (*P* 172; *B* 423). Having given the story in the vehicle of prose, Zukofsky also turns it to song in *"A"*-13 (*P* 171).

19. It is worth noting that this emphasis on the importance of pleasure and variety would no doubt have been familiar to Shakespeare, given its currency in Mannerist esthetics (see Shearman).

20. The play on "all" and "part" in the last poem in the book, "Finally a Valentine," recalls the biblical (Hebraic) usage of "all" to mean "majority" or "most," rather than the Greek totality (*CSP* 240; see Handelman 65).

21. Zukofsky's use of French to characterize Mallarmé's book, with the pun on *livre* = pound = Pound, implies that his critique is also aimed at Pound's enterprise (*"A"* 421).

22. The "encore" of *"A"*-19 also points to this materiality, with its pun on "en corps."

23. A complete list of the poems Zukofsky read is given in *Prepositions*, 37.

24. My discussion of this "An" song was originally published in *Sagetrieb* 5.1

(Spring 1986). For other perspectives, see Leggott (34–48) and Quartermain ("Only is order othered" 958–60).

25. The lines are derived from Act IV, sc. 1. "Foison" is from Ceres' line, "Earth's increase, foison plenty"(11). Except for "to," the other words are taken from an exchange between Ferdinand and Prospero:

> Fer. Let me live here ever.
> So rare a wondered father and a wise
> Makes this place Paradise.
> Pro. Sweet, now silence!

As elsewhere, Zukofsky omits the context despite its relevance.

26. Another meaning of "initial" is relevant here: in music, it denotes "each of the prescribed notes on which a Plain-song melody may begin in any given mode" (*OED*). Once again a turn to song.

27. Zukofsky does provide a key to this method in the short poem, "The Translation," an etymological meditation on his wife. See *CSP* 234.

28. Another hidden connection spans these two stanzas: "aching nerve" plus "feed and feed back" gives cybernetics, which Norbert Wiener coined from Greek Κυβερνήτης, "helmsman" or "steersman." Still another meaning of "initial" is also relevant here, providing another bridge across the "yet": "a primordial cell that determines the basic pattern of derived tissues" (*Webster's New World*).

29. The family is also woven into the final stanza of this music: the violin signals Paul's presence, "thawed" puns on Celia's maiden name, Thaew, and "three-fingered chord" suggests Zukofsky's perception of familial harmony. It is important to note that this Eden does include imperfection: fear is thawed, not banished; and "summer happy" acknowledges that some are happy, not all, and also that happiness may be seasonal, i.e., temporary.

Sources

Works by Ezra Pound

A Lume Spento and Other Early Poems. New York: New Directions, 1965.

America, Roosevelt and the Causes of the Present War. Money Pamphlet no. 6. London: Peter Russell, 1951. Translation of *L'America, Roosevelt e le Cause della Guerra Presenta*. Venice, 1944.

The Cantos of Ezra Pound. New York: New Directions, 1986.

Collected Early Poems of Ezra Pound. Ed. Michael John King. New York: New Directions, 1976.

"Communications." *Townsman* 2.6 (April 1939): 12–13.

Confucius: The Unwobbling Pivot, The Great Digest, The Analects. Translation and Commentary by Ezra Pound. New York: New Directions, 1969.

"Data." *Exile* 4 (Autumn 1928): 104–17.

A Draft of XVI Cantos. Paris: Three Mountains, 1925.

Ezra Pound and the Visual Arts. Ed. Harriet Zinnes. New York: New Directions, 1980.

Ezra Pound Reading His Poetry. Vol. 1. Caedmon, TC 112. 1960.

"Ezra Pound Speaking": Radio Speeches of World War II. Ed. Leonard W. Doob. Westport, Conn.: Greenwood Press, 1978.

Gaudier-Brzeska: A Memoir. New York: New Directions, 1970.

Guide to Kulchur. New York: New Directions, 1970.

Jefferson and/or Mussolini: L'idea statale: Fascism As I Have Seen It. New York: Liveright, 1970.

Literary Essays of Ezra Pound. Ed. T. S. Eliot. New York: New Directions, 1954.

"A National Poetry." Beinecke Library, Yale University.

Pavannes and Divagations. New York: New Directions, 1958.

Personae: The Collected Shorter Poems of Ezra Pound. New York: New Directions, 1950.

Poems 1918–1921. New York: Boni and Liveright, 1921.

Pound/Joyce: The Letters of Ezra Pound to James Joyce, with Pound's Essays on Joyce. Ed. Forrest Read. New York: New Directions, 1967.

Selected Cantos. New York: New Directions, 1970.

Selected Letters, 1907–1941. Ed. D. D. Paige. New York: New Directions, 1971.

Selected Poems. New York: New Directions, 1957.

Selected Prose: 1909–1965. Ed. William Cookson. New York: New Directions, 1973.

The Spirit of Romance. New York: New Directions, 1968.

Translations. New York: New Directions, 1963.

Works by Williams Carlos Williams

The Autobiography. New York: Random House, 1951.

The Collected Poems of William Carlos Williams. Volume I: 1909–1939. Ed. A. Walton Litz and Christopher MacGowan. New York: New Directions, 1986.

The Collected Poems of Williams Carlos Williams. Volume II: 1939–1962. Ed. Christopher MacGowan. New York: New Directions, 1988.

"A Cry in the Night." Beinecke Library, Yale University.

The Embodiment of Knowledge. Ed. Ron Loewinsohn. New York: New Directions, 1974.

"Excerpts from a Critical Sketch: The XXX Cantos of Ezra Pound." *Symposium* 2 (April 1931): 262.

Imaginations. Ed. Webster Schott. New York: New Directions, 1970.

In the American Grain. New York: New Directions, 1956.

I Wanted to Write a Poem: The Autobiography of the Works of a Poet. Ed. Elizabeth Heal. New York: New Directions, 1958.

"The Later Pound." *Massachusetts Review* 14.1 (Winter 1973): 124–29.

"Let Us Order Our World." Ed. Augustus M. Kolich. *The William Carlos Williams Newsletter* 8.2 (Fall 1982): 15–22.

"A Note on the Art of Poetry." *Blues* 1.4 (May 1929): 77–79.

"A Note on Paterson: Book III." *Paterson: Book III*. New York: New Directions, 1948. Dust jacket.

Paterson. Rev. Ed. prepared by Christopher MacGowan. New York: New Directions, 1992.

Pictures from Brueghel and Other Poems. New York: New Directions, 1962.

"The Poem as a Scene of Action." Beinecke Library, Yale University.

A Recognizable Image: William Carlos Williams on Art and Artists. Ed. Bram Dijkstra. New York: New Directions, 1978.

Selected Essays. New York: New Directions, 1954.

The Selected Letters of Williams Carlos Williams. Ed. John C. Thirlwall. New York: McDowell, Obolensky, 1957.

Something to Say: William Carlos Williams on Younger Poets. Ed. James E. B. Breslin. New York: New Directions, 1985.

"The Turn of the View Toward Poetic Technique." Beinecke Library, Yale University.

"War the Destroyer." *Harper's Bazaar* no. 2762 (March 1, 1942): 49.

Works by Louis Zukofsky

"A". Berkeley: University of California Press, 1978.

All: The Collected Short Poems, 1923–1964. New York: W. W. Norton, 1971.

An Era. A Poetry Post Card. Santa Barbara: Unicorn Press, 1970.

Bottom: On Shakespeare. Repr. Berkeley: University of California Press, 1987.

Collected Fiction. With a Foreword by Gilbert Sorrentino, and an Afterword by Paul Zukofsky. Elmwood Park, Ill.: Dalkey Archive Press, 1990.

Complete Short Poetry. With a Foreword by Robert Creeley. Baltimore: Johns Hopkins University Press, 1991.

First Half of "A"-9. New York: Privately Printed, 1940.

Initial. New York: Phoenix Bookshop, 1970.
It Was. Kyoto: Origin, 1961.
Louis Zukofsky. N.E.T. Outtake Series.
Pound/Zukofsky: Selected Letters of Ezra Pound and Louis Zukofsky. Ed. Barry Ahearn. New York: New Directions, 1987.
Prepositions: The Collected Critical Essays. Expanded Edition. Berkeley: University of California Press, 1981.
A Test of Poetry. New York: Jargon/Corinth Books, 1964.

Other Works

Adams, John. *Works*. Ed. Charles Francis Adams. 10 vols. Boston, 1850–56.
Bacigalupo, Massimo. *The Forméd Trace: The Later Poetry of Ezra Pound*. New York: Columbia University Press, 1980.
Bakhtin, M. M. *The Dialogic Imagination: Four Essays*. Ed. Michael Holquist. Trans. Caryl Emerson and Michael Holquist. Austin: University of Texas Press, 1981.
Baldwin, Neil. "Zukofsky, Williams, and *The Wedge*: Toward a Dynamic Convergence." In *Louis Zukofsky: Man and Poet*, 129–42. Ed. Carroll F. Terrell. Orono, Maine: National Poetry Foundation, 1979.
———. "Varieties of Influence: The Literary Relationship of William Carlos Williams and Louis Zukofsky." *Credences: A Journal of Twentieth Century Poetry and Poetics* 2.1 (1982): 93–103.
———. "The Letters of William Carlos Williams to Louis Zukofsky: A Chronicle of Trust and Difficulty." *Library Chronicle of the University of Texas*. Vol. 23 (1983): 37–49.
Bataille, Georges. *Visions of Excess: Selected Writings, 1927–1939*. Ed. Allan Stoekl. Trans. Allan Stoekl and others. Minneapolis: University of Minnesota Press, 1985.
Beckett, Samuel. *Proust*. New York: Grove Press, 1970.
Benjamin, Walter. *Illuminations*. Ed. Hannah Arendt. Trans. Harry Zohn. New York: Schocken, 1969.
Bernstein, Charles. *A Poetics*. Cambridge: Harvard University Press, 1992.
Bernstein, Michael André. *The Tale of the Tribe: Ezra Pound and the Modern Verse Epic*. Princeton: Princeton University Press, 1980.
Berrone, Louis, ed. and trans. *James Joyce in Padua*. New York: Random House, 1977.
Blake, William. *Complete Writings*. Ed. Geoffrey Keynes. London: Oxford University Press, 1966.
Boyers, Paul. *By the Bomb's Early Light: American Thought and Culture at the Dawn of the Atomic Age*. New York: Pantheon Books, 1985.
Breslin, James E. *William Carlos Williams: An American Artist*. New York: New Directions, 1970.
Brodie, Bernard, ed. *The Absolute Weapon: Atomic Power and World Order*. New York: Harcourt, Brace, 1946.
———. *Strategy in the Missile Age*. Princeton: Princeton University Press, 1959.
Bryson, Norman. "The Gaze in the Expanded Field." In *Vision and Visuality*, 87–

113. Dia Art Foundation Discussions in Contemporary Culture 2. Ed. Hal Foster. Seattle: Bay Press, 1988.

Bush, Ronald. *The Genesis of Ezra Pound's Cantos*. Princeton: Princeton University Press, 1976.

Carpenter, Humphrey. *A Serious Character: The Life of Ezra Pound*. Boston: Houghton Mifflin, 1988.

Casillo, Robert. *The Genealogy of Demons: Anti-Semitism, Fascism, and the Myths of Ezra Pound*. Evanston, Ill.: Northwestern University Press, 1988.

Certeau, Michel de. *The Practice of Everyday Life*. Trans. Steven F. Rendall. Berkeley: University of California Press, 1984.

Chaucer, Geoffrey. *The Complete Poetry and Prose*. Ed. John H. Fisher. New York: Holt, Rinehart and Winston, 1977.

Cohn, Norman. *The Pursuit of the Millennium: Revolutionary Millennarians and Mystical Anarchists of the Middle Ages*. St. Albans: Granada, 1970.

Comens, Bruce. "Soundings: The 'An' Song Beginning 'A'-22." *Sagetrieb* 5.1 (Spring 1986): 95–106.

The Compact Edition of the Oxford English Dictionary. Oxford: Oxford University Press, 1971.

Corbin, Henry. *The Concept of Comparative Philosophy*. Trans. Peter Russell. Golgonooza Press.

Cousins, Norman. "Modern Man is Obsolete." *Saturday Review of Literature*. August 18, 1945. Enlarged version in *Modern Man is Obsolete*. New York: Viking, 1945.

Creeley, Robert. *The Collected Prose*. Berkeley: University of California Press, 1988.

Dasenbrock, Reed Way. *The Literary Vorticism of Ezra Pound and Wyndham Lewis: Towards the Condition of Painting*. Baltimore: Johns Hopkins University Press, 1985.

Deleuze, Gilles. *Nietzsche and Philosophy*. Trans. Hugh Tomlinson. New York: Columbia University Press, 1983.

Deleuze, Gilles, and Félix Guattari. *A Thousand Plateaus: Capitalism and Schizophrenia*. Trans. Brian Massumi. Minneapolis: University of Minnesota Press, 1987.

Dembo, Louis. "Louis Zukofsky [Sincerity and Objectification]." In *Louis Zukofsky: Man and Poet*, 265–81. Ed., Intro. Carroll F. Terrell. Orono, Maine: National Poetry Foundation, 1979. Rpt. from "The 'Objectivist' Poet: Four Interviews," *Contemporary Literature* 10 (Spring 1969): 155–219.

Derrida, Jacques. "Of an Apocalyptic Tone in Recent Philosophy." *Studies in Ancient Letter Writing. Semeia* 22, 63–98. Ed. John L. White. Society of Biblical Literature, 1982.

———. "No Apocalypse, Not Now (full speed ahead, seven missiles, seven missives)." *Diacritics* 14.2 (1984): 20–32.

Duncan, Robert. *The Truth and Life of Myth: An Essay in Essential Autobiography*. Fremont, Mich.: Sumac Press, 1968. Rpt. in *Fictive Certainties*, 1–59. New York: New Directions, 1985.

Eccles, Henry E. *Military Concepts and Philosophy*. New Brunswick, N.J.: Rutgers University Press, 1965.

Eliot, T. S. *For Lancelot Andrewes: Essays on Style and Order*. Garden City: Doubleday, 1929.

———. *Four Quartets*. London: Faber and Faber, 1959.
———. *"Ulysses*, Order and Myth." *Selected Prose*, 175–78. Ed. Frank Kermode. London: Faber and Faber, 1975.
Flory, Wendy Stallard. *Ezra Pound and The Cantos: A Record of Struggle*. New Haven: Yale University Press, 1980.
Ford, Ford Madox. *The English Novel: From the Earliest Days to the Death of Joseph Conrad*. Philadelphia: J. B. Lippincott, 1929. Rpt. Folcroft, Pa.: Folcroft Press, 1969.
Foucault, Michel, and Gilles Deleuze. "Intellectuals and Power." In *Language, Counter-Memory, Practice: Selected Essays and Interviews*, by Michel Foucault. Ed. Donald F. Bouchard. Trans. Donald F. Bouchard and Sherry Simon. Ithaca: Cornell University Press, 1977.
Froula, Christine. *To Write Paradise: Style and Error in Pound's Cantos*. New Haven: Yale University Press, 1984.
Fussell, Paul. *The Great War and Modern Memory*. London: Oxford University Press, 1975.
Hall, Donald. "Ezra Pound: An Interview." *Paris Review* 28 (Summer–Fall 1962): 22–51.
Handelman, Susan A. *The Slayers of Moses: The Emergence of Rabbinic Interpretation in Modern Literary Theory*. Albany: State University of New York Press, 1982.
Heidegger, Martin. *Poetry, Language, Thought*. Trans. Albert Hofstadter. New York: Harper and Row, 1971.
Hobhouse, L. T. *The Metaphysical Theory of the State, A Criticism*. London: George Allen and Unwin, 1918.
Howard, Michael. *The Causes of Wars*. 2nd Ed., enlarged. Cambridge: Harvard University Press, 1984.
Jakobson, Roman, and Morris Halle. *Fundamentals of Language*. 2nd Ed. The Hague: Mouton Publishers, 1971.
Jay, Martin. "Scopic Regimes of Modernity." In *Vision and Visuality*, 3–27. Dia Art Foundation Discussions in Contemporary Culture 2. Ed. Hal Foster. Seattle: Bay Press, 1988.
Jones, David. *In Parenthesis*. London: Faber and Faber, 1963.
Joyce, James. *A Portrait of the Artist as a Young Man*. New York: Viking, 1968.
Jung, C. G. "*Ulysses*: a Monologue." Trans. W. Stanley Dell. *Nimbus* 2.1 (1953): 7–20.
Kearns, George. *Guide to Ezra Pound's "Selected Cantos."* New Brunswick, N.J.: Rutgers University Press, 1980.
Kenner, Hugh. "Ezra Pound's Commedia." In *Dante Among the Moderns*, 39–56. Ed. Stuart Y. McDougal. Chapel Hill: University of North Carolina Press, 1985.
———. *The Pound Era*. Berkeley: University of California Press, 1971.
Klein, Richard, and William B. Warner. "Nuclear Coincidence and the Korean Airline Disaster." *Diacritics: A Review of Contemporary Criticism* 16.1 (Spring 1986): 2–21.
Leggott, Michele J. *Reading Zukofsky's 80 Flowers*. Baltimore: Johns Hopkins University Press, 1989.
Levinas, Emmanuel. *Totality and Infinity*. Trans. Alphonso Lingis. Pittsburgh: Duquesne University Press, 1969.

Levy, Hyman. *A Philosophy for a Modern Man.* New York: Knopf, 1938.

Lewis, Wyndham. "The European War and Great Communities." *Blast* 2 (July 1915): 15–16.

Lewis, Wyndham, Ezra Pound, and others. "Manifesto II." *Blast* 1 (July 1914): 30–43.

Lyotard, Jean-François. *The Postmodern Condition: A Report on Knowledge.* Trans. Geoff Bennington and Brian Massumi. Minneapolis: University of Minnesota Press, 1984.

McFarlane, James. "The Mind of Modernism." In *Modernism 1890–1930*, 71–93. Ed. Malcolm Bradbury and James McFarlane. Harmondsworth: Penguin, 1976.

Mackenzie, John L., S.J. *Dictionary of the Bible.* New York: Macmillan, 1965.

McGann, Jerome. "Contemporary Poetry, Alternate Routes." *Critical Inquiry* 13.3 (Spring 1987): 624–47.

Mallarmé, Stéphane. *Igitur. Divagations. Un coup de dés.* Paris: Editions Gallimard, 1976.

———. *Selected Poetry and Prose.* Ed. Mary Ann Caws. New York: New Directions, 1982.

Mariani, Paul. *Williams Carlos Williams: A New World Naked.* New York: McGraw-Hill, 1981.

Merleau-Ponty, Maurice. *The Visible and the Invisible.* Ed. Claude Lefort. Trans. Alphonso Lingis. Evanston, Ill.: Northwestern University Press, 1968.

Miller, J. Hillis. *The Linguistic Moment: From Wordsworth to Stevens.* Princeton: Princeton University Press, 1985.

———. *Poets of Reality: Six Twentieth-Century Writers.* Cambridge: Belknap Press, 1965.

Milton, John. *The Complete Poetical Works.* Ed. Douglas Bush. Boston: Houghton Mifflin, 1965.

Nicholls, Peter. *Ezra Pound: Politics, Economics and Writing: A Study of The Cantos.* London: Macmillan, 1984.

Norman, Charles. *Ezra Pound.* New York: Macmillan, 1960.

Olson, Charles. *Charles Olson and Ezra Pound: An Encounter at St. Elizabeths.* Ed. Catherine Seelye. New York: Grossman, 1975.

———. *Human Universe and Other Essays.* Ed. Donald Allen. New York: Grove Press, 1967.

———. *The Special View of History.* Ed. Ann Charters. Berkeley: Oyez, 1970.

Ong, Walter J. *Fighting for Life: Contest, Sexuality, and Consciousness.* Ithaca: Cornell University Press, 1981.

Pearlman, Daniel D. *The Barb of Time: On the Unity of Ezra Pound's Cantos.* New York: Oxford University Press, 1969.

Perloff, Marjorie. *The Poetics of Indeterminacy: Rimbaud to Cage.* Princeton: Princeton University Press, 1981.

Power, Arthur. *Conversations with James Joyce.* Ed. Clive Hart. Chicago: University of Chicago Press, 1974.

Quartermain, Peter. " 'Actual Word Stuff, Not Thoughts for Thoughts': Louis Zukofsky and William Carlos Williams." *Credences: A Journal of Twentieth Century Poetry and Poetics* 2.1 (1982): 104–22.

———. " 'Only is order othered. Nought is nulled': *Finnegans Wake* and Middle and Later Zukofsky." *ELH* 54.4 (Winter 1987): 957–78.

Rachewilz, Mary de. *Discretions*. Boston: Little, Brown, 1971.

Rainey, Lawrence S. *Ezra Pound and the Monument of Culture: Text, History, and the Malatesta Cantos*. Chicago: University of Chicago Press, 1991.

Rapp, Carl. *William Carlos Williams and Romantic Idealism*. Hanover, N.H.: Published for Brown University Press by Univerity Press of New England, 1984.

Redman, Tim. *Ezra Pound and Italian Fascism*. Cambridge: Cambridge University Press, 1991.

Reich, Steve. "Steve Reich In Conversation with Jonathan Cott." *The Desert Music*. Nonesuch Digital 79101-2.

Riddell, Joseph. *The Inverted Bell: Modernism and the Counterpoetics of William Carlos Williams*. Baton Rouge: Louisiana State University Press, 1974.

Rieke, Alison. " 'Quotation and Originality': Notes and Manuscripts to Louis Zukofsky's 'A'." In *Lawrence, Jarry, Zukofsky: A Triptych—Manuscript Collections at the Harry Ransom Humanities Center*, 77–105. Ed. Dave Oliphant and Gena Dagel. Austin: Harry Ransom Humanities Research Center, 1987.

Robbins, Keith. *The First World War*. Oxford: Oxford University Press, 1985.

Robinson, Douglas. *American Apocalypses: The Image of the End of the World in American Literature*. Baltimore: Johns Hopkins University Press, 1985.

Rorty, Richard. "Foucault and Epistemology." In *Foucault: A Critical Reader*, 41–49. Ed. David Couzens Hoy. Oxford: Basil Blackwell, 1986.

Rosenfield, Isaac. *The Strange, Familiar, and Forgotten: An Anatomy of Consciousness*. New York: Knopf, 1992.

Saussure, Ferdinand de. *Course in General Linguistics*. Ed. Charles Bally and others. Trans. Wade Baskin. Rev. Ed. New York: Fontana/Collins, 1974.

Schafer, Murray. "Ezra Pound and Music." In *Ezra Pound: A Collection of Critical Essays*, 129–41. Ed. Walter Sutton. Englewood Cliffs: Prentice-Hall, 1963.

Schneidau, Herbert. *Ezra Pound: The Image and the Real*. Baton Rouge: Louisiana State University Press, 1969.

Serres, Michel. "Knowledge in the Classical Age: La Fontaine and Descartes." *Hermes: Literature, Science, Philosophy*, 15–28. Ed. Josué V. Harari and David F. Bell. Baltimore: Johns Hopkins University Press, 1982.

Shearman, John. *Mannerism*. Harmondsworth: Penguin, 1967.

Stein, Gertrude. *Brewsie and Willie*. London: Brilliance Books/Plain Edition, 1988.

———. "My Last About Money." In *Look at Me Now and Here I Am: Writings and Lectures 1909–45*, 336–37. Ed. Patricia Meyerowitz. Harmondsworth: Penguin, 1971.

———. "Reflection on the Atomic Bomb." In *Reflection on the Atomic Bomb*. Vol. 1 of the Previously Uncollected Writings of Gertrude Stein. Ed. Robert Bartlett Haas. Los Angeles: Black Sparrow, 1973.

Stein, Gertrude, and Robert Bartlett Haas. "A Transatlantic Interview 1946." In *A Primer for the Gradual Understanding of Gertrude Stein*, 15–35. Ed. Robert Bartlett Haas. Los Angeles: Black Sparrow, 1971.

Stock, Noel. *The Life of Ezra Pound*. Harmondsworth: Penguin, 1985.

Terrell, Carroll F. *A Companion to the Cantos of Ezra Pound*. 2 vols. Berkeley: University of California Press, 1980–84.

Virilio, Paul. *War and Cinema: The Logistics of Perception*. Trans. Patrick Camiller. London and New York: Verso, 1989.

Webster's New World Dictionary. 2nd College Ed. Cleveland: William Collins, 1980.

Wells, H. G. *The War That Will End War.* New York: Duffield, 1914.

―――. *The World Set Free: A Story of Mankind.* New York: E. P. Dutton, 1914.

Whitman, Walt. *Complete Poetry and Selected Prose.* Ed. James E. Miller, Jr. Boston: Houghton Mifflin, 1959.

Wittgenstein, Ludwig. *Philosophical Investigations.* Trans. G. E. M. Anscombe. 3rd Ed. New York: Macmillan, 1968.

―――. *Tractatus Logico-Philosophicus.* Trans. D. F. Pears and B. F. McGuinness. New Ed. London: Routledge and Kegan Paul, 1972.

Woodward, Anthony. *Ezra Pound and The Pisan Cantos.* London: Routledge and Kegan Paul, 1980.

Wyschogrod, Edith. *Spirit in Ashes: Hegel, Heidegger, and Man-Made Mass Death.* New Haven: Yale University Press, 1985.

Yeats, W. B. *A Vision.* London: Macmillan, 1962.

―――. *The Collected Poems.* Definitive Ed. New York: Macmillan, 1956.

Index